the DIVINE
EMBRACE

the DIVINE EMBRACE

Recovering the Passionate Spiritual Life

ROBERT E. WEBBER

BakerBooks
Grand Rapids, Michigan

Published by Baker Books
a division of Baker Publishing Group
P.O. Box 6287, Grand Rapids, MI 49516-6287
www.bakerbooks.com

Printed in the United States of America

Library of Congress Cataloging-in-Publication Data

Webber, Robert.
    The divine embrace : recovering the passionate spiritual life / Robert E. Webber.
        p.   cm. — (Ancient-future series)
    Includes bibliographical references (p.   ) and index.
    ISBN 10: 0-8010-6555-0 (pbk.)
    ISBN 978-0-8010-6555-2 (pbk.)
    1. Spiritual life—Christianity. 2. Spirituality. I. Title.
    BV4501.3.W39 2006
    248—dc22   2006018844

CONTENTS

Introduction to the Ancient-Future Series

This book, *The Divine Embrace: Recovering the Passionate Spiritual Life*, belongs to the Ancient-Future series. In each book of the series I present an issue related to faith and Christian practice from a particular point of view, namely, that of drawing wisdom from the past and translating these insights into the present and future life of the church, its faith, worship, ministry, and spirituality.

In these books I address current issues in the context of three very significant quests taking place in the church today. First, these books speak to the longing to discover the roots of the faith in the biblical and classical tradition of the church. I affirm the Bible as the final authority in all matters of faith and practice. However, instead of disregarding the developments of faith in the church, I draw on the foundational interpretation of the church fathers and the creeds and practices of the ancient church. These are sources in which Christian truth has been summarized and articulated over against heretical teaching.

Second, this series is committed to the current search for unity in the church. Therefore, I draw from the entire history of the church together with its many manifestations—Orthodox, Catholic, and Protestant— particularly the Reformers and evangelicals like John Wesley and Jonathan Edwards. I weave insights from these traditions into the text so the reader will understand how other deeply committed Christians have sought to think and live the faith in other places and times.

Finally, I use these biblical, ancient roots together with insights and practices from Christian history to constitute the foundation for addressing the third issue faced by today's church: how do you deliver the authentic faith and great wisdom of the past into the new cultural situation of the twenty-first century? The way into the future, I argue, is not an innovative new start for the church; rather, the road to the future runs through the past.

These three matters—roots, connection, and authenticity in a changing world—will help us to maintain continuity with historic Christianity as the church moves forward. I hope what I cull from the past and then translate and adapt into the present will be beneficial to your ministry in the new cultural situation of our time.

ACKNOWLEDGMENTS

No one is fully able to acknowledge all the sources and people who contribute to the writing of a book. Many unnamed books, people, and even institutions have formed my life and challenged me to be sensitive to the work of the church as it moves into a post-Christian world. The fact that I mention only a few of these people and institutions here in no way diminishes my appreciation for the unnamed.

First, I need to thank Northern Seminary for my appointment as the William R. and Geraldyne B. Myers Professor of Ministry. This generous chair has substantially reduced my teaching load, allowing me more time to write. I am equally grateful to Baker Books, to Robert Hosack for freedom to develop this book in a way that reflects my convictions and to Paul J. Brinkerhoff for his editorial skills that made the book read more clearly.

Next, there are those special people who have encouraged me and helped me with the research and the process of many rewrites and editorial changes. A special word of thanks to the editors at Baker Books for their careful editing.

Early on in the process of writing, two friends read, discussed, and provided some helpful advice and insight—Sherry Schaub and Rev. John Carlson. Also, a number of people responded to the summaries I presented in "Ancient-Future Talk." Some of the email responses appear in the text. I owe a special word of thanks to these people, and also to the many unnamed people who provided me with their stimulating thoughts. Numerous books were helpful, particularly Mark McIntosh's *Mystical Theology*, whose panoramic interpretation of spirituality provided me with a paradigm to think about the unique nature of Christian spirituality. Thanks, also, to my friend and colleague Amanda Gambony, whose searching interaction has forced me toward greater clarity. Then there are my Northern Seminary students, whose response and interaction I value greatly. And this project could not have been completed without the constant attention of Ashley Gieschen to the frequent twists and turns of my evolving grasp of God's embrace and to the constant unannounced rewrites. And, of course, my wife, Joanne, who suffered through my frustrations, the early morning to late evenings, and the endless discussions. Thanks to these and many unnamed contributors who through the years have challenged my mind and heart with God's truth.

The Divine Embrace

Lord Jesus Christ, you stretched out your arms of love

on the hard wood of the cross that everyone might come

within the reach of your saving embrace: So clothe us in

your Spirit that we, reaching forth our hands in love, may

bring those who do not know you to the knowledge and

love of you; for the honor of your Name. *Amen.*

The Book of Common Prayer, 101

1

INTRODUCTION

A Dinnertime Conversation on Spirituality

I was talking to two young couples during dinner when a question changed the conversation rather abruptly. "What are you writing on these days?"

"I'm writing on spirituality," I responded. Immediately they responded with an explosion of ideas. For the next half hour I listened to each person express his or her range of thoughts about spirituality.

"I'm spiritual," said Isabel. "There has to be something more than the material world. I don't know what it is—a power, an energy, a mystery. There is something there, something more than meets the eye."

"Not me," said John.

"Are you an atheist?" I asked.

"No. I'm not really an atheist. I just don't think you can know."

"Then," I said, "you must be an agnostic."

Alexandra chimed in, "I remember when I was a little girl, I saw a sign on a building that said, 'All paths lead to God.' I thought to myself, 'That makes a lot of sense.' There are many religions and everyone has their own path to God, and that's okay."

The fourth person, Jack, declared, "What I can't stand is someone who thinks they have truth, that their view is the right one and everyone else is wrong."

This statement drew a chorus of "Yeahs" and resulted in an extended discussion affirming the validity of all spiritualities. The idea that anyone

could affirm that there is such a thing as universal truth for everyone
was clearly anathema, a bad idea in today's world of relativism, of *no
absolutes*.

I asked a few questions, but mainly I just listened.

Finally, Jack, who was seated to my left, asked, "So what do you
believe?"

"I'm a committed Christian," I answered, "and as a matter of fact, I'm
one of those Christians who believes Jesus to be 'the way, the truth, and
the life.' Jesus declared himself to be the way to God, so I affirm that
spirituality is uniquely connected to Jesus. But that doesn't mean that I
don't have respect for other spiritualities," I added.

These two couples were surprised to hear those words, especially
since they had condemned anyone who thinks that there is such a thing
as universal truth. After a few moments of embarrassed silence I asked,
"So, what are you going to do with me?"

After a brief pause, Jack said, "Explain yourself. I'm willing to hear
you out."

"Okay," I said, "but to explain myself I have to tell you a story." I
sensed a puzzlement on his part, so I quickly added, *"All spiritualities
are based on a story. You have to know the story of a particular religion to
understand its spirituality."*

This statement aroused the curiosity of everyone. "Tell the story," said
Jack. "Maybe I don't know the story; as a matter of fact, I don't think
I've ever heard Christianity told as a story."

"Okay," I responded, "but I have to tell you I can't prove the story."[1]

"I like that! I don't like it when religious people try to prove their faith.
Just the fact that you say that we shouldn't try to prove the story with
history and science makes me want to listen."

It took me about an hour to sketch out the story. There was lots of
laughter, interaction, and interfacing. I did not try to prove the faith
with historical facts or scientific data or build a presuppositional case.
Instead I simply told the story of God: how God created us to be in
union with himself, how this unity was broken, and how Jesus, by God's
Spirit, brought us back into union with God by becoming one of us, by
living to show us what true humanity looks like, by dying to destroy all
that is death in the world, and by rising to lift us up into a new life in
God. "Consider," I suggested, *"that Jesus really is the way to God, that he
really does disclose the truth about life, and that through Jesus the vision
for humanity and all of history is revealed."* After I finished the story of
how Jesus by God's Spirit unites us to God and calls us to a new way of
seeing and *living* life, the first question was:

"What God did in Jesus, did God do that for everybody?"

"Yes," I said, "he did."

"For Buddhists?"

"Yes."

"For Hindus?"

"Yes."

"For Muslims?"

"Yes."

"For all people?"

"No exceptions. Everybody."[2]

"I got it!" said Jack. "I got it! I got it! I've never heard spirituality expressed that way before. That's incredible."

With a look of astonishment on her face, Isabel said, "That is a *good* story! What are we to do?"

I had already begun the writing of *The Divine Embrace* when this conversation took place. I was, as I think my dinner guests were, impacted by this conversation. Consequently, I rewrote what I had already written to make this book a response to our discussion, to engage the conversation on a deeper level. I invite you, the reader, to join the dialogue and think with me about a spirituality that is rooted in the story of God.

CHRISTIAN SPIRITUALITY IS . . .

What is Christian spirituality? There is a great deal of confusion about Christian spirituality today. For many who have been reared in the faith, like these two young couples, and for many outside of the Christian faith, spirituality in the Christian tradition seems to be misunderstood.

For example, the cover story of a recent *Newsweek* magazine titled "Spirituality in America" and bearing the subtitle, "What we believe, how we pray, where we find God," defines spirituality as the "passion for an immediate, transcendent experience of God."[3] The various articles show how this transcendent experience is realized in religions as various as Islam, Pentecostalism, Catholicism, and the Jewish Kabbalah as well as in environmentalism. The writers make no real distinction between the story or vision of each of these religions, simply describing all spiritualities as the search for experience.

Of course spirituality has an experiential dimension, but the experience is always in keeping with the story from which it arises. So the Christian experience will differ from that of Islam, Buddhism, or New Age religions because it is based on a different story. This book is about the Christian story of the *divine embrace*, the spirituality that proceeds from it, and how this spirituality may be recovered in a relativistic, postmodern world where spirituality is viewed as a common, content-less experience of otherness.

WHERE DO WE START?

The heart of biblical and ancient Christian spirituality is *our mystical union with God accomplished by Jesus Christ through the Spirit*. God unites with humanity in his saving incarnation, death, and resurrection. We unite with God as we receive his new life within us.

Christian spirituality then, simply put, is *God's passionate embrace of us; our passionate embrace of God*. These two aspects of Christian spirituality are like the two sides of a coin—inextricably linked together, unable to exist apart. On one side we find the *divine initiative*, referring to what God does to make us spiritual. On the other side we find *our response*, referring to our reception of the union. These two sides of a single coin tell us that *God makes us spiritual, and we live the spiritual life*. But to understand these two aspects of spirituality, we must place them in the setting of God's story of the world.

GOD'S STORY

What is God's story? *It is the story of God's purposes for humanity and the world*.[4] God created us in his image and likeness, to live in union with himself, to be what he created us to be, and to do what he created us to do: take care of the world and make it the place of his glory.

But we failed both assignments. We rebelled against God and sought the meaning of life by following the course of evil in our personal choices, resulting in the world as a place of violence, greed, and lust.

We can't change ourselves or the world. So God does it for us.

God's story is the story of how God reversed the human condition, broke the hold of sin and death—which separates us from God, and restored us to the original vision of *becoming the person God created us to be* and *making the world the place of God's glory*.

Christian *spirituality*, then, does not fall into what *Newsweek* describes as a contentless "transcendent experience" but is God's gift of a redirected life in union with God's purpose for life. Our *spiritual life* then, is union with God fulfilled in a life of *contemplation* and *participation* in God's vision for life in this world. Contemplation and participation, it turns out, is our worship of God.

This description of spirituality contains four crucial words. Two of these words refer to God's way of union with us: *story* and *mystical-union*; two refer to the way of our union with and worship of God: *contemplation* and *participation*. The first two words speak to the *source* of spirituality; the second two words speak to the *actions* of the spiritual life.

The Source of Spirituality

It is God who makes us spiritual, not ourselves. God's embrace is the passionate outworking of God's vision to reunite us to himself and re-direct our lives to fulfill his original purposes for us and the world. The two words that express the divine initiative that restores our spiritual condition are *story* and *mystical-union*.

Story

In recent years there has been a great deal of discussion about story-telling as a prime form of communication. This emphasis on story is a result of the shift from modernity to postmodern times. In modern times people were much more interested in argument. The emphasis was on setting forth your premise, then developing the arguments that proved your case.

I was trained in the modern method of apologetic argument. In sem-inary I took a course on presuppositional thinking. "Your basic presup-position," I was told, "is that there is a God who created the world and revealed himself to the world. Ask your opponent to set forth his or her presupposition, then show the logic of your opponent's presupposition and the logic of your own, and then persuade him or her that Christi-anity must be embraced as true." Christian theologian and philosopher Francis Schaeffer was a master of this approach, and many of us became his pupils and sought to do what he did, but none of us did it nearly as well.

But we no longer live in the modern world that privileges reason, science, and the empirical method of proving this or that to be true. Some bemoan the shift from the modern world. Some even hang onto the modern world because their theology is dependent on it. For them, the thought of thinking differently is threatening, so they do not want to go there.

But in the postmodern world, the way of knowing has changed. *We now live in a world in which people have lost interest in argument and have taken to story, imagination, mystery, ambiguity, and vision*—and it was Christianity as *story* that compelled my dinner guests to listen with interest.

However, this does not mean or at least should not mean the complete loss of reason. Reason has a place in story. It is Christian rationalism that has failed, not intelligent discourse. So there is no need to be afraid of story. Story is neither irrational nor relativistic. Spirituality is about God's story—how God reunites us to God's own purposes for our life in this world and the world to come.

Mystical-Union

The story of God is the story of how God unites with us so that we may be united to him. My dinner friends and I spent a great deal of time conversing about the universal human desire to be in union with God. We acknowledged that every religion in the world expresses the longing to be in union with God in one way or another. But Christianity presents a particular way that union with God is achieved. The Christian Scriptures teach that God created people to be in union with him and his purposes for creation. The early chapters of Genesis picture the union God enjoyed with Adam and Eve in the Garden of Eden. But the union between God and humanity was broken when Adam and Eve turned away from God and God's purposes for life. We, like them, have done the same.

How is this union with God recovered? The texts of the Christian faith tell us no matter how hard we try, there is nothing we can do to restore our union with God. That is the *bad news*. But the *good news* is that God does for us what we cannot do for ourselves. God became a man and lived in our skin, so to speak, to accomplish once again the union between God and humanity that was lost by Adam. The ancient fathers speak of God restoring our spiritual union with him by his own "two hands"[5]—Jesus and God's life-giving Spirit. *So spirituality is not a self-generated achievement but a gift given to us by God. This gift sets us free to see life in a new way and to live life as God intended, in union with the purposes of the Creator and Redeemer of the world.*

The Christian concept of union with God is not a new or novel idea. It is the most common description of spirituality throughout the entire history of the church. Veli-Matti Kärkkäinen, professor of systematic theology at Fuller, asks, "What is the way back to God, to live with God, to live in God and share in the divine?" From the beginning of the Christian faith, he asserts, the answer has been "union with God."[6] Philosopher and popular author on spirituality Dallas Willard declares, "God's desire for us is that we should live in him. He sends among us the way to himself. That shows what, in his heart of hearts, God is really like—indeed what *reality* is really like."[7] Philip Sheldrake, vice president of Sarum College in Salisbury, England, and a renowned historian and theologian of spirituality, points out that "spirituality is the whole human life viewed in terms of a conscious relationship with God, in Jesus Christ, through the indwelling of the Spirit, and within the community of believers."[8]

I don't doubt that for many spirituality as *union with God* is a new insight. And that is because *union with God* has become lost in the twentieth century. Spirituality has been wrenched from its origins in the story of God and set adrift to become just about anything. In this free-float state, spirituality has been more influenced by culture than by God's vision. Current spirituality, having asserted its independence from God's vision for the world, is expressed more as "a journey into self" than "a journey into God." Nevertheless, union with God does have to do with self, not as in the narcissistic self but as the challenge to be the new self—re-created to be all that God intends us to be in our restored nature and new state of being. For when God lives in us and we in him, we lose ourselves through a surrender of ourselves to the purposes of God. We become transformed selves.

Because this union is a *mystical*-union, I need to make clear how I am using the word *mystical* throughout this book. Bernard McGinn points out that we can distinguish "between two senses of mysticism: the implicit, general or objective mysticism of the new life 'hidden with Christ in God' (Col. 3:3), and explicit, special or subjectively realized mysticism, that is, the conscious experience of God's presence in the soul."[9] In both uses God's union with us is a mystery even as our union with God is a mystery. I use the words *mystical* and *mystery* throughout this book to refer, not to an esoteric spiritual experience, but to the mystery of our union with God.

God's union with us is referred to by Paul as a mystery. He speaks of "the revelation of the mystery hidden for long ages of the past, but now revealed and made known" (Rom. 16:25–26). He identifies this mystery in his letter to the Ephesians as "insight into the mystery of Christ" (Eph. 3:4). Christ is God's mystery made known. The plan of God to reunite the world is now revealed and known in Jesus. The mystery, then, applies to the story of God.

That God's story is a mystery doesn't mean that it can't be grasped in the heart or even in the mind, for it is a *revealed* mystery, a mystery that God "so loved the world, that he gave his only begotten Son" (John 3:16 KJV). It is the mystery of God's love that, while not subject to rationalism, is comprehended by us as an unbelievable, astonishing wonder, an awesome, incredible vision of the entire world, of all history, and of the meaning and purpose of all humanity. So also the mystery of God as triune—eternally dwelling in the community of Father, Son, and Holy Spirit—is the mystery in which our desire for relationship in community is situated. The mystery that God, overflowing with love, created a universe as a place of his glory tells us who gives meaning to nature, to the rhythm of life, to the seasons of beauty. That humanity rebelled against God and broke union with him is a mystery. The story of Abraham and Israel is the mystery of God's self-revelation. The mystery of the Virgin Mary proclaims that God became earthed for our sake, that God and man were united in Jesus, that God entered our suffering on the cross, and that Jesus rose from the grave, conquering death.

These events are the mysteries that change the way we see the world, the mysteries that compel our self-giving. That this God now lives in us and that God, at the end of history, will put away all evil and restore his heaven and earth—cleansed from all rebellion—and restore creation to what God originally intended is the mystery that fills our lives with hope. Thus, to regard God's story as a mystery does not mean we cannot talk about it, think about it, or explore its meaning. But it does mean that we must come to it with the worshiping mind of Paul who cried:

> Oh, the depth of the riches of the
> wisdom and knowledge of God!
> How unsearchable his judgments,
> and his paths beyond tracing out!
> "Who has known the mind of the Lord?
> Or who has been his counselor?"
> "Who has ever given to God,
> that God should repay him?"
> For from him and through him and to him are all things.
> To him be the glory forever! Amen.
>
> Romans 11:33–36

The term *mystery* also applies to our subjective experience. McGinn calls this mystery "the conscious experience of God's presence in the soul."[10] It is the experience of the union of God dwelling in us and we in him. And the way to experience this mystery is to live in it, to *embody* it through the spiritual life of contemplation and the way of participation.[11]

THE ACTIONS OF THE SPIRITUAL LIFE

If it is true that we are made spiritual because of God's union with us, it is also true that our *spiritual life* is the living out of God's union with us through contemplation and participation: the worship of God as a style of life.

The Way of Contemplation

In the spiritual life we choose to contemplate the mystery of the Triune God who creates and has entered into our history to reconcile the world through his mighty acts of salvation culminating in Jesus Christ. Contemplation is a prayerful pondering of the mystery, a wonder, a sense of astonishment and awe before the glory of it all.

The biblical image of contemplation that we are to follow is found in Mary, the mother of Jesus. After she was told of the mystery of God being united with the man-child Jesus in her womb, she responded in worship: "May it be to me as you have said" (Luke 1:38). She then "treasured up all these things and pondered them in her heart" (Luke 2:19). St. Augustine, the fifth-century father of the Western church, says, "Mary conceived the Word first in her mind and then in her body." He adds, "It would have been worth nothing to her to have carried Christ in her womb if she had not carried him with love in her heart."[12]

Our contemplation, like that of Mary's, is not a mere intellectual assent to God's story but "a free penetrating and fixed gaze,"[13] "a loving look at God."[14] It differs from meditation, which is the *search* for God. It is instead *"delight* in the found truth."[15] It is a real, genuine, internal delight in the story of God's rescue of creatures and creation. This delight in God expresses itself in the worship of God translated as a love for the story, a love for life, a love for this world.

Delight is the hope that swells up within us because this is such a good story, such an incredible drama of how God overcomes evil and establishes his kingdom throughout all creation. This world is not doomed to always be as it now is. There is hope, and in this hope we take great delight. Peter, a disciple of Jesus, put it this way: "Blessed be the God and Father of our Lord Jesus Christ! By his great mercy we have been born anew to a living hope through the resurrection of Jesus Christ from the dead" (1 Peter 1:3 RSV). To contemplate the story of God that is captured in this single verse is to delight in it, to simply love it, and to be energized by it, and this is a vital aspect of the Christian spiritual life. When Isabel, one of my four dinner guests, responded with, "That is a *good* story! What should we do?" those words expressed delight, wonder, awe, and faith.

The Way of Participation

The spiritual life of contemplation on God's story leads us to the second aspect of our spiritual life: choices we make to participate in God and God's purposes for life in this world. When we, like Isabel, upon hearing the story desire to participate in God, we are no longer preoccupied with self, the welfare of the self, the indulgence of the self, and the preservation of the self. Instead the focus is on God's purposes for our life and the life of the world.

Participation in God affirms life. To worship God through participation means to live life intentionally, choosing to live God's way in our personal life, in all of our relationships within the family, in the institutions of society, and in our vocations. This life in God in the world is shaped by an interior disposition—a heart that constantly wills to do what God desires for creatures and creation. To participate in God's story is to live a transformed life, a life that brings glimpses of the ultimate transformation of all creation when all that God has made is now in union with God's purposes and heaven and earth breaks forth in praise of its Creator and Redeemer.

The primary biblical example of participation in God is Jesus himself. Jesus, the incarnate Word, is the only man who "got it right." In Jesus God shows us what humanity should look like, for he reversed the disobedience of the first Adam, who rebelled against God's purposes for life, and gave us in his life the true image of a restored humanity. Jesus's life was a perfect participation in God. He himself expressed this union in the words of his prayer spoken on the night of his death: "As you are in me and I am in you" (John 17:21). Jesus died for us to destroy the ultimacy of death over us. He was resurrected from the grave so that a new life could be birthed in us. He now lives in us and unites us to God.

Our own spiritual lives are a participation in God through Christ, for it is "no longer I who live, but Christ who lives in me" (Gal. 2:20 RSV). God, who became human by the Spirit to unite himself with us, actually takes up residence within us and lives in us! So Christian spirituality is the experience of God living in us and the challenge of our living in God. It is as simple as that, but it goes deep, very deep, not only into the heart and soul of every person but into the heart and soul of God and of life itself.

The Divine Embrace

I capture this ancient understanding of spirituality—God's union with us and our union with God—in the image of the divine embrace found in the following words of *The Book of Common Prayer*: "Lord Jesus Christ, you stretched out your arms of love on the hard wood of the cross that everyone might come within the reach of your *saving embrace*: So clothe us in your Spirit that we, reaching forth our hands in love, may bring those who do not know you to the knowledge and love of you; for the honor of your Name. *Amen.*"[16]

I use the image of the divine embrace throughout this book to express both God's divine initiative and our human response. In this image I call for a spirituality that is not a mere search for a transcendent experience but a spirituality that is rooted in the unique story of God. I ask you not to subscribe to the relativism that all paths lead to God but to a countercultural affirmation that God, the Creator of the universe, has cut a path into our history and, having become one of us in Jesus, unites us with himself. Look in all the religions of the world and you will find no better story than this. God has come to us in Jesus so that we may come to God through Jesus. That is Christian spirituality. And living in that union, that divine embrace, that is the spiritual life.

How to Read This Book

The writing of *The Divine Embrace* has been a daunting task, a stretch, you might say. The problem for me was the need to bring a vast amount of material together under the cover of a single book. It would have been easier in some ways to write a multivolume introduction to spirituality. I found myself asking:

What does the Bible teach about spirituality?

How has what the Scriptures taught been developed theologically?

How has this biblical-theological spirituality been changed as it has bumped up against the ancient, medieval, Reformation, modern, and now postmodern cultures?

How has evangelicalism expressed or not expressed this spiritual tradition?

How does the present spiritual culture of New Age and Eastern religions affect Christian spirituality?

How do we experience and live out a biblical-theological spirituality?

Once I had a sense of these questions, I asked, "How do you present all this material in a coherent way, a way that will make a difference in the life of the reader?" After numerous false starts, I realized that I needed to approach the structure of the book as a story developed through Christian history. After all, *ancient-future* means that the road to the future runs through the past. So to know the future of spirituality, we need to know its past—its origins, its formation, the road it has traveled, its present state, the challenges that lie ahead. That's what Ancient-Future, which is the overall title of this series of books, means.

So part 1 tells the story of spirituality from the ancient church to the present day. In chapter 2, I briefly summarize God's story of creation, incarnation, and re-creation and show how the biblical story was challenged by the Gnostics, the Arians, the Nestorians, Pelagius, and those who insisted Jesus had only a divine will. Through these challenges I show how God's story was defended and clarified by the creeds and common writings of the ancient fathers of the church, who affirm our union with God as a gift and the spiritual life as contemplation and participation. I then show how this life-affirming spirituality became modified by Platonic dualism, which separated spirit and matter and redefined union with God to necessitate a renunciation of the world. I also show how late medieval mysticism separated spirituality from God's story and redefined the spiritual life as a journey into the interior self.

Chapter 3 continues the story of spirituality from the Reformation era through the nineteenth century. The Reformers, mindful of the late medieval separation of spirituality from God's story for the world, returned to the consensus of the ancient church and affirmed with slight variations the ancient, life-affirming union with God. But again, ancient spirituality affirmed by the Reformers was modified by new cultural movements in the modern world. The first movement is a turn toward an intellectual union: influenced by rationalism, the contemplation of God's embrace and participation in God's purposes for the world is replaced by knowing God through an embrace of right doctrine. A second modification of spirituality is found in an overemphasis on experience. The revivalists, influenced by romanticism, shifted the focus of contemplation from the story of God to a preoccupation with personal experience.

Then chapter 4 concentrates on the story of spirituality only within the evangelical history of the twentieth century. Evangelical spirituality, having lost union with God, draws primarily from the rational and the experiential approaches to spirituality developed in the eighteenth and nineteenth centuries. These views dominated the expressions of spirituality enunciated in the first two-thirds of the century. In the last thirty years of the twentieth century, evangelical spirituality has been shaped by the culture of narcissism, romanticism, and consumerism.

Now, what about the future? Chapter 5 addresses the need to be deeply concerned about the future of spirituality because of the new spiritual context in which we live. In this, the final chapter of part 1, I address the issue of the new spiritualities, especially the New Age movement and Eastern religions. I argue that the new pluralistic and relativistic world in which we live demands us to recover a spirituality grounded in the biblical and theological tradition of the early church or else Christian spirituality will continue to be shaped by the cultural narrative and become one among many attempts to achieve an "experience of transcendence."

I recognize that part 1, especially the historical material of chapters 2 and 3, will be a difficult read for some. You can skip those two chapters if the details bog you down. But do come back to them later, for they show how Christian spirituality became redefined by the new mysticism and other forms of spirituality from which Christians need to be rescued.

Part 2, where I concentrate on the recovery of a biblical and historical spirituality, can be understood without the historical background. But it will be significantly more clear with the historical perspective in mind.

Part 2 addresses a different set of questions. Part 1 asks, "How has spirituality been separated from the biblical-theological tradition of the ancient church?" or, "What does spirituality need to be rescued from?" In part 2 I ask, "How can we return spirituality to the biblical-theological convictions in which it was originally situated?" The story of part 2, then, is a story of reconstruction. My hope is that we can move beyond intellectual, legalistic, experiential, or culturally conditioned spiritualities to affirm once again our union with God in the divine embrace.

I have chosen to develop this story out of two sets of paradoxes. The words listed below capture both God's initiative and our response expressed in the divine embrace. You may want to memorize these paradoxes, contemplate their meaning, and participate in the reality they present. They represent the basic features of our return to an ancient spirituality:

God's Story
My Story
His Life in Mine
My Life in His
Life Together

God's Story, which I present in chapter 6, is God's incarnate embrace. When God created the world, he had a vision for us humans and for the whole creation. This vision was rejected at the fall, but God became involved in history to restore his vision. *His Story* deals with God's recovery of his vision for the world through his own two hands—Jesus and the Spirit. I ask you to approach God's incarnational embrace through three great typologies of Scripture: (1) creation/re-creation, (2) the first Adam/second Adam, (3) the Exodus event/Christ event. I then close this chapter with the biblical and ancient understanding of *recapitulation*. God does his work of creation over again. He re-creates and makes all things new in Jesus Christ. God's embrace in Christ calls us who are *in him* to return to God's original purposes in creating us and the world. Our spiritual life is situated in this embrace of God. Because God embraces us, we *embrace God* and God's vision for our lives and the world.

My Story, the subject of chapter 7, deals with: "How do *we* embrace God's story? How do *we* enter God's story in order to live the spiritual life?" Acts 2:38–46 gives us insight into the oldest answer to this question. In this passage of Scripture, Peter tells his listeners to do three things: (1) repent, (2) be baptized for the forgiveness of sins, and (3) receive the gift of the Holy Spirit. In contemporary evangelicalism, too little is made of Peter's instruction. Repentance has been replaced in some circles

by a "feel good about yourself" mentality; baptism is ignored by some
and interpreted as "my witness" by many others; and confusion seems
to reign about the Holy Spirit. I seek to restore the ancient view that
(1) repentance is continual, (2) baptism is the sign of God's re-creative
power, and (3) the Spirit is the living seal of God. The *rites* connected
to these three aspects of coming into God's story bring us into a contemplation of God's work in history through which God's vision for the
world has been restored. Consequently, the focus of spirituality is not
a contemplation of self but a contemplation of God, who gifts us with
a restored spiritual calling to be what he created us to be and to make
the world the place of his glory.

His Life in Mine, the subject of chapter 8, moves from the contemplation of the wonders of God's mystery known in Jesus Christ to a
participation in God's embrace in life where we live, move, and have
our being. This chapter asks, "How do we live out God's embrace? How
do we become the person God created us to be?" (The second overarch-
ing question of this book, "How do we make this world the place of
God's glory?" is not the primary subject of this book. But it is obvious
that when we become the person God created us to be, it will make an
impact on every aspect of life. Another book needs to be written to address that question.)

So, how do you participate in God's embrace for your life? The biblical key is baptism—immersion into the life, death, and resurrection of
Jesus Christ. This is the pattern of spirituality—putting *off* the *old* person
who has been buried with Christ in his death; putting *on* the *new* person
raised to the new life of the Spirit.

My Life in His, the concern of chapter 9, tells us how to stay in the
baptismal pattern of death and resurrection. I draw from the rule of St.
Benedict to show how this rule calls on us to make vows of stability,
fidelity, and obedience; to commit to the disciplines of study, prayer,
and work; to encounter Christ in daily life, in material things, and in
people. The discipline of the monastic life is not only for monastics but
is applicable to all Christians in their daily union with God.

The fifth aspect of the spiritual life is *Life Together*, the nourishment
of the whole person through the Christian church and its worship—the
subject of chapter 10. In this chapter I present how the church is the
continuation of the presence of Christ and, as such, is to be the community of God's embrace through which and in which the spiritual
purposes of God in the world are made manifest. Worship proclaims
and enacts God's embrace of us and the world in his incarnation, death,
and resurrection and nourishes us in the spiritual life. Worship points
to the ultimate purpose of all history: the eternal worship of God by
creatures and creation.

Finally, I end with some concluding comments titled: *No Story but God's; No God but the Father, Son, and Spirit; No Life but the Baptized Life.*

At the end of each chapter is *a summary for reflection and conversation.* There are several uses for this summary. First, if you are the kind of person who likes to see the whole picture of a book, how it is organized internally and developed into a perspective, you can gain this insight by reading the summaries at the end of each chapter before reading the book in detail. Having the entire story of the book in mind, you can read each chapter more profitably. Second, the summaries are there for your personal reflection to stimulate your own spiritual life toward deeper contemplation of God's mysteries and to move you toward a more intentional participation in the purposes of God for your life and the life of the world. Finally, the summary is a guide for group discussion and, if followed, will keep the conversation focused and applicable.

I have also added suggestions for extensive reading in theological areas not fully developed in the text in the *notes with commentary,* and in the *selected bibliography.* I am an endnote reader myself and almost always read endnotes before I read a book. I want to see who has influenced the author's thought and where this book intends to take me. Because *The Divine Embrace* will take you into some very old places of thought that are now being rediscovered, I point to a broad and rich reading list in the *bibliography* for a more comprehensive study than what I am able to do in a single synthesized writing.

CONCLUSION

The concern of this writing is to go back to the earliest convictions of Christian spirituality. Why go back? Because the Roman culture in which Christianity first emerged is very similar to the culture of today's world. It was a culture of political unrest, a world of numerous religious options, a time of moral confusion and poverty. The religions of the day made no demands on believing, behaving, or belonging. In this context the Christian message was not presented as one more spirituality among the spiritualities but as Alan Kreider points out, Christians proclaimed, "We believe, we behave, we belong."[17] One would think that the clarity of union with God in the context of the plurality of religions would doom it to failure. But it was that very union with God—lived out in belief, behavior, and belonging—that resulted in the rapid spread of the Christian faith throughout the Roman Empire.

Today our world culture is very similar to the culture in which the Christian faith first emerged—worldwide political unrest, competing world religions making their way to everyone's doorstep and into everyone's home through television, unprecedented poverty, and the complete breakdown of moral standards. Is it possible that the spirituality that took root in the Roman world can do the same in today's world? Is it possible to once again narrate the world by God's story?

The writing of this book has made a great impact on my own spiritual life. God's story, which I have always known at least in outline form, began to take on new meaning for me as I researched, reflected, and wrote. It is a great story no matter how you look at it, but I think my tendency has been to see God's story as a mere intellectual worldview. But the day-by-day study, the chewing on this story and on its implications for my life, has warmed my heart and has done what real contemplation ought to do—burst within me a new and deeper delight, not just in the story of God but in God himself. So I invite you, the reader, to not only read this book but to let it lead you into a new delight in God. For God's story is not a *thing* apart from God but the very life of God in the life of the world. Consequently we are called to this story, not as an idea that needs to be defended with intellectual argument as if its validity depends on proof, but we are called to enter the story by delighting in it and participating in it. For true spiritual life is not an escape from life but a passionate embrace of life itself, which, it turns out, is an embrace of God and God's purposes for our life here in this world and in the eternal praise of God in the new heavens and the new earth.

A SUMMARY FOR REFLECTION AND CONVERSATION

Summary	Reflection
Spirituality is our mystical-union with God through Jesus Christ by the Spirit.	Spirituality is grounded in the triune nature of God.
Christian spirituality is situated in the *story* of God.	God is creating, incarnating, re-creating a habitation for himself, a people to be his family. God unites us to himself by "his own two hands."
God is *united* to humanity in order to unite humanity to himself through his death and resurrection.	Incarnational spirituality—God dwells in us and we in him.
Contemplation	A delight in the mystery of God creating, incarnating, and re-creating by his own two hands.
Participation	Be what you were created to be; make this world a habitation of God's glory.
The divine embrace	The appropriate image for biblical and ancient spirituality.

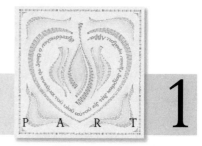

P A R T 1

THE CRISIS

*How Spirituality Became Separated
from the Divine Embrace*

THE CRISIS: HOW SPIRITUALITY BECAME SEPARATED FROM THE DIVINE EMBRACE

Chapter 2   *The story of God's divine embrace in the incarnation, death, and resurrection of Jesus was defended by the ancient creeds and debates of the church. Spirituality and the spiritual life, situated in the divine embrace, was modified by Platonic dualism, which saw spirituality as an escape from this world, and late medieval mysticism, which interpreted spirituality as a journey into self.*

Chapter 3   The Reformers returned spirituality to the divine embrace with some modification. In the modern era spirituality as the divine embrace was redefined by a spirituality preoccupied with a forensic justification combined with sanctification guided by gratitude, and a spirituality that focused on the conversion experience followed by a flight from the world.

Chapter 4   Twentieth-century evangelical spirituality inherited the modifications of the past and developed privatized spiritualities of legalism, intellectualism, and experientialism.

Chapter 5   The present evangelical practices of spirituality, separated from the divine embrace, are inadequate to the challenge of the widespread popularity of New Age and Eastern spiritualities grounded in an impersonal, pantheistic conception of God and the world. The challenge before us is to recover a spirituality and spiritual life situated in the divine embrace.

2

A HISTORICAL PERSPECTIVE 1 (AD 30–1500)

Rescuing Spirituality from Dualism and Mysticism

B ecause I will tell the story of how spirituality became separated from God's story in so few pages, I ask you to approach this chapter as a person throwing a stone into a body of water, watching it skim across the water, rising here and there, perhaps a half dozen times before sinking. Standing before two thousand years of history, determined to comment on how Christian spirituality became separated from God's story is like throwing that stone. We can only watch it hit the surface now and again.[1]

The relationship of spirituality to God's story has a long history in Christian thought. This relationship has been affirmed, challenged, distorted, lost, and regained in various epochs of history. Today spirituality is separated from God's story. In his crucial work, *Spirituality and Theology*, Philip Sheldrake points out that "contemporary spiritual writing is open to the accusation that it amounts to little more than uncritical devotion quite detached from the major themes of Christian faith."[2] In order to understand this separation, I will comment briefly in this chapter on (1) how God's story was affirmed in the ancient Christian church and (2) how the story was lost through Platonic dualism and in late medieval mysticism. In chapter 3 I will address how ancient spirituality was regained with some moderation by the Reformers and how Christian spirituality was lost again in the modern shifts toward intellectual and experiential spiritualities together. We will look at these points in Western history where the stone skims the water and through this history gain a perspective on the crisis of spirituality in the twentieth and twenty-first centuries (treated in chapters 4 and 5).

What I offer is a brief interpretation of the history of spirituality. I recognize the complexity of the subject and realize the events and persons I choose to look at are not comprehensive. My goal, therefore, as the title of these chapters suggests is *perspective*.

HOW GOD'S STORY AND SPIRITUALITY WERE AFFIRMED IN THE ANCIENT CHURCH

The ancient church fathers understood that "attempts to speak about our understanding of God (theology) and our efforts to live in the light of that understanding (spirituality) cannot be separated."[3] Spirituality is a *lived theology*. We too must understand that the Christian convictions about God and God's truth are not mere philosophical abstractions. Theology is actually meant to be *lived wisdom*.

I have already mentioned that the key to understanding spirituality as lived theology is found in God's vision of creation, incarnation, and re-creation. The Triune God creates a world in which to dwell and a people to be his family. He gives them the task of making the world the theater of his glory. They rebel (the fall) and turn against their Creator, and the culture they make reflects their rebellion against God's purposes for themselves and the world. God becomes involved in creation to reverse the order of things, to redeem the world, and to restore his rule over creation. God accomplishes his restoration of creation in the incarnation, in which he unites with humanity, taking into himself the sin and suffering of the world so that humanity may be united with him once again. By his death and resurrection he triumphs over sin and death and begins the new creation that will be fulfilled in the new heavens and earth. This message is captured in the words of Paul to the Corinthians:

> But Christ has indeed been raised from the dead, the firstfruits of those who have fallen asleep. For since death came through a man, the resurrection of the dead comes also through a man. For as in Adam all died, so in Christ all will be made alive. But each in his own turn: Christ, the firstfruits; then, when he comes, those who belong to him. Then the end will come, when he hands over the kingdom to God the Father after he has destroyed all dominion, authority and power. For he must reign until

he has put all his enemies under his feet. The last enemy to be destroyed is death. For he "has put everything under his feet."

1 Corinthians 15:20–27

The key truth that Paul proclaims is that God in Christ reclaims the entire creation from the tyranny of a disordered world brought about by the rebellious nature of the human condition. Because we have been united with God through Jesus Christ, our spiritual life is to live in this union, to passionately embrace God's vision of a renewed world.

This Scripture story of creation, incarnation, and re-creation was challenged in the ancient church by the emergence of various heresies. But it was also this vision of God that was defended by the ancient Christian creeds. Christian spirituality, as we will see, is unequivocally situated in the doctrines challenged by the heretics. So it is within the creedal statements about God that we find a biblical spirituality articulated, defended, and preserved.

GOD AS CREATOR CHALLENGED

The first challenge came from the Gnostics, who rejected God as Creator. There were many Gnostic sects that emerged in the New Testament period and grew in great numbers in the second century. Although there were differences between these groups, they shared a common theology based on a nonbiblical dualism between two Gods: the spirit God and the creator God. This dualism was based on Paul's contrast between "flesh" and "spirit," which the Gnostics argued referred to an eternal conflict between two sources of good and evil. The evil God was Yahweh, the creator God, the God of the Old Testament. The good God was the spirit God. The soul, the Gnostics argued, came from the spirit God and is imprisoned in the material body, which came from the evil God. The soul wants to do what is good, but the flesh, our bodies, do evil.

In Gnosticism, spirituality is, as Bengt Hägglund points out, "the freeing of the spirit from its bondage in the material realm."[4] It is Jesus who sets us free. He was sent by the spirit God as an apparition (not a physical incarnation, or Jesus would also be imprisoned in a body). Gnostics taught that the path of spirituality is to *deny the body in order to release the soul to live in the spiritual realm.*

This battle raged in the latter half of the second century. It was no small disagreement consuming the energies of the major defenders of the biblical story, especially the work of Irenaeus in the East and Tertullian in the West. By the end of the second century the biblical vision of only *one* God, Father, Son, and Holy Spirit, who *creates* all things visible and invisible and *redeems* the physical creation through the Word incarnate and the Spirit, won the day and resulted in the Apostles' Creed. In the ancient church the Apostles' Creed was no abstract doctrine but spiritual life itself. It was taught as a weapon in spiritual warfare, and all persons coming to baptism were required to memorize it and *live in its truth*.

Apostles' Creed

I believe in God, the Father almighty,
    creator of heaven and earth.
I believe in Jesus Christ, his only Son, our Lord.
    He was conceived by the power of the Holy Spirit
        and born of the Virgin Mary.
    He suffered under Pontius Pilate,
        was crucified, died, and was buried.
    He descended to the dead.
    On the third day he rose again.
    He ascended into heaven,
        And is seated at the right hand of the Father.
    He will come again to judge the living and the dead.
I believe in the Holy Spirit,
    the holy catholic Church,
    the communion of saints,
    the forgiveness of sins,
    the resurrection of the body,
    and the life everlasting. Amen.[5]

The creed affirms God as Creator and confesses that God became incarnate in our history to re-create the world and bring it under his reign.

In the ancient church the Apostles' Creed was essential to spirituality. It was confessed at all baptisms and to this day is known as the baptismal creed, the faith of those who embrace Christ. At a recent baptism I heard the minister cry out, "This is the faith of the church, and we are proud to proclaim it." For this pastor and congregation, the creed is no dry intellectual statement. Over against Gnostic dualism in the ancient church and New Age and Eastern religions today, the Apostles' Creed proclaims that the only God—Father, Son, and Holy Spirit—creates, enters into our history to redeem it from its fallen condition, and will come again to restore creation to its original purpose. So the spiritual conflict of this world is not between the spirit and physical flesh. Instead, this world's spiritual conflict is a life lived under God's reign versus a life lived in rebellion against God's purposes for creation.

This is why the ancient church required new Christians to memorize the Apostles' Creed as a "weapon of spiritual warfare."[6] Because spirituality is the living out of God's purposes for creation, creational theology is essential to Christian spirituality. The Scriptures affirm the unity of spirit and matter and embrace creation not only as the imprint of the creativity of God but also the place where God's will is to be done even as it is done in heaven. Dualism separates spirit and matter and seeks to be *spiritual* through the renunciation of life in this world. The Apostles' Creed, the earliest creed of the church, keeps the world God created and our union with him together. The spiritual life is emphatically life in this world—the world that God has created and loves.

THE INCARNATION OF GOD CHALLENGED

The second challenge to a spirituality situated in God's story occurred in the fourth century. The issue up for debate focused on the second article of the Apostles' Creed: "I believe in Jesus Christ, his only Son, our Lord." The questions were: "What is the relationship of the Son to the Father?" "Who was it who became incarnate in our material world?" "Is the Son of God God, or is the Son of God a creature appointed by God to become incarnate?"

According to Arius, a presbyter (minister) and the chief architect of the debate, God could not become incarnate in the flesh because spirit and matter could not be united.[7] Therefore Arius taught that the Son of God was not God. He was not even "like God" but instead was declared to be "unlike God." Because God the Father could not unite with matter, God's first act of creation was to bring a son into being, who was a different essence than himself. Arius's famous slogan was "There was a time when he was not," indicating, of course, that the Son was a creation of God and not God. So here is the picture according to Arius: God did create. There was a rebellion against God, and the world has been redeemed. But God did not become incarnate himself. He created a Son different than himself, who became incarnate to save the world.

Arius's interpretation of God's story undermined the biblical teaching that it was God himself who became incarnate in his own creation to restore it (John 1:14). Athanasius, the chief opponent to Arius, argued that the Son was the "same as" the Father. His argument was that "if the Son was not the same essence as the Father, then God did not save us." His famous slogan, "God became one of us that we may become God," means God became one of us in the incarnation to restore his original purposes for creation and humanity. God renewed the union of himself and humanity in his incarnation, died, and was raised for our reconciliation.

The incarnation, therefore, is the thread that ties creation and re-creation together. "It was the almighty creator Himself who carried out the work of salvation, so that fallen creation might be restored to its original destiny."[8] God, as a man, reversed the curse that hangs over creation because of the rebellion of man. In Jesus Christ, God is made our sacrifice for sin; he is victor over the powers of evil; he begins again his original purposes in creating the world. In Jesus Christ all God's purposes for humanity and creation are fulfilled. Therefore God, being made man, not only unites us to God but reveals how humans are to live in this world. In this way God both gifts us in spiritual union with himself (spirituality) and models how we are to live (the spiritual life).

Ultimately the Athanasian view was affirmed because it was consistent with the biblical teaching that the incarnate Word is God. He is not *like* God; he *is* God. He who is the very essence of God is united with the very essence of humanity. This Arius/Athanasius debate produced the Nicene Creed, which was originally written in AD 325 and ratified by the church in the Council of Constantinople, AD 381. (Note that I have put in italics the phrases affirming that the Son of God is God.)

Nicene Creed

We believe in one God,
    the Father, the Almighty,
    maker of heaven and earth,
    of all that is, seen and unseen.

We believe in one Lord, Jesus Christ,
    the only Son of God,
    eternally begotten of the Father,
    God from God, Light from Light,
    true God from true God,
    begotten, not made,
    of one Being with the Father.
    Through him all things were made.
    For us and for our salvation
        he came down from heaven:
    by the power of the Holy Spirit
        he became incarnate from the Virgin Mary,
        and was made man.
    For our sake he was crucified under Pontius Pilate;
        he suffered death and was buried.
        On the third day he rose again
            in accordance with the Scriptures;
        he ascended into heaven
            and is seated at the right hand of the Father.
    He will come again in glory to judge the living and the dead,
        and his kingdom will have no end.

We believe in the Holy Spirit, the Lord, the giver of life,
    who proceeds from the Father and the Son.
With the Father and the Son he is worshiped and glorified.
He has spoken through the Prophets.
We believe in one holy catholic and apostolic Church.
We acknowledge one baptism for the forgiveness of sins.
We look for the resurrection of the dead,
    and the life of the world to come. Amen.[9]

Once again we see the very structure of God's story—creation, incarnation, re-creation—was affirmed. The creed answers the question, "Why has God been united to our humanity?" The answer: "For us and our salvation he came down from heaven." God's story, the Nicene Creed affirms, is not about a creature God makes and sends to restore us and the world. God's story is about God, God of very God, the very essence of God uniting with the very essence of man to save us. The spiritual union we enjoy with God is not of our own making, it is initiated by God, accomplished by God, and given to us as a gift from God because God united our humanity with his in the relationship established in the incarnation. The implication for spirituality is clear: we earnestly *contemplate* (delight in) the mystery of God revealed in the incarnation and choose to *participate* in the purposes of God for humanity revealed originally to Adam, now fulfilled and modeled for us in Jesus.

THE DIVINE INITIATIVE CHALLENGED

It was the message that God saves us and gifts us with spiritual life that created the third challenge to God's story: "Why do we have to come to God through Jesus and the Spirit? Don't we in and of ourselves have the capacity to choose the holy life?" This challenge was raised by the monk and itinerant preacher Pelagius. He argued against the fall of all humanity insisting that "it is possible for a man to be without sin," that it is therefore possible for a person to do "a good work" that would be pleasing to God, although he does admit that all good works are "by the help of his grace" who "ever assists this very possibility." Pelagius's teaching, however, denies the giftedness of spirituality. Instead he places the achievement of spirituality within the will of the person enabled by God to actualize his own spiritual state of being. "We distinguish three things and arrange them in a definite order. We put in the first place *'posse'* [ability, possibility]; in the second, *'velle'* [volition]; in the third, *'esse'* [existence, actuality]. The *posse* we assign to nature, the *velle* to will, the *esse* to actual realization. The first of these, *posse*, is properly ascribed to God, who conferred it on his creatures; while the other two, *velle* and *esse*, are to be referred to the human agent, since they have their source in his will."[10]

It was Augustine, the great Western father of the church, who became the main opponent of Pelagius in the fourth century. Augustine argued that "a man's free choice avails only to lead him to sin, if the way of truth be hidden from him."[11] The doctrines of Pelagius were rejected in AD 407 at the Council of Carthage, and again in the Council of Orange, AD 529, the notion was rejected that "God's grace can be bestowed in response to human invocation."[12] By rejecting Pelagianism, the church affirmed that our spirituality is not accomplished by our initiative but by God, who became incarnate as Jesus Christ, his Son, the second Adam, to do for us what we are unable to do for ourselves—unite us to God. So the spiritual life, that is union with God and walking in his way, is not what we do, *not our works*, but *the enablement of the Spirit to do God's purposes in the world*.

THE UNION OF GOD AND MAN CHALLENGED

A fourth challenge to God's story revolved around the interpretation of John 1:14, "The Word became flesh and dwelt among us" (RSV). How are divinity and humanity united in Jesus?

Again, there were differences of opinion. All recognized that a union between the human and divine took place in the womb of the Virgin Mary. But what was the relationship of divinity and humanity in this union? And does this even matter? Some argued for a view in which the divine nature overshadowed the human nature. The human nature, this view proclaimed, was a real and true human nature, but it was absorbed into the divine nature. This view was defeated by the argument that if Jesus's humanity was absorbed into the divine nature, then our human nature was not fully united with God through the incarnation, and therefore Jesus was not properly the second Adam. It was not really one of us, then, who died for sin and was resurrected for us all.

Another group argued for the relationship between the human and divine this way: instead of absorbing the human nature into the divine nature, the two were separated and turned into two centers of activity. In this two-nature theory Jesus was truly a man, but his divinity, they said, was only called upon to do divine things—like divine insights, miracles, and such—while his normal, day-to-day life was lived out of his humanity. The criticism leveled against the "two separate nature theory" was that it was not a complete union of the human and the divine but a mere association of the two natures. If the human was only associated with divinity, then God was not completely united to humanity. God could not have fully entered our suffering on the cross nor fully participate in the resurrection of humanity.

In time it became clear that the union of God and man in the incarnation was not correctly expressed in anything other than the paradox of a union of 100 percent God with a union of 100 percent man. Jesus Christ, it was taught, was really God because "only God could save." But Jesus Christ was fully man because "only man could undo what man had done." The Scriptures speak clearly on this matter. In regard to the divine, it is *God* who is "reconciling the world to himself in Christ" (2 Cor. 5:19). In regard to the human, "Since death came through a man, the resurrection of the dead comes also through a man. For as in Adam all die, so in Christ all will be made alive" (1 Cor. 15:21–22). In Jesus Christ God is acting in union with us to restore our union with him.

The answer to the question "What is the relationship of the two natures of Jesus?" was answered this way: "He is *God* who has become one of us; he is a *man* who is in union with God." This paradox of Jesus as the God-man was affirmed in the Chalcedon Creed of AD 451, which summed up the debate but left it in the realm of mystery, not completely explainable:

> Therefore, following the holy fathers, we all with one accord teach men to acknowledge one and the same Son, our Lord Jesus Christ, at once complete in Godhead and complete in manhood, truly God and truly man, consisting also of a reasonable soul and body; of one substance (*homoousios*) with the Father as regards his Godhead, and at the same time of one substance with us as regards his manhood; like us in all respects, apart from sin; as regards his Godhead, begotten of the Father before the ages, but yet as regards his manhood begotten, *for us men and for our salvation*, of Mary the Virgin, the God-bearer (*Theotokos*); one and the same Christ, Son, Lord, Only-begotten, recognized in two natures, *without confusion, without change, without division, without separation*; the distinction of natures being in no way annulled by the union, but rather the characteristics of each nature being preserved and coming together to form one person and subsistence, not as parted or separated into two persons, but one and the same Son and Only-begotten God the Word, Lord Jesus Christ; even as the prophets from earliest times spoke of him and our Lord Jesus Christ himself taught us, the creed of the Fathers has handed down to us.[13]

The key to the Chalcedon Creed is the union of the human and the divine in the "one person and subsistence." These are Latin words not found in the Bible but words used to preserve the biblical teaching of the incarnation of God and humanity as a real union between the fullness of divinity and the fullness of humanity. Divinity and humanity were united in one single person, Jesus Christ. This never happened before, and it will never happen again. Jesus Christ is the one man who saves all.[14]

The Chalcedon Creed, like the Nicene Creed, states the reason for this incarnation of God into our humanity. It was "for us men and for our salvation." The implication for spirituality is this: In the incarnation God and man were united. In the incarnation God lifted humanity into union with himself in Jesus. The union humanity once had with God, lost in Adam, is now restored. God has restored union with humanity through his own two hands. God, the incarnate Word, united with our humanity by the Spirit, reverses the human condition through his death and resurrection.

Spirituality situated in the theology of creation, incarnation, and re-creation is captured in this early Christian prayer—a prayer that because of its theological depth stirs the heart to delight as it contemplates the great mystery of God who renews all things to his glory:

> Unceasingly do we adore thy life-giving Cross, O Christ our God,
>   and glorify thy Resurrection on the third day; for thereby, O
>   Almighty One,
> thou didst renew the nature of man, which had become corrupt,
>   and didst restore to us the way to heaven: For thou only art
>   good and lovest mankind.
> Thou hast done away with the penalty of the tree of disobedience,
> O Saviour, in that thou, of thine own good will, wast nailed to the
>   tree of the Cross; and when thou hadst descended into Hell, O
>   mighty One, thou didst break the bonds of death, in that thou
>   wert God: For which cause we worship
> thy Resurrection from the dead, joyfully crying unto thee: O Lord
>   Almighty,
>   glory to thee.
> Thou hast destroyed the gates of Hell, O Lord, and by thy death
>   hast annihilated the kingdom of Death, and hast freed the
>   human race from corruption, giving life and incorruption and
>   great mercy unto the world.
> Glory to the Father, and to the Son, and to the Holy Spirit,
>   now and ever, and unto ages of ages. Amen.[15]

THE HUMAN WILL OF JESUS CHALLENGED

There is one more theological controversy from the ancient church that is crucial to our understanding of spirituality: does Jesus have a human will? The monothelite (one will) controversy, which emerged in the seventh century, taught that Jesus had only one will—the divine will.

The argument was that Jesus was motivated in all his human actions by the divine will.

This notion that Jesus had only one will was rejected at the Council of Constantinople in AD 681. This council affirmed the unity of the two wills, the human and the divine, in Jesus in the same way that the Chalcedon Creed (AD 451) had affirmed the union of the two natures in the one person. This debate was crucial for spirituality. It affirmed that Jesus, as a man, totally and fully acted on our behalf to reverse the rebellion of Adam through the submission of his own free will to the will of God. Just as Adam willed to rebel against the will of God, so Jesus willed to be obedient to the Father, restoring our will, so that we too may will to do the will of the Father. Because Jesus has attained our spirituality, our union with God, through his own will by the Spirit, so our spiritual life is expressed through the constant free identification with the divine will. The spiritual life is lived in the passionate choice to will God's will in all our living. The exercise of Jesus's will to always do the will of the Father is the key to our participation in God. Like Jesus, we participate in God by submitting our will to do the purposes of God perfectly modeled for us and even already accomplished for us by Jesus.[16]

THEOSIS

The Eastern fathers, following the creeds of the church, championed a spirituality of *theosis* or *deification*. These words are unfamiliar to Protestants, but their meaning is not. They refer to a participation in God through Jesus Christ by the power of the Spirit, based on the classical doctrines explained above.

The word *theosis* is a combination of the Greek *theo* (God) and *osis*, a causative verb that refers to an action or a process. *Theosis* is the state or process of participation in God. On the other hand, the Latin word *deification* means essentially the same thing. It is a combination of *deus* (God) and *ficare*, which means to make. To be deified is to be made one with God and God's mission and purposes in the world.

The fathers of the church and later Eastern writers very clearly state that *theosis* and *deification* do not mean that the spiritual state brings the believer into the very essence of God. Only one person shares in the essence of God, and that is the incarnate Word, who also shares the essence of man. The fathers are clear that the essence of our humanity is not lost or absorbed into divinity through the union of man with God.

Perhaps a better way for us to grasp the meaning of *theosis* and *deification* is to use the word *relationship*. However, the word *relationship* may not be strong enough to express the Eastern grasp of participation in Jesus and through him a participation in the very communal life of the Father, Son, and Holy Spirit that *theosis* and *deification* imply. In Eastern thought, the goal of the Christian is to so commune with God that he or she is made more and more in the image of Christlikeness, fulfilling God's purposes for humanity in God's creation.

Gregory of Nyssa, a fourth-century Eastern father, captures both the distinction between God and man and the spiritual process of divinization when he writes, "The soul grows by its constant participation in that which transcends it; and yet the perfection in which the soul shares remains ever the same, and is always discovered by the soul to be transcendent to the same degree."[17] This quote translated into common Christian language means:

1. We are in Christ and through him in God.
2. We are to continually grow in the likeness of Christ, who is the image of God.
3. The more we grow, the more we discover how far removed we are from the perfection of God.
4. So the spiritual life is a constant movement toward Christlikeness,
5. and the spiritual life of each of us results in a collective good for the world.

The conviction of *deification* has been basic to Orthodox Christians throughout their history. It is found in the desert fathers and developed in Evagrius of Pontus (d. 399), Macarius (d. 389), and Gregory Palamas (1296–1359), the theologian of the prayer tradition of *Hesychasim* (named after John the Hesychast, AD 400), which teaches union with God through unceasing prayer. Modern-day Kallistos Ware presents *deification* this way: "To be deified is, more specifically, to be 'christified': the divine likeness that we are called to attain is the likeness of Christ. It is through Jesus the God-man that we men are 'ingodded,' 'divinized,' made 'shares in the divine nature' (2 Peter 1:4)."[18] This unity between theology and spirituality has been maintained in the major spiritual writings of orthodoxy to this very day, as illustrated in the quote from Ware.

SUMMARY: ANCIENT SPIRITUALITY IS A THEOLOGICAL SPIRITUALITY

I want you to see that these theological issues constitute the primary theological convictions of spirituality. Some may ask, "Why bother with all this theological stuff? Isn't it sufficient to simply follow Jesus?" Philip Sheldrake answers this question by showing us that we are called to *live this theology*. God's story is no abstract, esoteric story that has nothing to do with life. God's story is the very essence of Christian living. Life is not a willy-nilly, "be nice to your neighbor" philosophy but a life to be lived in the way God designed it to be lived. This new life is to be a very reflection of God's own being and nature. Philip Sheldrake notes:

> Any version of Christian spirituality that is individualistic in tone fails to reflect the communion of equal relationships that is God-in-Trinity. It is not surprising that the nature of the Christian life was always an issue at the heart of early debates about the doctrine of God. To think of God as Trinity is fundamentally to assert, among other things, that within God there is society or relationship. To affirm that human beings are created in the image of that God implies that they are called to share more and more in the deep communion that is divine life itself. The crucial is the intimate link between the fundamental nature of God and God as revealed through creation and salvation.
>
> Spiritualities that are disengaged from the world rather than committed to it, and to its transformation, fail to reflect the irrevocable commitment of God to the world in Jesus Christ. This is what the doctrine of the incarnation seeks to express. Belief in the incarnation also invites people to adopt a balanced approach to human nature and especially to its material dimension, the body. This should be neither radically pessimistic or naively optimistic. The incarnation is more than a defence of the reality and importance of the human nature of Jesus Christ. It is a governing principle of Christian living; of God's way of relating to creation and our way of response. This means that the Christian vision of God, and God's self-disclosure, forces spirituality to accord a fundamental importance to human history and material existence.[19]

Here then is the very focus of our spiritual life. First we *contemplate* the reality of God incarnate, taking into himself our humanity and in that humanity being our sacrifice for sin on the cross, rising from the grave victorious over the power of evil, and thereby restoring creatures and creation to himself. This is the central contemplation of the spiritual life. We contemplate God's wonderful works in our personal devotion and in our communal life in the church, in worship, in Scripture, in Eucharist, and in prayer.

Throughout history thousands of believers have produced great works of art inspired by that contemplation—church architecture, icons, hymns, paintings, sculpture, dance, oratorios, drama. Who of us has not delighted in God through the music of Handel's *Messiah*, or in the icons of a Byzantine chapel that proclaim God's story of salvation, or in the simplicity of the hymn "Of the Father's Love Begotten," or in the moving words of Bernard of Clairvaux's "O Sacred Head Now Wounded," or in the mystery of baptism or the powerful celebration of the resurrection in the great

Paschal vigil. These expressions, as well as a myriad of others, draw us into a contemplative delight of God whose love for his creatures and creation is so great that his Son and his Spirit worked together to regain union with us sinners.[20] The contemplation of this great truth results in a spiritual enlightenment, a deep and inner delight of the soul, and a passionate commitment to participate in God through an obedience to the purposes of God revealed in Jesus Christ.

The second part of the spiritual life is to *participate* in the purposes of God in history. We live in a theological consciousness of life shaped by the mystery of the Triune God reconciling all of life to himself. The spiritual life arises from the cluster of biblical teachings that form the Christian vision of reality.

It is a *trinitarian spirituality* because it proclaims God to be a person in the community of Father, Son, and Holy Spirit who calls us to participate in the communion and fellowship that the Son has with the Father by the Spirit.

It is a *creational spirituality* because God created the material world as a place of his dwelling and glory and put humanity in the world to be the caretakers of the world doing his purposes.

It is an *anthropological spirituality* because it understands humanity as created in the image of the Triune God, called to live under God, fallen, but now restored to live in the original purposes of God.

It is an *incarnational spirituality* because it confesses that he who made heaven and earth became one of us and demonstrated to us what humanity united to God looks like.

It is a *Christological spirituality* because it calls on us to surrender our human will as Jesus did, to the divine will.

It is a *cruciform spirituality* because God in Christ entered our suffering to reconcile us to God, calling us to live the cruciform life.

It is a *resurrection spirituality* because as Jesus was resurrected from the dead to new life, so we become a new creation in him.

It is a *Pentecost spirituality* because as the life-giving Spirit was active in creation, God's involvement in history came upon Jesus at his baptism, ministry, death, and resurrection and came upon the church, so the Spirit—the hand of God—empowers our life.

It is a *baptismal spirituality* because we are united to Christ in baptism in faith and called to live in the pattern of death and resurrection.

It is a *communal spirituality* because, like God who dwells in community, we too are to live out our lives in the community of Christ's body, the church.

It is a *liturgical spirituality* because here in worship we proclaim and enact God's saving deeds for the world.

It is a *eucharistic spirituality* because in the union of the spiritual and material at bread and wine the vision of the world is before our very eyes, taken and ingested into our bodies.

It is a *prayer spirituality* because it is here, in utter dependence upon God, that we live out our life.

It is a *social spirituality* because as Jesus ministered to the needs of the poor, the needy, and the weak, we too are called to be like Jesus to others.

It is an *ethical spirituality* because God has displayed in Jesus the life of morality and justice.

It is a *vocational spirituality* because all our work is under God and his purposes in history.

It is a *revelational spirituality* because God has made all this known to us in his mighty deeds, culminating in his Son, who is the Alpha and Omega of the universe, the one who reconciles all things to himself—authoritatively recorded for us in the inspired texts of Scripture.

There is a straightforward simplicity about this theological spirituality. It is not speculative. It does not require a renunciation of life, a rigorous asceticism, the monastic life, deep feelings, agonizing prayers, fasting, dreams, or visions. It simply proclaims that God has taken the initiative to unite us and the world to himself and calls on us to *see* and *live* our life out of this vision of reality. Irenaeus put it well: the "glory of God, is the human person fully alive."[21] The goal of the Christian life is to affirm God's truth in the heart and, following Jesus, to live in the purposes of God revealed in his life.

This vision of life is the common conviction of the ancient church. This is the great mystery of our union with God, a mystery that in contemplation can never be exhausted and in participation can never be equaled. Athanasius himself wrote, "In proportion as I thought I apprehended it, in so much I perceived myself to fail in doing so."[22] Because we cannot fully grasp what we seek to understand in contemplation, we ought the more to live in the mystery itself so that we may become in participation that which we seek to contemplate. As Orthodox theologian Vladimir Lossky states, "We must live the dogma expressing revealed truth, which appears to us an unfathomable mystery, in such fashion that instead of assimilating the mystery to our mode of understanding, we should on the contrary, look for a profound change, an inner transformation of Spirit, enabling us to experience it mystically."[23]

This view of reality stands on its own. It is a vision of God, the world, human existence, history, and the goal of creation. When this story is modified by other philosophies, reduced to one or more of its parts, made dependent on reason or science, refocused on a mere intellectual construct, a private experience, or a set of legalistic rules, its very nature is changed. Our task, then, is to look at a few examples of how the original biblical and theological vision of spirituality has been modified. Our goal is to gain a perspective that will help us understand the crisis of a spirituality no longer situated in God's story.

SPIRITUALITY MODIFIED BY DUALISM AND MYSTICISM

I have already referred to contemplation as one of the two realities of the spiritual life, the other being participation. I have identified Christian contemplation with Mary who "pondered . . . in her heart" (Luke 2:19). Christian contemplation ponders, reflects, gazes, and delights in the wonders and the mysteries of God active in this world "reconciling the world to himself"(2 Cor. 5:19). In Christian contemplation God is the subject who acts in history; *contemplation* enters God's vision of the world and is stunned, filled with wonder, amazed, full of inner delight and joy. This contemplation is, in sum, an experience of God's presence. The realization of his presence in the world, creation, incarnation, death, and resurrection and the ultimate presence of God in the fulfillment of history in the new heavens and the new earth is the subject of our *contemplation*.

The First Shift in Contemplation: Platonic Dualism

Contemplation shifted away from the mystery of God creating and becoming incarnate to re-create through the influence of Platonic philosophy. At the end of book seven of the *Republic*, Plato calls people to contemplate, not the God of history, but an "outside of the world essence" known as "universal light" or "the absolute good":

> Those who are to be the guardians of the state and the upbringers of the coming generation, after having been in early manhood exercised in all the civic functions of peace and war, when they have reached fifty years, let those who have distinguished themselves in every action of their lives and in every branch of knowledge, come at last to their consummation: *the time has now arrived at which they must raise the eye of the soul to the universal light which lightens all things, and behold the Absolute Good* (τὸ αγαθὸν αὐτό); for that is the pattern according to which they are to order the State and the lives of individuals, and the remainder of their own lives

also; *making philosophy their chief pursuit*, but, when their turn comes, each one devoting himself to the hard duties of public life and holding office, not as a desirable but as an unavoidable occupation.[24]

Plato sees contemplation as focused on the object that is above the material world. The contemplation of this object is to be the "chief pursuit" of life. Plato speaks of the superiority of this contemplation in *Phaedrus*: "*In the heaven above the heavens there abides Being Itself with which true knowledge is concerned; the colourless, formless, intangible, essence, visible only to mind.* The mind which is capable of it rejoices in beholding reality and in gazing upon truth. It beholds knowledge absolute in existence absolute, and the other true existences in like manner, and feasts upon them."[25]

The contemplation introduced by Plato is characterized by a dualism between matter and spirit. It separates God from his activity in the world and makes God the object of contemplation. The Greek concept of God is an "up there, out there" God. God is the essence who sits in the heavens, the remote God of total otherness who cannot be known because he dwells in the dark, in the "negation of existence." So God, in the Greek philosophical context, becomes an "idea out there," not the biblical God whose mystery is revealed in his creating, incarnating, and re-creating actions in history.

The first shift in contemplation is from God as subject to God as object. Here is the key difference. The biblical God is the subject who creates ("I believe in God the Holy Spirit, the giver of life"—Nicene Creed); the biblical God is the subject who becomes incarnate in the womb of the Virgin Mary to initiate union with his rebellious creatures ("True God from True God. . . . through him all things were made. For us and our salvation he came down from heaven . . . and was made man"—Nicene Creed). In this vision of the world the union of God and man for the reversal of the human condition is already attained for all humanity. God did it. Spirituality *contemplates* the wonder of it all and *participates in this life in this world*, according to the original purposes of God displayed in his own incarnation among us.

When God through our thinking is turned into an object who in a sense "sits in the heavens," spirituality takes on the form of a dualism between God and creation. In spiritual dualism God is no longer the subject who becomes involved in the history of the world. Instead, in dualism God dwells in the realm of the spirit and we humans dwell in the realm of the material. Spirituality, therefore, becomes *our* effort to transcend our material existence because, as this thinking goes, we are the subject and God is the object. In dualistic spirituality the spirit within me needs to escape this world, this life, this burden of humanity and to achieve union with God, the spirit, who dwells outside the earthly, material place of human existence. Unfortunately, it was this dualistic perspective that greatly influenced Christian spirituality in late antiquity and the medieval era. The result is a shift that not only reshapes God into "the object out there" but also creates a new focus on *my efforts* to attain union with God through a *rejection of life in this world*, so that *union with the God who dwells in the realm of the spirit might be achieved.*

Traces of dualism are found in monastic spirituality—both Eastern and Western. While Eastern monasticism is found chiefly in the desert fathers, who seek to escape the world by living in the desert, Western monasticism is dominated by the Benedictine tradition. There is a difference between the two. The Eastern monastic tradition is influenced more by a Platonic view of contemplation, whereas the rule of St. Benedict is closer to the biblical vision of contemplation and participation. Let me explain.

Desert spirituality (Eastern monasticism) arose after the conversion of the Roman Empire. Christianity lost its countercultural edge and, having become the only legitimate religion of the Empire, began to luxuriate in "wealth and privilege." Desert spirituality "renewed the prophetic ministry of ancient Israel in the church" by bearing witness "against a bourgeois and worldly church." But the downside of the desert fathers, claims John Meyendorff, is that they "learned to use Neoplatonic language, which was that of contemporary philosophy, but which was hardly compatible with Christianity."[26] However, to be fair, Meyendorff points to the influence of Macarius on the later desert fathers whose mysticism "is entirely based on the Incarnation." For Macarius and many other desert fathers, spirituality is based not on "freeing the spirit from the impediment of the flesh" but an entrance "into eschatological reality, the Kingdom of God, which embraces him, his spirit and his body, in a divine communion."[27] So the desert fathers constitute a mixture of Platonic philosophical contemplation and biblical contemplation. Later I will draw on their biblical contemplation, especially in spiritual warfare and prayer.

On the other hand, Western monasticism was primarily shaped by the rule of St. Benedict, the founder of the Benedictine tradition and author of the monastic rules. (The actual rule of Benedict was composed in the sixth century by St. Benedict of Nursia.) The rule contains direction for the monastic life including how to form a monastery, how to administer it, and what the daily spiritual life of the monk should look like.

The purpose of the monastic life is to continually seek God, to live only for God through the practice of the disciplines. Monastic spirituality, which is a separation from an ordinary life in this world, expresses union with God through the solitary life or within community life. A key to the experience of union with God is *listening prayer*. "This means that the monk must be very quiet and still within himself, but also very alert and attentive if the word of God is to resonate properly with his innermost depths so that he is nourished and enlightened by it."[28]

While monastic spirituality and especially the rule of St. Benedict has made a significant contribution to the spiritual life of the Christian church, there are two ways it differs from the spirituality that is rooted in God's story. First, it presents a retreat from ordinary life as the primary and superior way of achieving union with God. Second, spiritual union with God is not always seen as a gift but appears to be an achievement gained through striving. Nevertheless, the monastic tradition produced men and women who were deeply committed to God through Jesus Christ and passionate in following Jesus through what the church refers to as the *spiritual disciplines*.

An affirmation of spirituality situated in the story of God does not mean that one should reject the contribution of monasticism to the church and to our day-to-day walk. It is possible to reject the dualism yet find insights of great value for the spiritual life based on truth. I will later draw lessons from the desert fathers on spiritual warfare and probe the rule of St. Benedict for disciplines of the spiritual life.

The Second Shift in Contemplation: Late Medieval Mysticism

The second shift in contemplation away from God's story occurred in the rise of late medieval mysticism. Here the shift is from the contemplations of God creating, incarnating, and re-creating to a contemplation on the experience of the self.

Ancient Christian contemplation, as we have seen, was based on the story of God uniting with man in the incarnation to die and to be raised, not only to re-create humanity but to bring the whole creation to its re-creation in the new heavens and the new earth. This ancient approach to contemplation of the mystery of God revealed in Jesus Christ is, says author and scholar Herbert McCabe, "not like an increase of knowledge, but, if anything, an increase in ignorance. We become more acutely aware of our inadequacy before the mystery as we are brought closer to it. So it is God's initiative that is needed. Not that we should speak more about him, but that *he* should speak to us."[29] In a similar manner Rowan Williams, former archbishop of Canterbury, speaks of truth as not that which we should interrogate but that which interrogates us. "The greatness of the Christian saint lies," Williams suggests, "in their readiness to be questioned, judged, stripped naked and left speechless by that which lies at the center of their faith."[30] This approach to the mysteries of God revealed in Jesus Christ is the dominant form of biblical and ancient Christian mysticism. In spite of the modification on contemplation made by a Platonic and Neoplatonic philosophy, historic mysticism remained prominent among the mystics of late antiquity and early medievalism. What remains mystical about the faith is "not the inner experience of the Christian, but the hidden meaning and transformative understanding discovered in Christ." This mystery is "God's plan to reunite creation with God's own existence." This mystery "is embodied in Christ, discerned in the scriptures, and sacramentally enacted in the Eucharistic community."[31]

The distinguishing mark of ancient Christian spirituality is that it focuses on God's journey into our history to redeem it. The distinguishing mark of the new mysticism is that it *focuses on the journey of the self into God*. What stands behind this shift in emphasis is the formation of theology as a science—a shift that resulted in the tragic separation of theology from spirituality.

The background to this divorce is found in the rise of scholastic theology. Scholastic theology separated spirituality from its previous connection with the creeds and made it a distinct discipline. In other words, the organization of theology into separate disciplines inadvertently separated spirituality from its home in the story of God. Aquinas, in the *Summa*, divided theology proper into three parts: (1) God as the first principle; (2) God as the end of creation; and (3) the incarnate Word as the connection between God and the end of creation. This division became dogma and one component of theology. But another component, separated from dogma, was titled *moral theology*. Unfortunately, moral theology was regarded as independent from dogma, and cut from its roots in theology, moral thought acquired a life of its own. Consequently, spirituality was removed from dogma and treated under moral theology as a "practical discipline." This separation of theology into compartments of "dogma over here" and "moral theology over there" proved to be disastrous for the unity that formerly existed between theological reflection and spirituality in the ancient church. Spirituality became separated from theology and eventually developed a life of its own. Mark McIntosh summarizes the tragedy of the divorce between theological reflection and spirituality in these words: "Coinciding with the growth of scholasticism, medieval spirituality's intensifying focus on individual experience and affectivity gave rise to a spiraling mutual distrust between spirituality and theology that lingers even today."[32]

For example, theological thinking prior to Aquinas was like a web of thought that made up the whole. A spiderweb is a beautiful web of interconnected strands. If you pull one strand, it is so connected to the whole that the entire web is disturbed. Ancient theology is like a complex web of interrelated ideas. Spirituality is connected to the whole—to

Trinity, creation, incarnation, death and resurrection, faith, church, worship and sacraments, and the end time. Spirituality in the ancient tradition is not a separate discipline but an intricate part of the whole vision of God's story. Scholastic theology looks less like a spider web and more like a set of building blocks. The result was disastrous for ancient theological spirituality. The new spirituality, mysticism, was no longer situated in God's story.

The creeds, like the strands of a spider web, had affirmed the mystery of God who creates and becomes incarnate to re-create. Thus ancient Christian spirituality was rooted in God's mystery, unfolding in history and culminating in Christ. The new mysticism differs from spirituality based on God's mystery in Christ, because it is now God's mystery taking place in *my* life. Even though mysticism is a "term used to cover a literally bewildering variety of states of mind,"[33] the new mysticism of the late medieval era can be clearly described as a "fascination in the West with subjective experience or with the development of a detailed itinerary for the spiritual journey."[34] Unfortunately, medieval mysticism was shaped as much by culture as it was by Christian themes. So, for example, the dominant theme of medieval mysticism was a romantic relationship with God, a love union, stimulated perhaps by the twelfth-century Renaissance of courtly love, the Arthurian myths, and the poetry and songs of the troubadours. A culture of romance and intimacy influenced Christians to turn to the Song of Solomon as a Christian expression of intimacy and to strive for a romantic relationship with God.

Because of the divorce between theology and spirituality, mysticism shifted from the ancient understanding of spirituality to a new approach. *Spirituality, which was once a contemplation of God's saving acts, now contemplated the self and the interior life.* What was once a journey into God became a journey into self. This new inward focus of a journey into self resulted in a new language of spirituality.[35]

First the language of spirituality moved from the "indescribable wonder of God" to the "wonderfully indescribable experience of God." Because spirituality now focused on the experience that occurs inside of me, spirituality expressed a movement away from "God's story," to "my story." Instead of contemplating on God's mighty acts of creation, incarnation, and re-creation, through which God restores all humanity and the entire created order, contemplation shifted to a focus on "my inward journey." God's *cosmic* story of redemption was exchanged for the drama of redemption that takes place *within me*, which is different from witnessing to God's saving acts, which embrace me and I in turn embrace. Consequently, participation in God shifted from *life-affirming* spirituality to a *life-denying* spirituality. The world, instead of being the theater of God's glory where God defeats death and evil to restore the world, now becomes Satan's domain from which we must be saved for another world—heaven. Consequently a new emphasis on spirituality arose: retreat from the world and cultivation of the inner private life alone. A new kind of mysticism was born—a mysticism that often escaped into intellectual fantasy and spiritual romanticism.[36] There are numerous mystical movements and traditions in which this shift can be illustrated. Space will only permit one example.

Richard Rolle (1290–1349), an English writer, summarized this new experiential spirituality in his classic work, *The Mending of Life*. Contemplation that was concerned with the journey inward took place in three ascending steps:

First, one must become free from all the "occupations of the world" to ready oneself to embrace the deeper meaning of life.

Second, "Contemplation is the free and sharp-sighted exploration of wisdom, raised with wonder."

Third, the above contemplation leads to "the penetrating observation of the soul opened wide in every direction for the discerning virtues."[37]

Mark McIntosh points out that what one finds among the mystics is "the superiority of intense religious feelings." Spirituality is "one's own affective reaction to God which must be cultivated."[38] Feeling has become the sign of true spirituality. Rolle proposes three identifiable experiences of the soul's relationship to God as "burning love, songful praise and inestimable sweetness." The true contemplative must, he writes, "rejoice sweetly and ardently in interior joys" and "is seized as if in ecstasy, by the sweetness of divine love, and then, snatched up marvelously, he is delighted."[39] In the case of Rolle and others who follow him, spirituality is the experience of an inner joy and sweetness and a mapping of the inner journey of faith.

This history of the new mysticism in the medieval church and its reemergence in today's world is a very complicated and detailed study. But the statement that spirituality shifts toward a focus on inwardness and feeling is clearly recognized by scholars of mysticism. Bernard McGinn writes, "New ways of understanding and presenting the direct consciousness of the presence of God became evident in the early thirteenth century."[40] These new ways of experiencing God directly became by the fourteenth century "autobiographies," that is, narratives in which the author presents aspects of her or his own life as a model of suffering in imitation of Christ's passion and the reception of "divine consolations."[41]

What needs to be clear here is that a real shift has taken place in the understanding and practice of spirituality. Biblical spirituality confirmed by the theological debates of the ancient church is a contemplation on the mystery of creation, incarnation, and re-creation. This contemplation produces a delight in God that is certainly an inward feeling producing love, joy, and even an inward sweetness. The historic focus of contemplation, however, is on God and God's actions, on God's story, and on God's vision and not on the feelings themselves that God's story or vision of the world generated. Certainly there were mystics who continued to focus on God, but in the main there is a discernable shift to a contemplation of one's own experience and to the search for a direct and immediate union of the self with God.

This kind of mysticism, I argue, differs from the ancient confession that "God was in Christ, reconciling the world unto himself" (2 Cor. 5:19 KJV). *The focus on* my inner life *rather than the mystery of the Triune God at work in history to redeem the world becomes narcissistic and even expresses itself in bizarre, direct encounters with God that are viewed as more important than the divine embrace of God, which took place on the hard wood of the cross.* When spirituality loses its connection with the incarnation and the subsequent death and resurrection of Jesus as the revealed way of union with God and instead searches for a direct experience of union with God, a shift away from a biblical spirituality has taken place. Usually spiritualities divorced from the story of God end, not only in the contemplation of the inward experience, but in a negation of the historic understanding of participation in God as the surrender of the will to the doing of God's purposes in the world, to some kind of negation or escape from the world. This seems to be true, too, of the tenor of the new mysticism of the middle ages.

CONCLUSION

Biblical and ancient spirituality is a theological spirituality. One lives by the biblical convictions of the Triune God, who creates and who becomes incarnate to re-create. Spirituality is to be *located* in God's story, living out of God's story in everyday life. In her work *The Mind of the Maker*, Dorothy Sayers puts it this way: "The Trinitarian structure which can be shown to exist in the mind of man and in all his works is, in fact, the integral structure of the universe, and corresponds, not by pictorial imagery but by a necessary uniformity of substance, with the nature of God, in Whom all that is exists."[42] On the spiritual side of the theological vision, "The doctrine of the Trinity, with its far-reaching practical implications, constitutes the heart and soul of Christian spirituality." It is "the cornerstone of Christian belief because it synthesizes the whole 'economy' of God's relationship with creation, including humankind,"[43] and, as James Torrance points out, "The patristic phrase 'one in being (*homoousios*) with the Father,'" betokens here that communion with Jesus Christ is communion with God. Therefore, to participate by the Spirit in the incarnate Christ's communion with the Father is to participate in the eternal Son's communion—a relationship that is both *internal* to the Godhead and *externally* extended to us by grace, established between God and humanity in the incarnation. The prime purpose of the incarnation, in the love of God, is to lift us up into a life of communion, of participation in the very triune life of God. Conversely, using Henry Scougal's phrase, in our communion with God we experience "the life of God in the soul of man."[44]

In summary, both Gnostic dualism and the new mysticism changed the nature of spirituality and the spiritual life of contemplation and participation. Dualism separated the spiritual life from this material life in the world. Gnostic spirituality renounced life and sought to free itself from its material prison through ascetic practices. Platonism, freeing itself from all worldly encumbrances, sought to contemplate the essence of the spirit, which was above and beyond matter.

Then, too, while the new mysticism of the medieval era continued to emphasize spirituality as union with God, there was a discernable shift from union with God achieved through Jesus and the Spirit to a focus on the self becoming united with God as a result of a direct experience, which then becomes the focus of contemplation.

This criticism does not mean that all the new mystics and their concern for an experience of union with God should be shunned. The biblical and historic mystery is God coming to the world and to us to restore the world. The best of the new mystics explore *our* experience of God's procession into history and into *our* lives. There are those like Bonaventura who root their quest for experience in union with the God of Scripture made known through his saving acts culminating in Jesus Christ. On the other spectrum there are those who were characterized by "madness, infinite longing, annihilation."[45]

The best of the new mystics call us to reflect on how God's mystery unfolding in history also unfolds in our own lives. But we must explore this reality with the primary interest on God, not self, so that the mystery of God "reconciling the world to himself" (2 Cor. 5:19) is always seen as the primary subject of contemplation, making awareness of God's presence the subject of contemplation, not our personal experience the center of our attentiveness.

We turn now to see how the theological spirituality of the ancient church was partially recovered by the Reformers only to be lost again in the modern era.

A SUMMARY FOR REFLECTION AND CONVERSATION

Summary	Reflection
Ancient spirituality	God in Christ reclaims the entire creation. We have been united with God through God's embrace in Jesus Christ. The spiritual life is to live in this union, to passionately embrace God's vision for humanity and the world.
Ancient spirituality challenged	The ecumenical creeds of the church defend the story of God from which spirituality derives.
Platonic dualism modifies ancient spirituality	God becomes the object of contemplation (not the subject), and participation becomes an escape from this world (not an affirmation of life).
The new mysticism modifies ancient spirituality	Contemplation shifts to a delight in one's experience (not the mystery of God reconciling the world). Participation shifts to an escape from this world through visions and esoteric experience (not an affirmation of God's divine plan for the world).

THE CRISIS: HOW THE SPIRITUAL LIFE BECAME SEPARATED FROM THE DIVINE EMBRACE

Chapter 2 The story of God's divine embrace in the incarnation, death, and resurrection of Jesus was defended by the ancient creeds and debates of the church. Spirituality and the spiritual life, situated in the divine embrace, was modified by Platonic dualism, which saw spirituality as an escape from this world, and late medieval mysticism, which interpreted spirituality as a journey into self.

Chapter 3 *The Reformers returned spirituality to the divine embrace with some modification. In the modern era spirituality as the divine embrace was redefined by a spirituality preoccupied with a forensic justification combined with sanctification guided by gratitude, and a spirituality that focused on the conversion experience followed by a flight from the world.*

Chapter 4 Twentieth-century evangelical spirituality inherited the modifications of the past and developed privatized spiritualities of legalism, intellectualism, and experientialism.

Chapter 5 The present evangelical practices of spirituality, separated from the divine embrace, are inadequate to the challenge of the widespread popularity of New Age and Eastern spiritualities grounded in an impersonal, pantheistic conception of God and the world. The challenge before us is to recover a spirituality and spiritual life situated in the divine embrace.

3

A HISTORICAL PERSPECTIVE 2 (1500–1900)

Rescuing Spirituality from Intellectualism and Experientialism

Today the Reformation and post-Reformation period is generally dated from 1500 to 1750, and the modern era runs from 1750 to 2000. These dates are somewhat arbitrary and must be viewed with flexibility. Nevertheless, these periods are characterized by distinctly different ways of thinking so that the division between the two periods, in spite of the flexibility in dating, stands.

The primary difference between the Reformation and the modern period of history is that the Reformation looked backward to regain the source of the ancient church while the modern era, shaped by an antihistorical attitude, looked forward. Consequently, the Reformers' view of spirituality is much closer to the spirituality of the ancient church, while the modern era with its antihistorical mentality developed new ways to think about spirituality.

This chapter treats the Reformers first, exploring their continuity in thinking with the past, and then looks at the new paths of spiritual thought created by the Protestants, particularly those movements that are the sources for the modern evangelical approach to spirituality. There are, of course, many other contributions made to spirituality among

Orthodox and Catholic Christians during the modern era, but a study of these movements is beyond the scope of this book.

REFORMATION SPIRITUALITY

The Reformers considered the late medieval church (AD 1300–1500), its doctrines, its practices, and its spirituality to be a departure from the ancient sources of Christianity. The late medieval church, we recall, embraced a mysticism that focused on self and upon a spirituality of works. This mysticism was not embraced by the Reformers, who essentially advocated a return to the biblical sources defended by the church fathers and summarized in the ecumenical creeds.

The specific principles of the Reformers are summarized in the Latin terms *Solus Christus, Sola Scriptura, Sola Gratia, Sola Fide*. These tenets express the fundamental conviction of the Reformers that our spiritual relationship to God is a gift from God that comes to us through Jesus Christ, by God's grace, grasped in faith. It was this message that theologian Louis Bouyer states won "in a world where religion seemed merely a matter of pious practices, prayers to recite, indulgences to be gained, relics to be venerated; and in all this, people saw only acts to be done by man, supplemented, it might be, by the divine *concurses*, but only as a subsidiary."[1] Justification by faith exploded in this context because it pointed a works-oriented people back to God, who is Savior not self. Medievalists only saw God as Judge. Now it became known, as David Neff of *Christianity Today* said to me, that in the day of judgment, the Judge was on their side.

The Reformers refocused attention on two central aspects of ancient spirituality: (1) the absolute inability of humanity to choose union with God and (2) the divine initiative in which God is united to humanity through the incarnation, death, and resurrection of Jesus by the Spirit. These two truths are captured by Luther:

> He, therefore, who does not wish to go astray with those blind men, must look beyond works, and laws and doctrines about works; nay, turning his eyes from works, he must look upon the person, and ask how that is justified. For the person is justified and saved not by works nor by laws, but by the Word of God, that is, by the promise of His grace, and by faith, that the glory may remain God's, Who saved us not by works of righteousness which we have done, but according to His mercy by the word of His grace, when we believed.[2]

In these words Luther summarizes justification through faith and the flowing forth of the spiritual life from the realization that works do not justify. Some suggest that Luther's recovery of the Pauline emphasis on justification and faith were *new* and that the church from the first century until Luther was apostate. This view misunderstands both the theology of the ancient church and the theology of Luther. First, the ancient church did have a place for justification in its teaching. St. John Chrysostom, the fourth-century bishop of Constantinople, wrote of justification in his commentary on the Epistle to the Romans:

> We have been freed from punishment, we have put off all wickedness, and we have been reborn from above, and we have risen again, with the old man buried, and we have been redeemed, and we have been sanctified, and we have been given adoption into sonship, and we have been *justified*, and we have been made brothers of the Only-begotten, and we have been constituted joint heirs and concorporeal with Him and have been perfected in His flesh, and have been united to Him as a body to its head.[3]

The charge often made by modern Protestants that the early church fathers knew nothing about being reborn or about justification or sanctification cannot be sustained. Chrysostom included justification as one of the *cluster of truths* that relate to the spiritual gift that is each person's by God's grace. On the other hand, the popular opinion that the Reformers did not locate God's saving action in the incarnation cannot be sustained either.

For example, recent Finnish scholarship, under the leadership of Tunomo Mannermaa from the Finnish Academy of Luther Studies argues that "the indwelling of Christ as grasped in the Lutheran tradition implies a *real participation in God* and it corresponds in a special way to the Orthodox doctrine [early church] of participation in God, namely the doctrine of *Theosis*."[4]

Mannermaa quotes Luther's Christmas sermon of 1514 to illustrate that Luther embraced the ancient doctrine of union with God through the incarnation, death, and resurrection. Luther wrote,

> Just as the word of God became flesh, so it is certainly also necessary that the flesh may become word. In other words: God becomes man so that man may become God. Thus power becomes powerless so that weakness may become powerful. The *Logos* puts on our form and pattern, our image and likeness, so that it may clothe us with its image, its pattern, and its likeness. Thus wisdom becomes foolish so that foolishness may become wisdom, and so it is in all other things that are in God and in us, to the extent that in all these things he takes what is ours to himself in order to impart what is his to us.[5]

According to Finnish scholarship, Luther stands in the ancient tradition of spirituality. Luther affirms the central meaning of the incarnation: "God becomes one of us so that we may be united to God." Like the early church fathers, Luther rejects the notion that we become the essence of God. Instead, this participation in God is so that we conform to Christ. He takes on "our form and pattern, our image and likeness" to transform us to his "image . . . pattern, and . . . likeness."[6] His life is imparted to us so that living in union with Christ we may look more and more like him. The life we live is that of the restored image, a real and genuine life in the family of God united into the community of God the Father, Son, and Holy Spirit.

Luther, like the early church fathers, also expresses the vital connection between baptism and spirituality. "It signifies," says Luther, "that the old Adam in us would, by daily sorrow and repentance, be drowned and die, with all sins and evil lusts; and again a new man daily come forth and arise, who shall live before God in righteousness and purity forever."[7]

Recent studies on John Calvin (1509–1564) suggest that, like Luther, Calvin also emphasizes spirituality as union with God. In the *Institutes of the Christian Religion*, Calvin writes,

> Christ by baptism has made us partakers of his death, ingrafting us into it. And as the twig derives substance and nourishment from the root to which it is attached, so those who receive baptism with true faith truly feel the efficacy of Christ's death in the mortification of their flesh, and the efficacy of his resurrection in the quickening of the Spirit. On this he founds his exhortation, that if we are Christians we should be dead unto sin, and alive unto righteousness.[8]

The same incarnational perspective is articulated in the Anabaptist wing of the Reformation. Alvin Beach speaks of Anabaptist spirituality as a "transforming divine energy" based on "a reversal of the incarnation in which the eternal Word becomes man in order that man may become God."[9] Dirk Philips, a colleague of Menno Simons, the primary leader of the Anabaptists, explains the relationship of spirituality to the incarnation in these words: "All believers are participants of the divine nature, yes, and are called gods and children of the most High. . . . They yet do not become identical in nature and person itself to what God and Christ are. Oh, no! The creature will never become the Creator and the fleshly will never become the eternal Spirit itself which God is. . . . But the believers become gods and children of the most high through the new birth, participation, and fellowship of the divine nature."[10]

Clearly the sixteenth-century Reformers did not neglect the implications of historic incarnational spirituality in their doctrine of justification.

Justification came as a result of the incarnation, death, and resurrection. The spiritual life was not a mere standing before God but was the direct result of baptism into Jesus for the forgiveness of sin, reception of the Holy Spirit (Acts 2:38), and a continuous living in the world in the pattern of death and resurrection.

However, it would be a mistake to equate the Reformers with the ancient church fathers. The Reformers were still under the influence of a scholastic kind of theology that hearkened back to Aquinas and behind him to Augustine. The ancient understanding of the Trinity was dynamic and communal as opposed to the more static view of God that developed in scientific theology. The Reformers, in spite of their return to the church fathers, were still influenced by the more mathematical view of God passed down through the scholastics.

What may be said of the Reformers is that they had one foot in the past and recognized that spirituality was not self-achieved but was the *gift* of God. They also acknowledged the spiritual life to be life in this world, not a renunciation of life as in the dualists or the new mystics. But the Reformers also had one foot headed toward the future.

By replacing contemplation and participation with justification and sanctification, the Reformers set up what was to become a severe problem in the modern era—the separation of spirituality from a relational, lived theology to a spirituality rooted in a forensic justification that did not encourage the mystery of contemplation or participation but instead turned spirituality toward intellectual knowledge. This turning eventually meant that justification became the focus of an intellectual spirituality and sanctification was turned toward a preoccupation with experience. Gradually verification of spirituality was sought for in intellectual understanding or in a dramatic conversion, in feelings, in legalism, and in a new kind of world renunciation. Reason and experience, now in conflict, produced two kinds of spirituality among modern Protestants: the spirituality of intellectualism and the spirituality of experientialism.

My own experience of spirituality follows this trajectory of experientialism and intellectualism. I grew up in the revivalist tradition that emphasized the need for a conversion experience that resulted in a *feeling* of forgiveness followed by a joy that was to transcend all earthly problems as I was to anxiously await the coming of Jesus and an escape from the world with all its woes to heaven and eternal bliss. However, as I studied the faith in seminary and then graduate school, I began to look to knowledge as the assurance of my relationship with God. I embraced the notion that I could know God intellectually. I could penetrate into the mysteries of God and know his inner working, his character, his wisdom, his reality through a thirst for knowledge.

If I was told about the divine embrace, I didn't get it. I looked to myself, to *my* experience, to *my* knowledge as the source for spirituality. All the time I knew there was something missing, but I didn't know what it was or how to get out of the quagmire of the search for God in experience and in intellect, going to and fro from one to the other or seeking to bring them together in some kind of spiritual synthesis. The journey into intellectualism and experientialism was never satisfying. It was only an exhausting spiritual roller coaster.

MODERN PROTESTANT SPIRITUALITY

This history of modern Protestant spirituality is very complex, and I make no pretension to cover it all. I will speak only to those movements that have shaped twentieth-century evangelicalism, namely, Protestant intellectualism and experientialism. My main concern is to critique the impact of these movements on the understanding and practice of spirituality.

Protestant Hymnody

Before taking you to these movements, however, I would be remiss if I did not say that the dominant contribution to spirituality in modern Protestantism is in its hymnody. Louis Bouyer, the famed Catholic critic of the Reformation and subsequent Protestantism acknowledges the enormous debt we all owe to Protestant Christianity for its history of song. He speaks of Luther's theology as the "basis of the real spiritual life of Protestantism" found "in its devotional literature, especially its hymns." Referring to "A Mighty Fortress Is Our God," Bouyer states, "Very few hymns express so directly and powerfully the truths dear to the heart of the devout Protestant."[11] Indeed, we owe a debt of gratitude to numerous hymn writers whose lyrics and music still impact the Protestant spiritual life—especially Isaac Watts (1674–1748), the two Wesley brothers, John (1703–1791) and Charles (1707–1788), George Whitefield (1714–1770), and a vast array of writers up to this very day.[12]

Space does not permit a lengthy discussion of the impact of hymnody on Protestant spirituality. But it should at least be noted that the hymnody of Charles Wesley in particular often refers to the ancient theme of Christ in me and my life in Christ. For example:

> Come, Father, Son and Holy Ghost,
> And seal me thine abode!
> Let all I am in thee be lost,
> Let all be lost in God![13]

A footnote claims this last line was originally "Let all I am be God." Clearly Wesley understood our union with God—his life in mine; mine in his—lifted up into a relationship with God in the very life of God.

Hymns such as the one below emphasize our mystical union with God:

> Steadfast let us cleave to thee,
> Love the mystic union be;
> Union to the world unknown,
> Joined to God in spirit one;
> Wait we till the Spouse shall come,
> Till the Lamb shall take us home,
> For his heaven the bride prepare,
> Solemnize our nuptials there![14]

A brief review of any hymnbook commonly used in evangelical churches will demonstrate the continued popularity of the themes of union with God. In those churches where these hymns are still sung, there is at least a remnant of the spirituality of our mystical union with God. However, the dominant spirituality of most evangelical churches focuses either on an intellectual acknowledgment of his union or seeks for an experience of union to verify its reality.

The Enlightenment and Intellectual Spirituality

Today we speak of premodern and postmodern histories and put the Reformation in the middle as the period of transition. In the shift from the Reformation to the modern era, a new world has been born, and with it a new kind of spirituality has emerged.

The shift is a new way of thinking. In the medieval world the church stood at the center of thinking: "If the church says it, I believe it." During the Reformation, the Bible emerged as the ultimate authority: "If the Bible says it, I believe it." Then in the modern world, reason and science emerged as the new authority: "If reason and science prove it, I believe it." Truth was now determined through what became known as the empirical method, introduced by Francis Bacon (1561–1626), coupled with rationalism, introduced by René Descartes (1596–1650). According to this method of arriving at truth, human reason was autonomous and could come to truth without the help of revelation. Furthermore, thinking was based on the distinction between the object and the subject.

This new kind of dualism based on Descartes took an *I-It* approach to life. Previously people saw themselves in an *I-Thou* relationship to creation, history, environment, culture, the church, and the like. They did not look at these areas of life as objects to be studied, analyzed, or dissected. But now the emphasis turned from the whole to parts and to the rational and scientific study of the parts. Life was compartmentalized.

The modern world also became preoccupied with facts. Moderns argued that reason and science yield facts that are objective, outside of the knower, and value free. Anything else was opinion. It was commonly argued by the increasing secularism of the Enlightenment that religion was not based on facts but on an alleged revelation that could not be proven, whether Christian faith or another religion. Consequently, all religions were relegated to opinion. Christian faith was regarded by these secularists as irrelevant. People were to live life not on the so-called vision of God but on the facts of reason and science.

The dismissal of the Christian faith as opinion was challenged by William Chillingworth (1602–1644), the father of rational Christianity. In his book, *The Religion of Protestants, A Safe Way of Salvation*, he wrote,

> Following the Scripture, I shall believe many mysteries, but no impossibilities; many things above reason, but nothing against it; many things which, had they not been revealed, reason could never have discovered, but nothing which by true reason may be confuted; many things, which reason cannot comprehend how they can be, but nothing which reason can comprehend that it cannot be. Nay, I shall believe nothing which reason will not convince that I ought to believe it; for reason will convince any man, unless he be of a perverse mind, that the Scripture is the word of God: and then no reason can be greater than this; God says so, therefore it is true.[15]

Following in the footsteps of Chillingworth's rationalism, John Toland (1670–1722) wrote the book *Christianity Not Mysterious: Or, A Treatise Shewing, That There Is Nothing in the Gospel Contrary to Reason, Nor Above It: And That No Christian Doctrine Can Be Properly Call'd A Mystery*. In this work Toland makes the claim that the Christian faith is completely defensible through reason: "The New Testament (if it be indeed Divine) must consequently agree with Natural Reason, and our own ordinary Ideas. The Apostles commend themselves to every Man's Conscience, that is, they appeal to every Man's Reason, in the Sight of God. . . . Wherefore, we likewise maintain, that there is nothing in the Gospel contrary to Reason, nor above it; and that no Christian Doctrine can be properly call'd a Mystery. . . . I acknowledge no Orthodoxy but the Truth."[16] This factual orientation to Christianity became evident in the conservative theology of American denominations, where an intellectual approach to the Christian faith was embraced.

These groups responded to the new way of thinking by developing the discipline of apologetics. Apologetics approached the faith through the common empirical method of thinking. Reason and science were applied to the Christian faith to show that Christianity was not opinion but fact. Creation was fact and could be proven to be true. Revelation was a fact and could be proven, and so on. But the primary fact of all facts that needed to be proven was Scripture. For all other doctrines stood or fell with one's view of Scripture.

The view of Scripture developed by modern conservatives differs from the view held by the Reformers. The Reformers did not seek to prove Scripture. They simply spoke out of a scriptural worldview. For them, the story of God did not need to be proven; it simply needed to be proclaimed. People were to live in the story that Scripture authoritatively delivered by the hand of God, even though the story was seen somewhat statically, as opposed to the ancient dynamic view.

But whereas Scripture was once over reason and science, the tables were now turned, and reason and science became the judge of Scripture. Hence, modern theologians, following the accepted way of thinking, brought reason and science to the aid of the Bible. This made reason and science the authority over the Bible. The conservatives sought to harmonize the Scriptures with reason and science. They rejected paradoxes and seeming contradictions and sought to explain everything with the tools of reason, science, and logic. In doing so, they took away the mystery that characterized the faith from the beginning. The church, for example, which in the ancient world was understood as the continuing presence of Jesus in the world, now became a *volunteer assembly*. It was humanized, so to speak. Worship, which in the past was the telling and enacting of God's story of the world from beginning to end, was reshaped into a time of teaching the Bible. Baptism and Eucharist were shed of the mystery of God's action. Now desupernaturalized baptism became *my testimony of faith*, and the Eucharist, shed of all divine presence, became *what I do to remember Jesus*. The doctrines of revelation, Trinity, creation, incarnation, atoning death, bodily resurrection, and second coming became *facts to be believed*. They were not shed of their supernatural character by the conservatives, but the mystery was gone and the relational character was lost.

The Christian liberals, due to Enlightenment thinking, used reason and science as their authority to reinterpret the Christian faith as myth. They did not accept the virgin birth, the atonement, the resurrection, the second coming, or revelation. These doctrines, they taught, resulted from an ancient Hellenization of Christianity. So they demythologized the Bible and Christian faith, humanized Jesus, and reduced Christianity to the religion whose unique character was the introduction of love.

An influential liberal leader, Adolph Von Harnack (1851–1930), was convinced that Paul had Hellenized Jesus and turned him into a cosmic supernatural figure. Along with other liberals, Harnack embraced the Jesus versus Paul construct and argued that Christianity had been based on Paul's distortion of Jesus. He presented this theory in his famous work entitled *What Is Christianity?* published in 1900. This popular work sold thousands of copies and persuaded many clergy and laypeople that the significance of Jesus was the teaching of love, that Jesus was not God incarnate, and that Jesus was not the Savior of the world. Thereby, the stage was set for the conflict between the conservatives and the liberals that took place in the early part of the twentieth century known as the fundamentalist-modernist controversy.

But what happened to spirituality? The Christian faith had been intellectualized. The faith was now sadly subject to reason, to the empirical method, and to facts. Christian faith also was compartmentalized, and theology had been turned into a science. Consequently, Christianity previously seen as a story grounded in the divine embrace now became the object of study. The faith now was put under the scrutiny of historical criticism, rational analysis, and literary critique.

In the liberal world of Christian thought, the study of Christian spirituality shifted toward a focus on the *moral influence of Jesus*. These progressive intellectuals argued that Jesus introduced the kingdom of God as "the organization of humanity through action inspired by love."[17] Christian faith became a social ideal, and the true spiritual agenda became to bring the kingdom of God to earth.

The architect of this approach to spirituality was Walter Rauschenbusch (1861–1918). For Rauschenbusch, Christianity was "the social redemption of the entire life of the human race on earth."[18] He argued effectively for changing society in his works *Christianizing the Social Order* (1912) and *A Theology for the Social Gospel* (1917). He linked God's work in this world through Christian action with Darwin's prevailing doctrine of evolution and the idea of progress. A slogan that captured the spiritual agenda of the liberals was "Getting better every day in every way," written during a time when social efforts were on the rise to solve humanity's ills.

In the conservative Christian world spirituality was taking a different turn and was now seen as *right belief*. It was an intellectualized faith that stressed adherence to doctrinal truth. Spirituality was also related to the Reformers' doctrines of justification and sanctification, however with a different emphasis than that given to it by the Reformers.

The Reformers, as we have seen, put justification and sanctification in the context of God's saving acts (creation, incarnation, and re-creation) and understood spirituality as a "union with God"—an actual indwelling of Christ by the Spirit. This shift into modern intellectual spirituality treated justification as a forensic fact, an objective work of God that resulted in a *standing* before God.

This scientific method compartmentalized theology in a way similar to the scholastic theology of the medieval era. Modern theological thinking separated theology proper from practical theology. Theological thinking was ordered around categories of thought such as God, creation, the fall, the person and work of Christ, the church, and end times. Each of these divisions were subject to rational and scientific analysis producing propositions of faith that were to be believed and defended. On the other hand, matters of ministry such as worship and spirituality were wrenched from the broader context of God's vision of creation; incarnation and re-creation ministry, divorced from God's story, developed a life of its own quite apart from theological reflection.

Let me illustrate this shift toward a spirituality disconnected from God's story by comparing historic spirituality to this new intellectual embrace of forensic justification.

Historic spirituality looks like this: God became one of us in the incarnation. When the Word became incarnate in Jesus by the Spirit, God lifted all humanity into himself and, by his death and resurrection, reconciled all to himself (Rom. 5:12–21). Spirituality is therefore a gift of God's grace. God has taken the initiative to unite with us so that we may be united with him. Baptism is the spiritual rite of conscious and intentional union with Jesus (Rom. 6:1–14) and reception of the Holy Spirit (Acts 2:38). The spiritual life is the freedom to live in the baptismal pattern of his death and resurrection, dying to sin and rising to the new life in the Spirit. In this ancient model of spirituality, Jesus is our spirituality because we are in union with God through our union with Jesus by the Spirit. His entire life from conception to resurrection is on behalf of humanity. He reverses our belonging to Adam (Rom. 5:12–21). He overcame sin for us (Col. 2:13–15). He destroyed the power of death (1 Cor. 15:35–59). He begins the new order of creation (2 Cor. 5:17). He does all this in the power of the Spirit. Christ now dwells in us by the Spirit and we in him.

Spirituality rooted in justification without the connection to the incarnation and Christology looks like this: We are justified by Christ who has done everything necessary to reconcile us to God. Christ is our righteousness. God looks at us through the righteousness of Christ and imputes or declares us righteous in Christ. (This is called the forensic or judicial view of establishing our relation to God.) Now that God has made us spiritual through Jesus Christ, we are called to respond to God in thanksgiving by living the sanctified life. The new emphasis in spirituality within Protestantism, in general, is this justification/sanctification model.

The ancient model of spirituality is situated in the story of God's vision for the world accomplished by the two hands of God—Jesus Christ and the Holy Spirit. The modern model of spirituality is taken out of

God's story and situated in God's forensic justification. Spirituality has become intellectualized.

Consider these differences between the ancient and modern intellectual approaches to the matters of spirituality: The incarnational model of the ancient church is relational. God relates to humanity by becoming one of us. We relate to God because, through the incarnation, we are lifted up into a relationship with the divine. In this ancient depiction of incarnational spirituality there is a divine indwelling of God, a mystical union between God and man, a relationship of continuous prayerful dependence. Contemplation of God and his wondrous story is characterized by the delight of the heart, an inner reality that proceeds from a union with God that is real. Participation in God also is real because as God participated in our life in Jesus we, like him, seek to bring our will under the will of God, doing the purposes of God in all of life and in all our relationships. In the incarnational spirituality, baptism also is more dynamic and relational. The mystery of baptism is an immersion into Jesus and his death and resurrection as the pattern of spirituality. Incarnational spirituality equally sets forth a relational model of the church as the body of Christ, the extension of Jesus in the world, the continuation of his presence in the world. Worship and the sacraments, too, are related to God's incarnation. Worship tells and enacts the story of God culminating in the incarnation, death, and resurrection, and the sacraments apply the mysteries of Christ to our day-to-day living.

By contrast, a justification/sanctification spirituality is less relational and more intellectual. The forensic notion of justification appears to be a transaction that changes only our standing or position before God. The words *forensic*, *transaction*, *standing*, and *position* do not adequately represent the Scriptures that speak of God dwelling in us and we in him and do not do justice to the doctrines of justification and sanctification as intended by the Reformers. The dynamic of God's incarnation into our life and the lifting up of our life into his life seems to be missing in the forensic model of spirituality. The mystery of our union with God seems to be taken out of spirituality. Then, too, sanctification eventually evolves into works. It is seldom connected to baptism and seldom described as "living in the pattern of the death and resurrection."

In summary, ancient spirituality is placed within the whole story of God and maintains the dynamic relational aspect of spirituality in union with God. On the other hand, the impact of the Enlightenment emphasis on justification and sanctification separates spirituality from the story of God (especially the incarnation in which humanity is lifted into God) and creates an intellectual spirituality that not only affirmed a forensic standing before God but one that equated spirituality with *right belief*. Spirituality ceased to be a *lived theology* and became faith as an intellectual construct. Clearly a separation from ancient spirituality has occurred in the development of intellectual spirituality.

The Romantic Movement and the Rise of an Experiential Spirituality

The second shift away from ancient spirituality resulted from the romantic movement and influenced spirituality toward a preoccupation with experience. Romanticism may be described as a reaction to the Enlightenment, a response that has enduring consequences to this day. The romantic movement is contrasted to the Enlightenment because it posits a new way of knowing. Romantics opposed the analytical method of knowing truth with its reason and science and called for a more intuitive, inner experience of knowing through the imagination, the senses, passion, and the will. They emphasized the return to wholeness over against compartmentalization and looked at reality organically rather than piecemeal.

The primary philosophical figure of the romantic movement was G. W. F. Hegel (1770–1831), and its primary theologian was Friedrich Schleiermacher (1768–1834). In his famous work *On Religion: Speeches to Its Cultural Despisers*, Schleiermacher emphasized faith as the feeling of absolute dependence. In his work *The Christian Faith*, which is based on the story of God (regarded as more liberal than his conservative counterparts), he sees "redemption" as "the fulfillment of true humanity as intended by God, and men are so constituted that no individual can be completely fulfilled until all are brought into harmonious and loving relationship with each other in the Kingdom of God."[19] Schleiermacher is still widely read and influential, especially among the theologians of immanence.

It is difficult to know exactly how the romantic movement directly impacted nineteenth-century evangelicalism. It is interesting to note, however, that movements such as pietism and revivalism focused, like romanticism, on an inner, experiential knowing. Whereas the rationalists argue that we know truth through the revealed facts of God's Word verified through reason and science, romantics insisted that truth was known in the heart through experience. This view is found especially in pietism and revivalism.

Pietism

Pietism began as a reaction against an intellectual Lutheranism that is now regarded by many to be "dead orthodoxy."[20] Pietism called for a heartfelt faith, a life of moral discipline, a recovery of the priesthood of all believers, and a cessation to denominational hostility. Pietists considered themselves to be the finishers of the Reformation, bringing spirituality to a heartfelt experience.

One of the pietist leaders, Philip Jacob Spener (1635–1705), called for reform in his work *Pia Desideria* (Pious Wishes, 1675). Spener advocated a return to a simple reading of Scripture and a literal following of its teaching as opposed to all the theological debates resulting from the scientific method of theology. Spener "declared a right feeling in the heart" to be "more important than pure doctrine."[21]

The spirituality of pietism differs from the intellectual spirituality of the era because it does not view spirituality as a mere cognitive grasp of one's relationship to God through justification by faith. The new emphasis was on spirituality as a "regeneration," a "new birth" that results in "an inner transformation." Faith is more than the acceptance of Christ's merits; it causes "Christ to dwell in the believer's heart."[22] This kind of transforming spirituality revolves around "the 'New birth' (regeneration, conversion), understood as a one-time decision to accept God's offer of grace and thus to experience a 'break through' from the lostness of sin to the new life of 'Christian perfection,' which many Pietists identified with becoming 'partakers of the divine' (2 Peter 1:4 RSV), though not with sinlessness."[23] This pietist emphasis on a *new birth spirituality* laid the foundations for a revivalist spirituality, which dominated nineteenth-century revivalism.

Revivalism

Evangelical revivalism and the spirituality spawned by this segment of the romantic movement is connected to John Wesley (1703–1791). Wesley was a man of his times, a minister in the Anglican church with roots in both the ancient church and the Reformation. Although Wesley was a reader of the mystical piety of Thomas à Kempis and the ancient author Macarius the Egyptian, Wesley was dissatisfied with his own spiritual condition. On a trip to America he met and became influenced by the Moravians, especially Peter Böhler, who persuaded him to "turn away from all dependence on his own works and to seek a true faith in Christ, which results in an inner sense of forgiveness." Wesley set out to *experience* the forgiveness of sin and a dynamic living faith, not a mere intellectual faith.

Wesley did experience this spiritual rebirth on May 24, 1738, and records in his *Journal* an experience at a society meeting in Aldersgate Street as the preface to Luther's commentary on the Epistle to Romans was being read: "In the evening I went very unwillingly to a society in Aldersgate Street, where one was reading Luther's Preface to the Epistle to the Romans. About a quarter before nine, while he was describing the change which God works in the heart through faith in Christ, I felt my heart strangely warmed. I felt I did trust in Christ, Christ alone for salvation, and an assurance was given me that he had taken away my sins, even *mine*, and saved *me* from the law of sin and death."[24]

Wesley stood in the tradition of justification by faith, and he was looking for something more than an intellectual spirituality grounded in a forensic faith. He wanted to experience God's forgiveness *within*, to experience a *feeling* and have an *interior* spirituality. John Tyson makes this observation about Wesley's longing for an interior reality of grace: "Justification is not simply the objective fact that God pardons, nor is it simply a cognitive belief that this is so. It involves an experience of being pardoned or knowing ourselves as pardoned—the sort of experience Wesley had at Aldersgate. It is not just the knowledge that Christ has taken away our guilt. It involves also becoming experientially free from that guilt."[25]

This *new birth* experience of Wesley in which his heart was *strangely warmed* catapulted Wesley into his new ministry of open-air preaching—a ministry that became a foundational model for his successors in evangelism, including Billy Graham. Wesley's ministry, unlike the Reformers before him and the Reformed emphasis on cognitive faith, stressed the affective side of faith, emphasizing the new birth as a life-changing emotional experience.

Doctrinally, Wesley's views were in keeping with an Arminian view of theology. He stressed the universal love of God, the offer of salvation to all, the freedom of the will to choose God's offer of salvation, the inner witness of the Holy Spirit that we are the children of God, a life of prayer, Bible study, worship, and growth in holiness, and the church as a community of accountability.

In his personal spiritual life Wesley remained an Anglican priest. He struggled to reconcile the influence of the ancient church, his Anglican heritage, and his experience of conversion and call to holiness. He continued throughout his life to keep the sacramental ministry of baptism and Eucharist and to maintain an ecumenical openness with people who differed with him. He was a man of enormous intellect and a prolific author who stands as one of the most influential and complex figures in the history of Christian thought. His influence is still widely felt among evangelicals to this day.

Jonathan Edwards

The emphasis on a revivalist spirituality has roots in John Wesley and Arminianism, and it also has roots in the Reformed theology of Jonathan Edwards (1703–1758). Like Wesley, Edwards had a life-changing experience, which he records in these words: "As I read the word, there came into my soul, and as it were diffused through it, a sense of the glory of the Divine Being; a new sense, quite different from any thing I ever experienced before. Never any words of scripture seemed to me as these words did. I thought with myself, how excellent a Being that was, and how happy I should be, if I might enjoy that God, and be rapt up to him in heaven, and be as it were swallowed up in him for ever!"[26]

In 1733 Edwards preached a stirring sermon titled "A Divine and Supernatural Light, immediately imparted to the soul by the Spirit of God, shown to be a spiritual and rational doctrine." In this sermon, considered by Edwards scholars to summarize his approach to spirituality, he writes of this spiritual and divine light as a "true sense of the divine excellence of the things revealed in the word of God, and a conviction of the truth and reality of them thence arising." This Light, Edwards taught, came upon the elect through grace and only this Light will "bring the soul to a saving close with Christ," and this Light "has its fruit in a universal holiness of life."[27]

Spirituality as the Changed Life

The emphasis on *holiness of life* in pietism and revivalism resulted in many transformed lives, especially among first-generation converts. The description of holiness by pietist William Law captures the nature of this transformed life:

Our blessed Saviour and His Apostles are wholly taken up in doctrines that relate to common life. They call us to renounce the world, and differ in every temper and way of life, from the spirit and the way of the world: to renounce all its goods, to fear none of its evils, to reject its joys, and have no value for its happiness: to be as new-born babes, that are born into a new state of things: to live as pilgrims in spiritual watching, in holy fear, and heavenly aspiring after another life: to take up our daily cross, to deny ourselves, to profess the blessedness of mourning, to seek the blessedness of poverty of spirit: to forsake the pride and vanity of riches, to take no thought for the morrow, to live in the profoundest state of humility, to rejoice in worldly sufferings: to reject the lust of the flesh, the lust of the eyes, and the pride of life: to bear injuries, to forgive and bless our enemies, and to love mankind as God loveth them: to give up our whole hearts and affections to God, and strive to enter through the strait gate into a life of eternal glory.[28]

The same kind of transforming emphasis is found in the writings of John Wesley. Wesley formed societies of Christians whose purpose it was to live holy lives and to keep each other accountable to right living. To this end Wesley carefully defined the spiritual life, birthing what came to be known as the holiness movement. The following rule is lengthy but worth taking the time to read because it expresses the piety that grew out of the experience of conversion:

> It is therefore expected of all who continue therein, that they should continue to evidence their desire of salvation,
>
> *First*; By doing no harm: by avoiding evil in every kind; especially that which is most generally practiced. Such as: the taking the name of God in vain; the profaning the day of the Lord, either by doing ordinary work thereon, or by buying or selling; drunkenness, buying or selling spirituous liquors, or drinking them (unless in cases of extreme necessity); fighting, quarrelling, brawling; going to law; returning evil for evil or railing for railing; the using many words in buying or selling; the buying or selling uncustomed goods; the giving or taking things on usury, that is, unlawful interest; uncharitable or unprofitable conversation, particularly speaking evil of magistrates or ministers; doing to others as we would not they should do unto us; doing what we know is not for the glory of God: as the putting on of gold, or costly apparel; the taking such diversions as cannot be used in the name of the Lord Jesus; the singing those songs, or reading those books, which do not tend to the knowledge or love of God; softness, and needless self-indulgence; laying up treasures upon earth; borrowing without a probability of paying for them.
>
> It is expected of all who continue in these societies that they should continue to evidence their desire for salvation,
>
> *Secondly*; By doing good; by being, in every kind, merciful after their power; as they have opportunity, doing good of every possible sort, and as far as possible, to all men:
>
> To their bodies, of the ability which God giveth, by giving food to the hungry, by clothing the naked, by visiting or helping them that are sick, or in prison:
>
> To their souls, by instructing, reproving, or exhorting all we have an intercourse with; trampling underfoot that enthusiastic doctrine of devils, that "we are not to do good unless our heart is free to it."
>
> By doing good, especially, to them that are of the household of faith, or groaning so to be; employing them preferably to others, buying one another, helping each other in business; and that so much the more because the world will love its own, and them only.
>
> By all possible diligence and frugality, that the gospel be not blamed.
>
> By running with patience the race that is set before them; denying themselves and taking up their cross daily; submitting to bear the reproach of Christ, to be as the filth and offscouring of the world; and looking that men should say all manner of evil of them falsely, for the Lord's sake.
>
> It is expected of all who desire to continue in these societies that they should continue to evidence their desire of salvation,

Thirdly, By attending upon all ordinances of God; such are: the public worship of God; the ministry of the word, either read or expounded; the supper of the Lord; family and private prayer; searching the Scriptures; and fasting, or abstinence.[29]

The emphasis on holy living in pietism and revivalism is clearly biblical and was very much needed in a world that was gradually moving toward industrialization and the growth of the city with its many temptations. However, it does differ from the experience of Christianity in ancient spirituality. Consider the following.

In the ancient church, experience was the act of baptism into union with Jesus in the pattern of his death and resurrection. The focus was not on an emotionally charged decision I made for Jesus but on the lifelong commitment to live in the pattern of dying to sin and rising to the new life of the Spirit. In ancient spirituality the focus of experience is that of God taking on our humanity, of God entering into our suffering, of God overcoming evil and death on the cross, of God restoring human nature, of God beginning a new act of creation in the resurrection, of God taking up a dwelling inside of us. Baptism into Christ was a lavish experience of union with God's experience for us and in us. The confidence in spirituality is not *my experience* but *my baptism into Christ*, with the focus on Christ embracing me in his death and resurrection.

In modern pietism and revivalism the focus of experience is certainly rooted in God incarnate, dead and buried; but the focus is on *my experience* of his death and resurrection. Testimonies of this experience do point to God in words like "I thank God that he saved me by the work of his Son," but then quickly move to "I know I have been saved because I gave my heart to Jesus, and he has filled my life with meaning and given me new joy in my life, and now I know I will go to heaven to be with him forevermore." The common emphasis here is a confidence in self. "*I* chose Jesus. *I* now have a better life."

Baptism has also shifted away from identity with Jesus in his death and resurrection and turned into "my personal testimony to others that I have given my life over to Jesus." The spiritual life in this case is not a passionate embrace of God signified by a baptism into *his* death and resurrection but a passionate embrace of my personal decision to follow Jesus signified by my conversion. In the outworking of this experiential spirituality, baptism into the death and resurrection of Jesus is replaced by confidence in my personal decision. And baptism no longer has any meaning.

However, as time marched on and the first generation of converts were replaced by a second, then a third generation, the guidelines, which were once fresh and full of life, became institutionalized into a set of rules that resulted in twentieth-century legalism. But that is the subject of the next chapter.

In summary, this turn toward experience greatly impacted evangelicalism. On the positive side it stimulated the evangelism movement of Billy Graham and others. On the negative side, like late medieval mysticism, the focus of spirituality eventually turned toward the journey of the self, toward the focus on experience, legalism, and a works mentality.

CONCLUSION

In the beginning of chapter 2 I wrote that trying to do a history of spirituality situated in God's story is like skipping a stone across a large lake. That is what I have done in chapters 2 and 3. Let us look back at those places where the stone briefly landed and examine the various sites.

I have attempted to show that the ancient church fathers situated spirituality in the divine embrace—God becomes united with his own creation in the incarnation in order to restore creatures and creation to himself. The spiritual life *contemplates* the mysteries and wonders of a God who dwells in our life that we may dwell in his. We *participate* in God by living out our baptism into Jesus by dying to sin and rising to the life of the Spirit. These mysteries are confirmed in the early church debates that affirmed God as Creator, God as incarnate in Jesus by the Spirit, the fullness of divinity and humanity in Jesus, the priority of grace, and the affirmation that Jesus accomplished our union with God through the surrender of his human will to the divine will of God. The spiritual life participates in God through the complete surrender of our own respective wills to the divine will of God in all areas of life.

In late antiquity and in the Middle Ages spirituality situated in God's story was challenged in two ways: First, Platonic dualism, found in the monastics who sought to achieve union with God through works and a renunciation of the material world, modified God's story. Second, late medieval mysticism shifted the contemplation of God's story to a focus on the personal experience of the story, a direct and immediate experience of God. Because of this change, the spiritual life that was once a participation in God's purpose to make this world a place of glory shifted to an escape from this world.

The Reformers returned spirituality to the story of God, to baptism into Jesus, and to a spiritual life of living daily in the pattern of death and resurrection. But the ground of spirituality, still in the incarnation of God dwelling with us so that we may dwell with him, began to shift toward justification as a transaction in which God imputes to us the righteousness of Jesus, forgiving our sins, and empowering us by the Spirit to live the sanctified life. Contemplation and participation in God took on the form of faith and obedience respectively.

The shift from incarnational reality to transactional salvation that began in the Reformation took a more cognitive form in the Protestant orthodoxy of the modern world. Justification was articulated in a forensic way. God acquits the sinner because of the work of Christ. Faith is cognitive—believing the fact and living out of its persuasion. Therefore faith is really lived out of an argument rather than within the story of God's divine embrace. *Sanctification*, the term now used for the Christian life, fails to emphasize the inner dwelling of God and the baptismal calling to live in the pattern of death and resurrection. In this rational spirituality the focus is on right thinking rather than on contemplation of God's mighty deeds of redemption and participation in God by the doing of God's purposes for humanity.

Pietism and revivalism reacted to the overintellectualization of Protestant orthodoxy and, using a language similar to the ancient doctrine of *theosis*, emphasized a *personal union with Christ*. But the personal union in pietism was not based on the incarnation, as it was in the ancient church, but rather on the personal experience engendered by faith in the crucified Christ, who now lives within. That this differs from the incarnate union of the ancient church can be seen in a number of ways.

First, in the biblical and ancient teaching, union is initiated by God in the incarnation. God becomes one of us, lifting humanity into himself. Pietism, while not denying the incarnation, essentially bypasses it and instead presents union with God as a result of the conversion experience. The *faithfulness of Jesus*, as the one man who unites us all to God and through whom we have access to God, disappointingly is exchanged for *our faith*, which unites us to God.

A second difference with the ancient understanding of union is that ancient spirituality focuses on the whole story of God, whereas pietism focuses on faith in the death and resurrection, reducing the story of God to less than its whole. A third difference is that in the ancient church we enter God's story in repentance, baptism, and the reception of the Spirit (Acts 2:38), whereas pietism emphasizes a conversion by faith that has no real place for the divine significance of the baptismal ritual. Baptism becomes *my response* instead of God's sign of creative power expressed through water.

There is a difference also in how the spiritual life is understood. In the ancient church the spiritual life is living in the pattern of death and resurrection, becoming fully human, following the model of Jesus, who united to God reveals humanity in the glory God intended. Pietism took on a negative attitude toward the world and taught a godliness not of affirming life in the way of Jesus, but a life that identified worldly activities and withdrew to a strict life that, at its worst, degenerated into legalism.

Experience has become the basis for certitude. Whereas the ancient and Reformation world called Christians to live in their baptism, pietism made continual experience in the faith the source of certainty. Philip Sheldrake points out that "Patristic 'mysticism' is not to be confused with later Western interest in subjective religious experiences or in detailed itineraries for the spiritual journey. 'Mysticism' was fundamentally the life of every baptized Christian who came to know God revealed in Jesus Christ through belonging to the 'fellowship of the mystery,' that is, the Church. This life was supported by exposure to Scripture and participation in the liturgy."[30]

Finally, and certainly by no means least, the language of Protestant spirituality shifted away from the language of contemplation and participation. The new language focused on justification and sanctification, faith and obedience, trust and obey, decision and rules. God's story stood behind these shifts, yet what became primary was *the right theological system* for rational intellectuals and *the born-again experience* and *living by the rules* for the romantic revivalists. These modern approaches to spirituality created the twentieth-century tension of a spirituality *arising within the self*. Whether the intellectual self or the experiential self, the problems resulting from these spiritualities, which have become divorced from the full story of God, now plague the evangelical spirituality developed in the twentieth century. It is to this subject we now turn.

A Summary for Reflection and Conversation

Summary	Reflection
Reformation spirituality	The Reformers, like the ancient fathers, situate spirituality in the divine embrace of incarnation, death, and resurrection. But they replaced contemplation and participation with justification and sanctification.
Modern intellectual spirituality	Christianity previously seen as a story grounded in the divine embrace now became the object of study. Liberals shifted spirituality toward the moral influence of Jesus. Conservatives emphasized spirituality as right belief—spirituality lost its ancient relational character grounded in the divine embrace. It was now based on a forensic transaction.
Modern experiential spirituality	Spirituality shifted from a contemplation of the divine embrace to a focus on the personal feelings derived from God's embrace. Participation in the purposes of God shifted to a negative emphasis of dying to worldly attachments.

THE CRISIS: HOW THE SPIRITUAL LIFE BECAME SEPARATED FROM THE DIVINE EMBRACE

Chapter 2   The story of God's divine embrace in the incarnation, death, and resurrection of Jesus was defended by the ancient creeds and debates of the church. Spirituality and the spiritual life, situated in the divine embrace, was modified by Platonic dualism, which saw spirituality as an escape from this world, and late medieval mysticism, which interpreted spirituality as a journey into self.

Chapter 3   The Reformers returned spirituality to the divine embrace with some modification. In the modern era spirituality as the divine embrace was redefined by a spirituality preoccupied with a forensic justification combined with sanctification guided by gratitude, and a spirituality that focused on the conversion experience followed by a flight from the world.

Chapter 4   *Twentieth-century evangelical spirituality inherited the modifications of the past and developed privatized spiritualities of legalism, intellectualism, and experientialism.*

Chapter 5   The present evangelical practices of spirituality, separated from the divine embrace, are inadequate to the challenge of the widespread popularity of New Age and Eastern spiritualties grounded in an impersonal, pantheistic conception of God and the world. The challenge before us is to recover a spirituality and spiritual life situated in the divine embrace.

4

A MODERN DISLOCATION
(1900–2000)

Rescuing Spirituality from Legalism and Romanticism

In twentieth-century evangelicalism we see the unfortunate result of separating spirituality from God's story. Spirituality has become situated in the narrative of the self. In this *privatized spirituality* evangelicals look to themselves for the confirmation of their spiritual condition. The self-focused spiritualities of the twentieth century have not emerged willy-nilly but are deeply rooted in the historical movements that separated spirituality from the vision of God, especially the modern developments of an intellectual spirituality and experiential spirituality discussed in the previous chapter. The problem of these dislocated spiritualities has been compounded by the current antihistorical, narcissistic, and pragmatic nature of evangelical Christianity. The evangelical orientation toward the self is evident also in the current attraction to the new mysticism which grew out of the late medieval era with its mystical emphasis on the journey into the self. But more about that later. First we must ask, "Who are we evangelicals who have embraced spiritualities of the self?"

Current evangelicalism can be conveniently organized into four phases: (1) the fundamentalist origins that dominated the first half of the twentieth century; (2) the emergence of traditional evangelicalism that is the primary story of the middle of the century; (3) the spread of a pragmatic evangelicalism appearing in the last third of the century; and now, (4) the current emerging church—the group I call the "younger evangelical"—is drawing a great deal of attention.[1] This exponential growth of evangelicalism in the last century has led sociologist Alan Wolfe to remark that "there is . . . a sense in which we are all evangelicals now."[2] My contention is that evangelicals, having separated spirituality from God's vision, practice spiritualities of legalism, intellectualism, and ex-perientialism. I will comment on these forms of spirituality.

SPIRITUAL LEGALISM

The first seven years of my life were spent in Belgian Congo, Africa, where my parents were missionaries under the Africa Inland Mission (AIM). I remember my father and mother as highly dedicated servants of God who gave their lives to proclaim the gospel in a remote part of the world. They were willing to turn away from the comforts of the Western world to live in a house made of mud with a grass thatched roof without the comforts of running water, electricity, or bathrooms. During the time they served as missionaries they translated large portions of the Bible, pastored, taught, farmed, counseled, and did whatever else was needed to bring the gospel of Jesus to people who had no knowledge of the faith. My parents were servants of the people as they embodied the faith and introduced Jesus to a whole village and beyond. In those days, which was just prior to the United States entering World War II, they demonstrated what may be considered a high point of older fundamentalist spirituality—the willingness to find themselves by forsaking their own self—dying to self to find their lives.

The world is full of evangelical servants like my parents—committed, passionate about ministry, and willing to serve. I thank God for their lives and for the many evangelicals like them who have passed down a godly heritage by their example of witness and sacrifice.

There was another side, however, to the spirituality practiced by my parents and demanded of my brother, my sister, and me. That was a spirituality embraced by many in their generation with a language of spiritual legalism, expressed in the ethic of dos and don'ts, and inherent in a rigid doctrinal legalism from which it was impossible to deviate without losing spiritual status.

The Legalistic Ethic of Dos and Don'ts

I wasn't conscious of the legalistic approach to the Christian faith embraced by my parents until we returned from Africa to the United States in 1940. My first conscious experience of evangelical legalism occurred when I was eight years old. During that summer I was sent to a YMCA camp for a month. Each week the kids were taken into town to see a movie. Since I didn't know better, I went. When my parents heard that I went to a movie, they were shocked and quickly instructed the camp leader that I was not allowed to attend any more movies. So for the rest of the summer, when others went to the weekly movie, I remained on the campground alone under supervision of a camp leader who was appointed to watch over me.

The question of whether or not to go to a movie is in itself not the issue. My parents' refusal to allow me to go to the movie was symptomatic of a much larger and pervasive issue within the evangelical world—its *legalistic mentality*.[3] A mentality constitutes a particular way of *seeing* reality. A legalistic mentality defines spirituality in terms of what a Christian *does not do*. Those who question the established dos and don'ts are regarded as rebels and are often ostracized in one way or another from the community. Unfortunately these dos and don'ts often get in the way of seeing the real ethics of Christian spirituality such as the growth of character, the concern for justice, and the care of the poor and the needy.

The origins of the dos and don'ts in American evangelicalism go back to the revivals in the frontier days of the nineteenth century. All of us have seen the western movies and the depiction of life in the western spread of the American frontier. The center of town is the bar with its heavy drinking, gambling, card playing, and lewd women. As Christianity spread west in the revival tradition, it was imperative for Christians to distinguish themselves from the crude, boisterous, drinking, smoking, dancing, card playing, gambling, and lascivious crowd. Christians, therefore, swung the pendulum to the other side and insisted on a cleaned-up life as a demonstration of a converted life and a spiritual walk with God. In time these outward expressions of a cleaned-up life turned from sin became the external marks of the spiritual life.

While abstinence from worldly practices was a genuine choice of an original generation of Christians, the dos and don'ts became for the second and especially the third generation of Christians an *imposed* structure of spirituality. The inner convictions that generated the original choice to refrain from worldly practices was lost. In its place now stood a legalistic ethos, that is, restraint from worldly practice became the sum and the substance of the spiritual life. Contemplation and participation was replaced by "keeping the rules," even if it was done only in an external manner.

Doctrinal Legalism

This spirit of legalism is true not only in matters of behavior but also in the approach to theology. Each evangelical subgroup has its fixed doctrines. For example:

All evangelicals agree that the Bible is the final authority in matters of faith and practice; legalism adds that biblical authority can be expressed only with full, plenary, verbal inspiration of the Bible.

All evangelicals agree that God is the Creator; legalists add a literal interpretation of Genesis 1 and insist that Scripture teaches that God created the world in seven days.

All evangelicals agree that the Bible is to be interpreted by God's people; legalists insist that there is only one valid interpretation of every text reached through the biblical, historical, theological methodology of interpretation.

All evangelicals agree that the church is called to reflect on Scripture and develop a theology of the Christian faith; legalists insist that there is only one kind of theology—propositional truth.

All evangelicals believe in the church; legalists insist that their church or fellowship is the pure church and all others are apostate.

All evangelicals believe in the second coming of Christ; legalists insist that their particular view of the end time (i.e., pretribulation rapture and premillenarian) is the one true understanding of Scripture.

All evangelicals believe in the ethical life supported by the theological virtues of faith, hope, and love modeled by Jesus; legalists deduce teachings from the ethical admonitions of Scripture and create a handy list of dos and don'ts to be followed scrupulously.

All evangelicals believe in the spiritual life; legalists define spirituality as reading the Bible daily, praying regularly, going to church every time the door is open, witnessing to everybody you meet, and maintaining the rules that define an evangelical spirituality.

Doctrinal legalism emerged in the struggle with liberalism in the first part of the twentieth century. The fundamentalist movement sought to protect historic Christianity through inerrancy, propositional theology, evidential apologetics, and the concept of a pure church. This resulted in a us/them mentality. By the time the battle with liberalism ended (because of the culture shift), the evangelical legalism created out of that situation had become sacrosanct, so that any questioning of it, even in the face of new issues and new battle fronts, was regarded as an unfaithfulness to truth.

This attitude created another legalism. What had been added to the faith as a way of protecting it now became the faith. Because legalists are passionate about their dos and don'ts and to the specific interpretations they add to the faith, they fight with people who don't agree with their ethos, their method, or the particular spin they give to biblical authority, theology, the church, behavior, or spirituality.

A Critique of Legalism

The problem with legalistic mentality is that it adds to the gospel and in some sense denigrates the Good News. It goes beyond biblical faith and practice to require adherence to systems of behavior and belief that go beyond the story of God and the freedom to live in the new life modeled by Jesus. These added features of the faith are usually systems of control that proceed from some historical movement when a group was forced to express its faith or lifestyle in a particular way at a particular time over against a movement that was threatening them. This is what happened to Christians on the American frontier. In order to distinguish themselves from the sinners, they developed their list of dos and don'ts as the sign of true spirituality. What may have been a genuine expression for the originators became a means of control in the next generation.

In the end legalism subverts the gospel. God's grace, which is the antidote to legalism, becomes so lost in the legalistic system that when grace is presented to those who are legalistic, grace is often rejected as untrue. Recently, for example, I spoke to a pastor who tried to bring his congregation out of legalism and into a fresh hearing of God's *freeing grace* by teaching God's story, only to be dismissed from his church and charged with teaching heresy. In this instance truth had been turned on its head and exchanged for the false security of legalism.

For a legalist, spirituality is tantamount to saying, "I think the right way, live the right way, associate with the right people, read my Bible, pray, go to church, and avoid worldly ways; therefore I am spiritual." This person might be a "good" person, live a straight and disciplined life, be a good friend and neighbor, and support the church and its ministries. But legalism is not true Christian spirituality, for in the end it looks to *self* to achieve a condition of spirituality by adhering to a predetermined set of rules and fixed doctrinal interpretations. It goes beyond what the Bible teaches and what the common tradition embraces.

Legalistic spirituality is not directly situated in God's story of creation, incarnation, and re-creation. Legalistic spirituality is situated in derivative rules and doctrines determined by a particular cultural expression of the faith. This sort of spirituality, instead of contemplating the mystery of God's vision and participating in the life purposed by God, measures a person's spiritual state by the secondary rules and doctrines that ask: "Are you keeping the rules?" "Are you adhering to the doctrinal particulars espoused by this particular church?" Legalism focuses on the self and how well the self adheres to the group expectations.

INTELLECTUAL SPIRITUALITY

Another kind of evangelical spirituality is the quest to *know* God. I encountered this emphasis in my seminary training. Like most seminarians, I did not know much about the Christian faith. In the early months of my seminary training, a concerned brother took me aside and said, "Bob, you have a great deal of zeal and passion for God, but you lack knowledge." He was right! So I took to my seminary studies like a fish to water. I loved all my courses and was determined that I was going to attain knowledge.

Knowing God in Systems of Theological Thought

I especially embraced the study of Calvin and in a short time became an "expert" on Calvin—or so I thought. I wanted to *know* God. I devoured the system of thought taught by Calvin. I studied the decrees of God and embraced supralapsarianism; I studied predestination and affirmed double predestination; I studied the nature of man and confessed belief in total depravity; I studied election and decided the case in favor of unconditional election; I studied God's grace and confirmed it as irresistible; I examined the atonement and became convinced that it was limited to the elect; and I studied perseverance and argued that all the elect would persevere until the end.

I had the Calvinist system down so cold that when I first started to teach I invited people who disagreed with my positions to come into my course and debate. I went so far with my Calvinism that I defended Calvin for burning Servetus at the stake for not believing in the Trinity. I thought my advanced knowledge made me more spiritual than those who did not "know" the full system of truth.

I am not the only one who has been influenced by an intellectual spirituality. Pat Allison writes the story of her husband, John, whom she describes as a "true blue conservative, influential type minister for 40 years." "One day," she writes, "while shaving he looked in the bathroom mirror and heard 'You're a phoney.' At first he disregarded this disclosure but as time went on he struggled constantly with these words finally recognizing 'I have prided myself in my excellent doctrine all these years.' Excellent doctrine," Pat writes, "had become an idol." For the next five years John rested and "came to know Jesus as he had never known him before."[4]

The Origins of Intellectual Spirituality

The origin of the modern notion of an intellectual spirituality as knowledge is rooted, as we have seen, in the Enlightenment emphasis on reason and science. Reason always has played an important role in

Christian thought, and it should. But the particular way evangelicals have used reason and science to affirm the spirituality of knowing is found in the seventeenth-century method of Descartes, whose vision of truth is caught in the statement he made famous: "I think, therefore I am." Christian intellectuals turned Descartes's dictum into something like, "I think about the knowledge of God, therefore I know God." Spiritual thinking became an intellectual spirituality.

For Descartes, knowledge was rooted in fact. And the way to get to fact was the scientific method of observation, analysis, and systematization. Evangelicals translated the method of Descartes into their study of Scripture and elevated knowledge to the level of participating in God. Whoever attained the greatest insight was the most intellectually spiritual. The method went something like this: The Bible is the mind of God revealed. God has created us in his image. Intellect, which distinguishes us from everything else God has made, is the highest aspect of our likeness to God. Therefore, if we wish to know God we must use our mind in the study of God's mind. God's mind and the human mind meet in the pages of Scripture.

In the pattern of Enlightenment methodology, evangelical scholars adopted the historical, grammatical, theological method of Scripture study. Scholars who had attained the knowledge of God told their students, "You have before you the tools to open up the Scripture and understand the mind of God." In evangelical circles this methodology led to a proof-oriented Christianity. The faith was to be regarded as true because it had been tested and proven to be true through the Enlightenment method of gaining facts in history and science. Consequently, Christianity became a fact to be believed, a truth upon which one could stake his or her life. The resurrection, for example, became an article of faith based on fact, diminishing the ancient emphasis that we are to live a new life through contemplation and participation in the resurrection of Christ. Adherence to the fact became more important than living into the resurrection of Jesus.

Unfortunately, the same Enlightenment methodology was used by the liberals. They went to Scripture and saw stories that reason and science could not prove. How could you prove that God and man were united in the womb of the Virgin Mary? How could you prove that Jesus's death was an atonement for sin? How could you prove that Jesus rose from the dead? For liberals, these mysteries of the faith, subjected to the Enlightenment method of reason and science, could no longer pass the test of facts. So the liberals had to find a new language for these mysteries. Such mysteries were, they said, myths. Rather than throw Christianity away, they argued that the myths must be demythologized; we must, they said, "get behind the myth to discover the truth." And what they found was love. Love alone is truth, and the myths, subjected to reason and science, took us to the one indisputable fact of the Christian faith: Jesus's message in a nutshell is "Love God and love your neighbor."

Factualism brought us to two spiritualities. The spirituality of "I know the truth of the mind of God, and here it is in these facts," and "There is only one discernable and trustworthy truth derived from the demythologized Jesus—love."

For me, being an evangelical in the 1950s meant that I embraced the intellectual spirituality of believing and arguing for the facts. It engendered a spirit of pride. I knew the facts about God, I thought, and to know the facts is to know God. *I cannot associate with those liberals who are wrong*, I thought. *And then there is all that Catholic witchcraft and Orthodox voodoo. What a shame that all those people think of themselves as Christian when they live in the darkness of tradition and falsehood. If only they could see things the true way—my way. If only they could have the true knowledge that we evangelicals have. We should pray for them and witness to them so they can see the light and come our way.*

This problem of pride and separation caused by a distorted view of spirituality through knowledge is certainly not a problem peculiar to the evangelical community. For example, early in my teaching career I was asked to teach a course on Protestant theology in a Catholic seminary. On the day of the first class I shared the typical evangelical attitude toward Catholics, none of which was very positive. When I was finished, they told me their stories of growing up with a negative view toward all Protestants, fearing that they were the heretics. I have had a similar experience talking with my Orthodox friends as well.

Knowledge is very important. As Christians we should think and study Scripture, the creeds, and the thoughts of great Christian thinkers. But knowledge in and of itself is not to be equated with the spiritual life. The problem with a so-called intellectual spirituality is that it is often a reflection of modern culture and not a true Christian spirituality.

This intellectualism spawned the discipline of apologetics—the attempt to defend Christianity with reason, science, philosophy, and other disciplines. In time conservative apologetic Christianity elevated an intellectually defensible Christianity to a state of supremacy. A person who can argue for the faith on the basics of evidence and can use logic to explain the Trinity or the doctrine of inerrancy or who can use science to prove creation or an "early earth" theory or who can argue from Scripture to prove predestination or its opposite, the freedom of the will, may feel himself or herself to be spiritually superior.

While knowledge is an important aspect of the Christian faith, it is not to be confused with the spirituality of our mystical union with God. Often the lust to embrace higher knowledge forms within us attitudes that are the opposite of Christian spirituality. Assuming that we have the "true system of knowledge," we may become divisive, judgmental, haughty, contentious, argumentative, arrogant, defensive, and proud. These are the attitudes the Scripture warns against. In my experience these attitudes show up in ecclesiastical separationism, which is usually based on the assumption that "I know the truth, and you don't, so I cannot have fellowship with you."

In the end an intellectual spirituality is situated, not in God's story, but in *my* knowledge about God's story, which is inherently limited. Eventually I came to the realization that my own knowledge was not a measure of my spirituality. I really didn't know God. I knew about God insofar as one system taught. But I fear it was knowledge for the sake of knowledge, knowledge that puffs up, knowledge that divides. Like other approaches to spirituality, this quest to know God through the mind was just another *self-focused spirituality*. My spirituality was rooted in *my* faith, *my* comprehension of a system of thought.

The contemplation of God, of his person, creation, incarnation, and re-creation of the world, is a different kind of knowledge. It is a contemplation on the *mysteries*, namely, the mystery of God creating, the mystery of God incarnate, the mystery of the cross and empty tomb, the mystery of God's presence in the church, and the mystery of Christ's return to claim his lordship over creation. The contemplation of these mysteries moves us to live into these mysteries, participating in God's life for the world.

EXPERIENTIAL SPIRITUALITY

Another kind of spirituality that has taken a foothold within various groups of evangelical Christians is the search for a defining spiritual experience. *Feeling* God has had a long and lively history within evangelicalism. It is presented as another way of *knowing* God. It is the opposite of knowing God through facts; it is a spirituality that claims God is known through intuition and emotion. Experience as the key to the spiritual life is often found in revivalism and among the Pentecostal, the holiness, and the charismatic movements.

The Origins of Experiential Spirituality

In the last chapter I discussed the origins of experiential spirituality in the romantic movement. Romanticism argued for knowledge based on intuition and feeling. Most of the romantics like Coleridge, Wordsworth, and Keats were pantheists. For them the universal mind was within creation. As we open ourselves to nature and to the impulses of the universal divine, we gain knowledge through feeling God. Friedrich Schleiermacher (d. 1834), the theologian of the romantic movement, taught that God was an "intuition of the universe" experienced in the unconsciousness of oneness achieved through the Spirit of utter dependence. Spirituality was a letting go in utter dependence upon the universe, a feeling of oneness with everything. Schleiermacher has been called the "father of modern theology" because of the unity he espoused between God and creation. One can see how close this view may be to a New Age spirituality that is based on oneness.

Evangelicals do not espouse this kind of feeling. Instead, the evangelical spirituality of experience is most clearly articulated in the *born-again* experience of John Wesley. No one should deny the validity of Wesley's experience. His life, ministry, and legacy that proceeded from that experience has resulted in an enormous impact on British and American evangelicalism and the subsequent growth of evangelicalism around the world.

But as I have pointed out, Wesley's experience was universalized into the defining mark of true spirituality. The goal of evangelism following Wesley's experience became that of bringing a person to the experience of *feeling* forgiven. A ritual known as the "invitation" was developed to facilitate this experience. At the end of the service the invitation is given to receive Christ as personal Lord and Savior. As the congregation sings "Just as I Am," the evangelist calls on people to "raise your hand" and "come forward," as at a Billy Graham crusade. Counselors are stationed to lead the new converts through several Scriptures and assure them of their salvation. They are admonished then to "read your Bible, pray, go to church, and tell others about Jesus."

My father was a pastor in this tradition. Every spring the yearly revivalist came to the church to preach and bring people to the experience of salvation. Just following World War II, in the year that I was fifteen, during the revivalist's invitation my dad came to me, grabbed me by the arm, looked into my eyes, and said, "Robert, are you sure?" I remember how disturbed I was by his question. I had been baptized at twelve and found baptism to be a highly meaningful expression of God's relationship to me. Why, I wondered, would my dad speak doubt into my heart by making a revival experience more important than my baptism?

Certainly many people have been resoundingly converted at an invitation ritual. But to make this experience a criterion for spirituality is a huge mistake. It elevates *experience* as the apologetic for faith. For example, I remember hearing of a mother who wrote to her daughter and said, "I'm putting the birth dates of your children in my Bible. But I don't know the dates of their second birth. Would you please send them to me so I can put them in my Bible." Besides being controlling, this gesture says: "I can know your kids are saved when I can affirm the date of each one's experience of repentance and forgiveness."

In this approach to spirituality the criterion for being a spiritual person is located in a particular experience that one must have at a particular time and place. Spirituality is situated in the experience. A person may then say, "I am spiritual because I raised my hand, walked forward, and asked Jesus into my heart." I do not want to deny the value of this experience. Certainly many people have had their lives completely changed through an experience of the conviction of sin and turning to God in a life-changing experience. For many this is a datable experience, a fond memory of a moment in which their life was altered forever.

What is questionable about the conversion is not the experience itself but situating spirituality in the experience. To suggest "I am a spiritual person because I *felt* the forgiveness of God in a particular experience" places confidence in my experience rather than in God's embrace of me on the hard wood of the cross. Consequently the spirituality of someone not having the experience is suspect and not confirmed until the person is able to testify to the facts of when and where the experience took place and witness to the changed life that resulted from it. In the end this kind of spirituality tends to center on the self, dwelling on the experience itself for the certainty of salvation and spirituality. Of this form of spirituality, Carol McDaniel rightly observes, "If we don't 'feel' something then we aren't being spiritual enough."[5]

Our Personal Relationship with Jesus

The notion of an experiential spirituality has several additional manifestations. A common expression is "Do you have a personal relationship with Jesus?" Usually when this question is asked we assume the person asking the question has a personal relationship with God and knows what that looks like! Merril Smoak's experience with this attitude, like mine, is concerned about this kind of question. He writes, "My evangelical, Baptist heritage has pushed me to have a personal relationship with Jesus. Personal quiet times, personal Bible studies, and discipleship programs were the formula to a personal relationship with Jesus and true spirituality. This approach has basically led to a 'works' mentality and an individual approach to Christianity"[6] as opposed to the ancient emphasis on union with God accomplished by the incarnate Word in his death and resurrection given to us as a gift.

When someone asks me the question, "Do you have a personal relationship with God?" I always answer, "You're asking the wrong question. What is important here is not that I in and of myself achieve or create a personal relationship with God, but that God has a personal relationship with me through Jesus Christ, which I affirm and nourish."

My student Marie Wonders understands why this question of a personal relationship with God must be turned on its head. Most everyone, she points out, talks about spirituality as "doing things to become a spiritual person." But Christian spirituality is "incarnational." "Christian spirituality," she writes, is "about receiving from God, rather than doing something for God. This is so countercultural!" She goes on to say, "Every time I hear that the Christian life is about receiving from God I am so excited to be a Christian, but I am also mindful that I often forget this and think the Christian faith is about things that I do for God. But if I forget that the Christian life is receiving from God, I am not understanding what makes the Christian religion different from all other religions out there."[7]

Marie has it right. Experience is not what *I feel or do* toward God but a reception of what God has done for me and for the whole world. But more about that in part 2.

Critique

My critique then of the three prominent evangelical forms of spirituality is simply this: *They all situate spirituality in the self.* "*I* keep the rules; *I* know God in a system of thought; *I* had a born-again experience." In contrast, historic spirituality situates spirituality in the story of the Triune God, who creates, became incarnate, took my humanity up into his, entered the suffering of the cross, and rose from the grave. God drew me up into himself and did for me what I could not do—*He himself restored my union with himself.* Now, having been baptized into this great mystery, I contemplate God's work for me and the whole world, and I participate in God's purposes for the world revealed in Jesus Christ. Spirituality is a *gift.* The spiritual life is the *surrendered life.*

TWENTY-FIRST CENTURY SPIRITUAL TRENDS DISLOCATED FROM GOD'S STORY

Toward the end of the twentieth century and now in the twenty-first century new shifts in spirituality have emerged. These shifts are related to the spirituality of the twentieth century in that they are either the opposite or they carry the twentieth-century spiritual tradition one step further. In the first category there are some who reject legalism in favor of a movement called *antinomianism.* Then there are those who reject intellectual spirituality in favor of an anti-intellectual spirituality, some going so far as to have what they consider to be a romance with God. These approaches to spirituality along with the adaptation of the church to the consumer mentality constitutes the new spiritualities emerging currently. Like the spiritualities of the earlier part of the twentieth century, these are also dislocated from God's story and situated in the self.

Legalism Exchanged for an Antinomianism Spirituality

One of the new spiritualities is the spirit of antinomianism. (*Anti* = against; *nomianism* = law. An antinomist is against all the rules.) Unfortunately, while my generation was brought up to keep the rules as a way of "knowing you are spiritual," the pendulum for some seems to have swung the other way. The rules against dancing, drinking, movies, smoking, and playing cards that once prevailed among evangelicals have been jettisoned for the sense of freedom in Christ. The worst form of this so-called spirituality that wrongly interprets Paul is "I'm free; I can do just about anything I want to do."

Recent surveys among teenage Christians seem to suggest that their lives are not very different from those of non-Christians. Dale Buss notes that "ninety-one percent of born-again teenagers surveyed a few years ago proclaimed that there is no such thing as absolute truth." Buss points out that teens are "following the moral breakdown of the broader American culture." "This Zeitgeist," he writes, "largely reflects a pseudo-faith that is fed by a steady diet of pop-culture feints, from the allegorical 'Lord of the Rings' movies to the t-shirt that recently adorned Pamela Anderson saying, 'Jesus is my homeboy.'"[8] What is needed is a recovery of the Pauline understanding of freedom. It is a freedom *from* legalism and a freedom *to live in Christ* and his purposes for humanity, not a freedom to do whatever I please.

I remember coming into the Pauline understanding of freedom in Christ, which is not licentiousness, in a graduate class where Romans 7 and 8 were being discussed. When the lecturer clarified Paul's meaning, it set me free. I saw my new freedom as a freedom from the need to keep the law as a way of assuring my eternal union with God in Christ. That insight set me free from the legalistic rules and ethos of the evangelical subculture. But I did not see the freedom from the law as a license to sin. Instead I saw my freedom as the freedom to live *in Christ*, who fulfilled the law in his perfect life and left me an example to follow.

Romans 7 is in a real sense an autobiographical account of Paul's struggle with the law. He writes of his own conflict saying, "I knew what I should do, but I couldn't keep the demands of the law and I couldn't get free of its condemnation. I have the desire to do what is good, but I cannot carry it out" (Rom. 7:18, author's translation). The demand of the law was an enormous source of frustration for Paul. He never found deliverance through the law by trying to keep it. The more he tried to keep the law, the more he discovered himself to be "a prisoner of the law of sin at work within my members" (Rom. 7:23). But Christ was found to be the end of the law. So freeing was this experience for Paul that he cried out, "Who will rescue me from this body of death?" (meaning the condemning power of the law). "Thanks be to God," he shouts, "through Jesus Christ our Lord!" (Rom. 7:24–25).

There is something very freeing about this Pauline insight. The lecturer was describing the role of the law. "The law condemns us because we cannot keep its demands," he said, "and then it brings us to Christ where we hear the Good News." This is Paul's message. "There is now no condemnation for those who are in Christ Jesus, because through Christ Jesus the law of the Spirit of life set me free from the law of sin and death" (Rom. 8:1–2). I am sure I had heard that message before the Lutheran lecturer explained it, but it now finally registered. "I'm free," I said to myself. "I'm free not to sin. And I'm free to live in the Spirit." This is what it means to participate in the life of God into which we have been baptized.

I should have known this truth, but I didn't, at least not clearly. Legalism had been such a part of my Christian experience that, like many others, I had become numb to grace. All I heard was "Do this; make an effort at that; achieve here." Legalistic spirituality was terrorizing me, making demands on me that I could not achieve. But my answer to legalism was not in an antinomian attitude of "I'm free to do whatever I want to do." Antinomianism situates freedom in the self, not in Christ, the central person of God's story. Spirituality grounded in Christ is simple and profound. It is simple because anyone can get it; it is profound because it has to do with all our living, all our values, all our relationships, all our work, all our leisure, all our worship, in fact, everything in life. It is a spirituality going deep, to the roots of our very being—living in God's pattern of death and resurrection 24/7.

Intellectual Spirituality Exchanged for an Anti-Intellectual Spirituality

The shift into postmodern culture is a shift from objective knowledge to subjectivity, to relativism, and to mystery. The new fashionable thing is to say phrases like, "I don't know. That is very complex. It is buried in mysticism." The mystery at work in the universe is the mystery of God creating, becoming incarnate, and re-creating. This Christian mystery and fashionable cultural mystery, however, are two different realities. The Christian who unthinkingly refers everything to mystery may be embracing cultural mystery, which is not at all the mystery of true Christian spirituality. Paul writes of the "mystery of Christ" that "has now been revealed" (Eph. 3:4–5). God's mystery in Christ can be freely explored, talked about, contemplated, and participated in.

Recently I was speaking at a conference designed to help younger people with the journey from modernity to postmodernity. During the question and answer time a person raised this question: "I have been told that we no longer know anything, that everything is mystery and ambiguity, but you seem to suggest there are some things that we do know. How do we know these things?"

I answered, "It is not that we do not know anything anymore. It is not like all that we have held to be true is simply up for grabs. Truth has not changed. It is our way of knowing that has changed and what we are willing to bleed and die for."

"The Christian way of knowing," I continued, "is reflection on Scripture within community." We in Christ belong to a community of faith connected with Israel that goes all the way back to the beginning of things. This community has been reflecting on what it perceives to be God's actions in history and on God's self-revelation in Scripture for centuries. Out of this reflection comes the *first order* truths that all Christians embrace—mainly the story of the Triune God, creation, fall, incarnation, death, resurrection, and re-creation of all things at the end of history. It is the *second order* systems that people now question as truth. These systems of theology (both conservative and liberal), rooted in the Enlightenment, attempted to answer all questions with certainty, leaving no room for ambiguity or mystery. Because these modern systems are now in question, we are able to get behind them to the narrative of faith from which they sprang. We do have truth. It is the story of God handed down in Scripture, in the church, and in its ministry of worship.

The antidote to an intellectual spirituality is not an anti-intellectual spirituality but a spirituality rooted in God's story that stands on its own. What I mean by this is that God's story is a vision of reality that does not need to be supported by reason, science, or any other discipline. Instead of interpreting God's story through the academic disciplines, God's story is the vision of reality through which the world, its history, and all the structures of existence are to be interpreted. So an anti-intellectual spirituality is as much rooted in the self as an intellectual spirituality. When we stand within God's story and interpret all of life, we see life through God's vision. And it is an intelligent vision that speaks the truth about life.[9]

Experiential Christianity Shifts into Narcissism

The third problem appearing now at the beginning of the twenty-first century is the shift toward narcissism. In his book, *The Culture of Narcissism*, Christopher Lasch points to the antihistorical attitude that is so prevalent today as a major cause of narcissism. He writes, "The devaluation of the past has become one of the most important symptoms of the cultural crisis to which this book addresses itself, drawing on historical experience to explain what is wrong with our present arrangements."[10]

The same devaluation of the past can be said of the church's current spirituality. The experiential message of pietism and revivalism, even in its early twentieth-century form, was more grounded in God's story than it appears to be in our current narcissistic culture. Evangelism's focus on God's story taking experiential root in our lives is in itself not narcissistic. It only becomes narcissistic when one becomes fascinated with his or her own journey and gives priority to self-reflection. Our contemplative wonder and awe is not to focus on the spiritual journey of the self but on the journey of God who creates and became incarnate in his own creation to re-create. And our participation in the spiritual life is not a continuous search for a transcendent experience but the transfiguration of this life through a life lived in the continual pattern of baptism—dying to sin and rising to the life of the Spirit.

Worship Narcissism

One place where a narcissistic preoccupation with the self is evident currently is in worship. The church's emphasis upon worship fits the *experience culture* in which we live today, and the expectations of the worship experience seem to be misplaced. I am not sure that anyone has defined the expected experience one should have in order to claim a spirituality formed by worship. But the current popular phrases surrounding the worship experience seem oriented around personal perception. "Did you *like* the worship?" But this may mean, "Did you like the sound?" "Did you like our performance?" "Did you like the preaching?" These questions have more to do with style and preference than the transformation of thought and action. Some have suggested turning the words toward God and asking, "Did God like our worship? Was God pleased with what we did today?" These questions, however, equally misunderstand the purpose of worship. In worship we proclaim and enact God's story of the world. Therefore, the more appropriate experiential question is "Did God's story, which was proclaimed and enacted today, make a transformative impact on your life?" Or, "How has the weekly rehearsal of the meaning of human life that is rooted in God's story changed the way you treat your family, your neighbors, the people with whom you work?"

Again, experience in worship is not *my immediate pleasure* or even *my immediate response*. The focus of experience is not on *my* experience of God but on how God as the subject of worship forms me through word and sacrament and thereby changes my life. I have been in one too many worship services where the focus was *cheerleading for Jesus*. I have done one too many hurrahs for Jesus because somebody made me feel guilty about cheering for a football team. Football cheering is not transferable to worship. Worshipers are not a cheering section for God. The problem with this kind of worship is not only that it is an accommodation to culture but that it is also a severe example of self-situated spirituality, especially when it emphasizes a romantic relationship with God through experiential mysticism.

Romantic Relationship with God

A romantic relationship to God is found frequently in contemporary music, poetry, and personal diaries. Certainly there is a valid place for feelings in our relationship to God, for God made us as emotional beings, just as there is a valid place for the use of reason because God made us with intelligence. But just as reason as "intellectual facts before which we bow" is not the spiritual use of reason, so also feeling as "a romantic relationship with God" is not the true embrace of spiritual feeling.

God is not my boyfriend or girlfriend with whom I sustain a romantic relationship. Yes, we are to love God, to have a relationship with God, but much of the current talk about "falling in love with Jesus" and the language that speaks of our relationship with God using sexual innuendo is derived from our current MTV culture that is obsessed with sexuality.

The true love of God and the true experience of God are not found in the languages of experience I have referred to above but in the act of contemplating God and of participating in God, which springs forth from our union with God in Christ. We do not contemplate our own experience of God or the romantic feelings we may experience. We contemplate the wonder, the marvel, the mystery, the glory of God creating and becoming incarnate to re-create the whole world and bring it back to himself. Worship is not measured by the depth of my feelings but the deep wonder of the God whose story is so marvelous that it does in fact create feelings of love and gratitude.

Spiritual Consumerism: McSpirituality

Another problem appearing in the late twentieth century that is rather new is the accommodation of the church to a kind of spiritual consumerism. Evangelical Pastor Mike Lueken comments on a "contemporary 'McSpirituality' that resembles very little the real deal." He feels that contemporary culture has shaped our view of spirituality into "our own image." In our consumeristic world, we have "reduced spirituality to attending a few religious classes, and having a few heart warming experiences." He goes on to say, "Those of us who pastor churches, particularly larger ones, have been swept up in the adrenaline rush of having more people coming to our church, attending our classes, buying our tapes and feeling good about our church—spirituality suffocates in this arid setting—but our pastoral ambition is ignited by these promising signs—our own unformedness and need for real spirituality is buried under the temporary thrill of a church that is making it . . . in quieter moments, when the noise and chaos of the church carnival stops, we hear different voices asking annoying questions like—maybe God isn't in this at all? Maybe we are manufacturing this growth—are people really changing?" Lueken asks a very hard question that articulates what many other evangelicals feel: "Have we substituted real spirituality with these various silly imitations and at the end of the day while we have many more people giddy about our church, not many of them are actually more like Jesus?"[11]

Current Influences

I know I have painted a rather bleak picture of spirituality among evangelicals. I have done this to accent the problem of situating spirituality in the self.

I would be remiss, however, if I did not mention the worldwide impact on evangelical spirituality expressed in the recent works of Richard Foster, Dallas Willard, and Eugene Peterson. These three authors, along with many whom they have educated and countless others whom they have influenced, have already initiated a return to spirituality arising from God's story, culminating in Jesus Christ, and articulated by the ancient fathers of the church.

Richard Foster, who treats the many historic models of spirituality in *Streams of Living Water*, confesses, "No one models these dimensions of the spiritual life more fully than Jesus Christ. If we want to see this river of life in its most complete form, it is to Jesus we must turn."[12] Dallas Willard writes similarly, "God's desire for us is that we should live in him. He sends among us the way to himself that shows what, in his heart of hearts, God is really like—indeed, what *reality* is really like."[13] Likewise, Eugene Peterson, translator of the well-known Bible paraphrase *The Message*, comments, "Spiritual theology is the attention we give to lived theology—prayed and lived, for if it is not prayed sooner or later it will not be lived from the inside out and in continuity with the Lord of life."[14] So following the spiritual disciplines, which has been recovered by thousands today, is not a me-centered attempt to grow my own spirituality from within me but an entrance into "Christ's character and power." The Spirit of the disciplines, then, is "nothing but the love of Jesus."[15]

CONCLUSION

I conclude this chapter on dislocated spiritualities by making a distinction between first-order spirituality and the second-order spiritualities. I explain this by drawing on a conversation I had with one of my students.

This student comes from a background of "keeping the rules" and was highly confused by the freedom exercised by several other students who gathered to discuss worship issues while drinking beer. "I don't get it," he said. "I am offended by it. Where I come from this matter of drinking is a mark of worldliness, a sure sign of not being right with God."

I answered him by drawing on a napkin a central circle and four other circles surrounding it. In the central circle I placed a cross and said, "This is the symbol of Jesus Christ. We both agree that Jesus is the center for the Christian faith." Then, I wrote four words, one in each of the four surrounding circles: *belief, belonging, behavior,* and *experience.* I told him there is a first order of conviction in each of these areas. We *believe,* for example, that Jesus is the Son of God; we *belong* to the church, which is his body; we *behave* according to the guidelines set forth in Scripture; and we affirm the primary *experience* of the spiritual life to be in union with God. All Christians of every persuasion have in common the first-order matters of belief, belonging, behavior, and experience. These are essential to the Christian faith and to the spiritual life of being in union with God.

I then drew another set of four circles. "Out there," I said "are second-order applications." These are derivative and not binding on all Christians. In *belief* it may be affirming a particular system of faith such as that of John Calvin, Martin Luther, Menno Simons, or John Wesley; in *belonging* it may mean belonging to the Catholic, Orthodox, or one of the Protestant denominations or fellowships; in *behavior,* a second order may mean no drinking, or a group may have a rule such as no driving SUVs; in *experience* it may be the insistence on a born-again experience or a "second blessing."

"What I am suggesting," I continued, "is that you need to make a distinction between what is central to the faith, what is first order, and what is second order. What is first order is common to all Christians; what is second order defines a particular Christian subculture. If you choose not to drink (keeping in mind the admonitions against drunkenness) or not to drive an SUV, that is a personal choice of discipline in the second order of behavior. You have no right to judge those who drink moderately or drive an SUV, and they have no right to judge you for choosing this particular discipline.

"In sum," I said, "in second-order matters there are many differences on how belief is to be systematized, how one expresses belonging to the community of Christ, how one behaves in matters not directly addressed in Scripture, or how one expresses experience. So in these matters we are to exercise freedom, but in love and respect to others who exercise freedom in ways different than we do."

The point, of course, is that the spiritual life is not determined by second-order commitments. Our spirituality is located not in self but in Jesus Christ. The spiritual life is contemplation of God's story and participation in the life of God in the life of the world. When second-order convictions are made primary, they confuse the true spiritual life. If we are to understand the spiritual life and talk convincingly to others, this distinction must be made.

What is absolutely central to the spiritual life is Jesus Christ. He alone establishes our spiritual life by the Spirit to the Triune God. First-order convictions of the spiritual life include the experience of union, the belonging to the church, Christ's body, living the Christian ethic, and

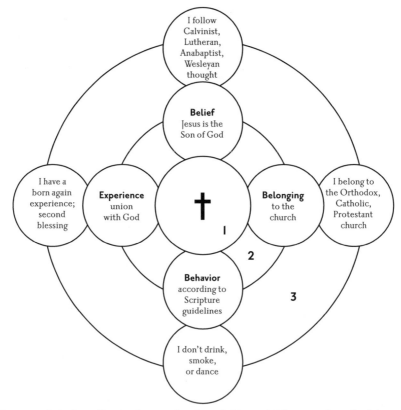

Diagram of circles—first and second order of things. 1. The central truth of the Christian faith is the person and work of Jesus Christ communicated through the biblical narrative. 2. The first order of truths are the common convictions of the church held always, everywhere, and by all Christians. 3. The second order interpretations pertain to this or that particular group.

affirming the beliefs commonly held by all Christians. All Christians are joined together in the first-order convictions.

Second-order convictions distinguish Christians from one another and include insistence on such things as having a particular experience, belonging to a particular denomination, following a set of rules, or believing in a specific system of thought. When we make second-order truths primary, the importance of first-order truth recedes into the background, and sometimes it even becomes lost. My contention is that the dislocated spiritualities discussed in this chapter are second-order convictions that are demanded by evangelicals, which in fact, distance us from the source of spirituality in God's story of Jesus and cause us to judge our spiritual state by second-order convictions, creating a dislocation from God's story and the first-order convictions derived from the story of God.

The consequence of this dislocation is not only a false privatization of spirituality but in the end the loss of God's story in a culture quickly sliding into pagan debauchery. The world, no longer inhabited by the story of God, is vulnerable to be shaped by another story. And this is exactly where we are in Western culture. We live in the presence of new stories that have set out to narrate the world, mainly New Age religion and the religions of the East. A privatized spirituality, wrenched from the story of God, will have little effect in our politically incorrect world now dominated by these new spiritualities. We turn to this subject in the next chapter.

A SUMMARY FOR REFLECTION AND CONVERSATION

Summary	Reflection
Spiritualities dislocated from God's story	Scientific theology drives a wedge between theology and practice. Spirituality is set free from the story and becomes what we make it to be.
Spiritual legalism	Measuring our spirituality by adherence to secondary ethical dos and don'ts and conformity to secondary doctrinal formations.
Intellectual spirituality	Measuring spirituality by knowledge acquired about God through the systems of scientific theology.
Experiential spirituality	Measuring spirituality by the intensity of feelings, the conversion experience, or other ecstatic experiences such as tongues, dreams, or the romancing of God.
Antinomian spirituality	Asserting one's freedom from all law. Testing God's grace.
Narcissistic spirituality	The focus on self in worship and spiritual experience. Making God the object of *our* affection.
Spiritual consumerism	The selling and purchasing of Jesus through gimmicks and techniques.

THE CRISIS: HOW THE SPIRITUAL LIFE BECAME SEPARATED FROM THE DIVINE EMBRACE

Chapter 2   The story of God's divine embrace in the incarnation, death, and resurrection of Jesus was defended by the ancient creeds and debates of the church. Spirituality and the spiritual life, situated in the divine embrace, was modified by Platonic dualism, which saw spirituality as an escape from this world, and late medieval mysticism, which interpreted spirituality as a journey into self.

Chapter 3   The Reformers returned spirituality to the divine embrace with some modification. In the Modern era spirituality as the divine embrace was redefined by a spirituality preoccupied with a forensic justification combined with sanctification guided by gratitude, and a spirituality that focused on the conversion experience followed by a flight from the world.

Chapter 4   Twentieth-century evangelical spirituality inherited the modifications of the past and developed privatized spiritualities of legalism, intellectualism, and experientialism.

Chapter 5   *The present evangelical practices of spirituality, separated from the divine embrace, are inadequate to the challenge of the wide-spread popularity of New Age and Eastern spiritualties grounded in an impersonal, pantheistic conception of God and the world. The challenge before us is to recover a spirituality and spiritual life situated in the divine embrace.*

5

A Postmodern Provocation (2000–)

Rescuing Spirituality from New Age Philosophy and Eastern Religions

Two very prominent words that were *not* from the language of my childhood or even in the 1950s when I was in college and graduate school are *secular* and *spiritual*. Originally the word *secular* meant to relate to the temporal (as in the Latin word *saeculum* from which the word is derived, which means "the present world"). However, by the 1960s the twentieth-century *secular* came to mean "a philosophy that is antagonistic to religion."

The word *spirituality* was not in the vocabulary of my youth either in my home or church. We used words such as *sanctification*, *holiness*, and *godliness*. So in this context someone might ask, "Are you living a godly life?" But no one ever asked, "Are you a spiritual person?" Nor were there any of the options for what we now call *spirituality*. There was never any talk of New Age spirituality, no focus on the psychology of the self, and no one talked about the spiritualities of the Eastern religions. Today, however, our language has completely changed. Seldom does one hear the language of sanctification or holiness or godliness in the culture let alone in our churches, but New Age language reaches beyond personal experience and extends into health, medicine, business, and even the pews of the Christian church. We speak of the triumph of the therapeutic or of discovering the self, and we engage the spiritualities of Buddhism, Hinduism, Tao, and many other Eastern religions.

In a relatively short period of five decades the landscape of our culture has changed from a fairly dominant presence of the Christian narrative to a culture that houses two new conflicting stories: that of secular perspective and that of the New Age point of view, the latter being the resurgence of Gnosticism. The challenge of Christian spirituality is to re-narrate the world and its culture in today's prevailing secular, quasi-spiritual culture.

But before addressing this challenge we must ask, "How could there be such a dramatic shift in such a short period of time?" A detailed explanation of this shift is far beyond the range of this book. Volumes have been written and continue to be written on the culture shift that has moved into a new post-Christian world. For that reason this chapter will focus on the trends that have brought us into the culture of secularism and the new spiritualities. To understand today's culture in which we live, we must acknowledge these two trends—one that undermined the Christian narrative; another that created a new kind of narrative. We turn now to look at these stories, to examine the way they have changed the landscape of American religion and spirituality, and to consider the challenge they pose to the Christian understanding and practice of spirituality.

THE UNDERMINING OF THE CHRISTIAN NARRATIVE: THE SECULARIZATION OF THE WEST

I define *secularism* as "a movement away from historic Christian sensibilities to a new condition of life." This definition contains three parts. First, the "historic sensibilities" refer to the Christian story that was the basis for the culture of the Western world. Second, "the new condition of life" refers to the new secular story that became prominent in the middle third of the twentieth century. Third, the "movement away" refers to the process that undermined the historic Christian worldview and paved the way for the secular condition of life that has swept through the Western world.

In order to understand our new cultural situation, I will briefly summarize (1) historic Christian spirituality, (2) the process by which this historic Christian spirituality collapsed, and (3) the emergence of secularism in the West, particularly in North America.

Historic Christian Spirituality

We have seen that historic Christian spirituality is situated in God's story. A brief review for the purposes of this chapter is in order. The key word in this story is *union*. God created creatures and creation for union with himself. Unfortunately they rebelled against God and refused to live in union with him or unfold culture according to his purposes. Therefore God became engaged in human history through the incarnation with the specific purpose to rescue humanity and restore the union of creatures with himself. The climactic point of God's mission was the reconciliation between God and man accomplished by Jesus Christ in his incarnation, death, and resurrection.

Spirituality is our union with God through our union with Jesus Christ accomplished by the power of the Spirit. The symbol of this union for the Christian is baptism. The spiritual life that results from this union is dying to sin and rising to the new life in Christ by the Spirit. The means by which this union is nourished is through contemplation on the mysteries of God and participation in the life of God through the doing of God's purposes. Thus the spiritual life is a calling to become fully human after the likeness of Christ, who, being united to God, has shown us what humanity, united to God, was intended to be. It is this story that literally shaped the Western world, resulting in great works of art, literature, philosophy, and public values.

This story and the spirituality it produced eroded, however, through the process of secularization. But how? What were the trends that undermined the Christian story? To answer this question, we turn to "the movement away."

The Movement Away

The movement away from historic Christian sensibilities is an extremely complex subject treated by the discipline of intellectual history. It was Francis Schaeffer who first introduced me to this discipline and awakened me to the erosion of the Christian view of reality and its view of spirituality.

Schaeffer's video series and book *How Should We Then Live? The Rise and Decline of Western Thought and Culture* shows how the Western world has gradually shifted its grounding in the Christian story to a secular perception of the world.[1] Since the publication of Schaeffer's work, many scholars, some under his influence, have written on the demise of the Christian story in the West. In this work I can only point to the major contours of this change and at best in only an introductory way. The rise of a secular worldview can be explained in the shifts of thought that took place in cosmology, science, epistemology, and psychology between 1700 and 1950. In this 250-year period the Western world shifted from a God-centered story of the world to a man-centered story, where humanity, not God, is the focus.

First, the cosmological revolution resulted in a new way of seeing the world. Historic Christianity saw the world as created by God out of nothing and dependent upon God to sustain its workings. The new understanding of the world, fueled by the discovery of the law of gravity and then the discovery of many other laws, resulted in what became known as the Newtonian world machine. Even though science was birthed out of the Christian story, the place of God in the story was eroded. God was no longer needed to sustain the world. It sustained itself. It was run by universal laws. A good example of those who lived out of this perspective were the deists, who believed in God but insisted he is like a clockmaker who made the world to run on its own mechanism.

Then, a new view of the world without God was birthed from the Darwinian theory of evolution. Evolution taught a new understanding of the origins of the human species. If God did not create the world, how did it come into being? Evolution out of chance provided a new explanation for the origin of the universe, but it raised new questions about the meaning of being a person. If humanity is not made in the image of God, what is the meaning of being a person?

By the first half of the twentieth century, a new meaning of personhood was found in the study of psychology, especially the work of Carl Jung and Sigmund Freud and later the work of Eric Fromm, Carl Rogers, and Rollo May. The new center for the meaning of personhood shifted from creation in the image of God to the self. Secular psychology advocated the actualization of the self. Finding the self became the "way of healing and salvation." J. Jacobi, a prominent student of Jung, points out that psychotherapy "has the power to cure . . . it has the means to lead the individual to his 'salvation' to the knowledge and fulfillment of his personality, which has always been the aim of spiritual striving."[2] If there is no God, where else would one look? The self is ultimate. One may say the self is God.

These three shifts—a world without God, the theory of a progressive evolution of the species, and the worship of the self—raised the epistemological questions: How do we know anything? Is there such a thing as truth? Revelation from God was rejected in favor of truth based on reason, experience, and science. These disciplines constituted the empirical method (knowledge based on observation) of arriving at truth. Since God and the supernatural are not observed, and since God is no longer needed to explain the cosmos and life within it, there must not be a God. Secularism, or life without God, had been birthed. Consequently in the sixties a movement known as the "God is dead" theory emerged and received serious attention by philosophers, theologians, and many thinkers in the general public. The "God is dead" theory was taken seriously enough to receive widespread attention, even making it to the cover story of *Time* magazine.

It was Francis Schaeffer who understood the full impact of a world in which there was no God. He rightly proclaimed, "If God is dead, man is dead." The Western world had arrived at a new condition of life, a condition which evangelicals first grasped in the late sixties and early seventies. The basic creed had shifted from, "I believe in God almighty, creator of heaven and earth," to, "I believe in myself, the measure of all things, master of my own destiny." Unfortunately, the emphasis on self apart from God began to kill the spirit and resulted in the torn fabric of society.

The New Condition of Life

The full force of secularism came to the surface in the social and cultural revolution of the sixties. During this time "Western civilization was suddenly thrown into a state of violent flux and from this turmoil emerged a strange new figure—the countercultural, anti-hero, enemy of authority, committed free thinker, impassioned free lover, obsessive searcher."[3] The shift in allegiance from God to self resulted in "urban riots and campus fury, [that] swelled alongside Vietnam War protests and a rebellious counter culture. It gave rise to feminist, environmental, and black power movements and to a steep rise in violent crime and family breakup."[4] It resulted in the breakdown of Christian institutions and values. It initiated an unraveling of the stable institutions and values of Christianity pouring forth a never-ending stream of protest against Christianity. The church came under attack; sexual mores underwent a dramatic shift; divorce changed the face of marriage; the value of law began to disintegrate; the educational system was weakened; Christian values were replaced by relativistic ethics.

This secular condition of life permeates our culture. The current struggle to get God out of public life is occurring in the media, in the political arena, in education, in sports, in entertainment, and in the interpretation of American history. The secularists want a state in which human beings reject any accountability to a higher power or to a revealed authority. In a secular society human beings are the final authority over life (as in abortion), over marriage (as in gay marriage), and even over death (as in euthanasia). The goal is to live only in reference to the individual and collective self as the final determiner of what is true for the common good.

It was in this context, a secularism that rejected God, that a new spirituality burst forth and spread throughout North America with surprising speed.

THE EMERGENCE OF A NEW SPIRITUALITY

We have just seen in the previous section that it is in the thorny soil of secularism that a new story has been birthed and God's story choked out. The new story I refer to is not a revival of a Christian worldview and its ethic but a story that combines New Age thought, Eastern religions, and the psychology of the self. This story presents a new spirituality to a world that is basically secular. This new story is content to be an intensely personal expression within a secular world living side by side with the secularist and usually agreeing with the relativistic ethic of the secular mind. This new story and the spirituality it presents permeates our culture and presents a major challenge to the Christian story and its spirituality.

For example, I recently made a trek to the spirituality section of a large book chain to see what was available for the reading public. The spirituality section consisted of a whole wall of books. Christian spirituality was the smallest shelf and included a variety of Bible translations, a few of the more solid popular books by Richard Foster and Dallas Willard, and a smattering of prayer books such as *The Book of Common Prayer*.

The overwhelming amount of books on spirituality—shelves and shelves of them—were books on New Age spirituality, books on the spirituality of world religions such as Islam, Hinduism, Confucianism, Taoism, Shinto, ancient religions from Egypt, as well as Mayan, Aztec, Native American, Neo-Pagan, and more recent religions like Krishna, Spiritism, and Wicca. All these books promised peace of mind, tranquility of spirit, and mystical experiences of transcendence. A few even suggested ways to achieve out-of-body experiences.

The presence of all these spiritualities within a secular world provides an interesting juxtaposition. Our world is thoroughly secular yet thoroughly spiritual. Renowned sociologist Peter Berger, who has written extensively on secularism, notes that our culture has been reenchanted. He writes, "The assumption that we live in a secularized world is false. The world today, with some exceptions . . . is as furiously religious as it ever was and in some places more so than ever."[5]

In secularism the focus was outward toward reason, science, and progress to make the world a better place. Secularists rejected God the Creator who became creation to re-create the world. They rejected God's intention for the world and decided they could restart the world and bring it to perfection through reason and science. But this narrative has collapsed with the world wars of the twentieth century and with the worldwide spread of poverty, disease, and violence.

The collapse of the secular dream has resulted in an inward turn. Rejecting the God who calls us to become what he created us to be, the new spirituality looks for God within the self, as if God and the self are one.

This turn inward has been portrayed as a kind of spiritual revolution. Wade Clark Roof described this phenomena in *Spiritual Marketplace*, setting out "to examine how the religious terrain itself is being transformed, and how trends now in place among members of this generation may be altering our most basic conceptions of religion and spirituality."[6]

Roof is right to speak of an alteration of religion and spirituality in the rise of the new spirituality. Therefore we turn to a brief examination of the new story to explore the challenge it poses to the Christian story and its practice of spirituality.

An Example of the New Story and Its Spirituality

Recently my wife, Joanne, and I were vacationing in the Caribbean. In the condominium we were renting I noticed a small stash of books placed there by the owner for casual reading. There was no Bible, nor were there any Christian books. But one book caught my eye, *Awakening to the Sacred*. So I took it to the beach and here is what I read in the first few pages:

> As seekers, you and I search for illumination and guidance. We want understanding—not only of our immediate problems but also of the great mysteries of the universe. We want to be able to move from murky illusion and confusion to wisdom, certainty, and clarity. We want to go from delusion to truth; we want the promise that we will be able to escape the darkness of the soul's infernal regions and make it to a place of infinite luminous peace, contentment, and divine unconditional love. We want to leave ignorance and unconscious as well as semiconscious behavior behind. We know that the antidote to ignorance isn't just more information. We know that our spiritual life depends on our being able to cultivate a higher consciousness—a mindful consciousness—as well as greater awareness. We know that our spiritual life depends on cultivating our own capacity to love. The joys and sorrows of human life are presenting you a tremendous opportunity. Taking the spiritual path to enlightenment implies some unconscious if not explicit belief in the possibility of deliverance, self-mastery, and transcendence. Others before you have plunged into the sea of spirit and bliss; others have found what they were seeking while drinking deeply of the immortal, elixir-like waters of enlightenment. Why should any of us spend our lives as onlookers at the seaside, nervously wading in the shallows? Life has a lot more to offer than that. Others have found freedom, satisfaction, and liberation. You can do it too. We can all do it. Together. The time has come to stride in and begin swimming in the deep waters. Surf's up.[7]

From this single quote it is possible to see the basic convictions of the story of the new spirituality. It is expressed in many phrases, all of which reflect the new story of Eastern religions, pantheism, the oneness of God and humanity, and the psychology of the self. According to the story spirituality, the primary predicament of the human person is the superficial grasp of life that results in "murky illusion, . . . delusion, . . . the darkness of the soul's infernal region, . . . ignorance, . . . unconscious[ness], . . . [and] semiconscious behavior."

Salvation from the imprisonment of self in this delusion of life is achieved through an "enlightenment," which is an "escape" into "the spiritual path, . . . the sea of spirit and bliss, . . . drinking deeply of the immortal, elixir-like waters, . . . swimming in the deep waters."

By taking the plunge into the enlightenment of the story of Eastern religions, the seeker will be brought to "illumination and guidance," understanding "of the great mysteries of the universe, . . . wisdom, certainty, clarity, . . . [and] truth," and "to a place of infinite luminous peace, contentment, and divine unconditional love." The more deeply we enter the Eastern story, the more we will be able to "cultivate a higher consciousness," develop a greater "capacity to love," and experience a "deliverance, self-mastery, and transcendence" that takes us into new levels of transcendence.

Finally, the appeal, the invitation to become a believer is extended. Do not be "onlookers at the seaside, nervously wading in the shallows." Make the plunge into the waters, into the community of *we* where it is done together and find "freedom, satisfaction and liberation." Don't wait! The time to do it is now—"stride in and begin swimming in the deep waters. Surf's up."

What is confusing for many people is that there are similarities of spiritual practice between Christians and other religions. How do we approach these similarities?

Similarities between Christian Spirituality and New Age and Eastern Spiritualities

In today's world of spiritual pluralism almost everybody is willing to talk about spirituality. Most people think of themselves as spiritual and are usually willing to share their viewpoint, not unlike my four dinner companions mentioned in chapter 1. When we engage in spiritual conversation, we need to keep in mind that *all religions will share a common vocabulary*.[8]

When a person says, "I am spiritual," or, "I have a spiritual life," what they are saying is, "There is more to me than meets the eye," or, "There is an invisible side to my life that is just as real as the visible side of my life." For this reason the word *spirituality* is used in the common speech of all religions—including Christians, Hindus, Muslims, Buddhists, or New Agers. So to begin, affirm that the word *spiritual* is common to the vocabulary of all people and all religions because it is used to refer to an unseen reality. Anyone who affirms there is more to the material world than what is seen by the eye can claim the word *spiritual* and say, "I am spiritual."

The experience of mystery in all religions is an encounter with something powerful and overwhelming. It creates a sense of awe, wonder, and reverence. Anyone can have this kind of ineffable, numinous experience. For example, it is entirely possible for an atheist, a Buddhist, a Christian, or a New Ager to be taken by the beauty of a sunset, to be moved by the eerie sound of the rainfall in the tropical forest, or be overwhelmed by the wonder, majesty, and beauty of the Grand Canyon and then to experience a mystery that lies beyond the seen world.

Another way the word *spirituality* commonly may be used is to describe the *experience of living the principles of one's faith*. All religious views, including that of Jews, Christians, Muslims, and adherents to Eastern religions and New Age philosophy are characterized by a way of life. For example, Hebrew spirituality lives by the Ten Commandments. Christian spirituality follows the ways of Jesus. Eastern religions call people away from material things to a life of simplicity and serenity. New Agers apply their principles to eating, to exercise, and to the care of the body. What people consider to be sacred has potential to shape one's whole way of living so that a person may say, "My whole life is spiritual."

Then also, *spirituality* refers to the *disciplines related to nourishing the spiritual experience*. These disciplines often pertain to communion or fellowship with God and include meditation, prayer, and contemplation, or they can extend to ascetic practices of renunciation to live under the rule of chastity, obedience, and simplicity.

In summary, these four characteristics are found in every religion among all the people of the world in all time and in every place:

1. The use of the word *spirituality*
2. The experience of mystery
3. A life lived by sacred principles
4. The embrace of disciplines

Nearly everybody affirms they have a spirituality, as spirituality is part of the human condition. So Isabel, from my dinner conversation on spirituality, summed up this universal condition of being human when she said, "I'm spiritual. There has to be something more than the material world. I don't know what it is—a power, an energy, a mystery. There is something there, something more than what meets the eye."

These universal common aspects of spirituality inevitably lead some to say, "All spiritualities are the same," or, "We are all united into one common experience of being spiritual." *However it is not true that all spiritualities are the same. And that is so because each spirituality is grounded in a particular story.* While Christians, Hindus, Muslims, Buddhists, or New Agers all speak of themselves as spiritual, the meaning of spirituality differs from one religion to another because each religion thinks about God, the world, and spirituality in different ways. That is why spiritual conversation needs to go deeper into the particulars of each religion.

Each Spiritual Tradition Is Situated in Its Own Particular Story

The principle that each spirituality is rooted in a particular way of thinking moves our thinking from general to the particular. To converse thoughtfully about spirituality, we must recognize spiritualities differ from one another because of the various convictions that lie beneath each particular spirituality. Each spirituality is rooted in a different story or worldview. The Christian story of the world and of human existence is very different from the New Age, Buddhist, or Hindu story.

We need to know the *why* that stands behind the practice found in a particular spirituality. Why do New Agers call their adherents to pray? Why do Buddhists renounce materiality? Why does Christian spirituality have a strong ethical side? The answers to these questions are found obviously in the philosophy or theology that gives shape to each spiritual tradition. So Christians, New Agers, and Buddhists all pray, but what prayer means within each tradition is determined by the story that stands behind the tradition. Consequently, because the study of any aspect of the story of each of the world religions is complex, the study of one aspect of religion—spirituality—is quite complex as well. The study of spirituality proceeds from a particular understanding of God. For example:

Is God personal or an impersonal, divine principle?

What are the world's origins, meaning, and destiny?

What is a human person?

What are the doctrines of sin and salvation (the problem of evil and redemption)?

How do we connect with God (e.g., worship, community, prayer, meditation)?

In matters related to justice, what is right, and how can we do what is right?

In a flight from San Francisco to Los Angeles I fell into conversation with a person from an Eastern religious tradition. We talked about spiritual things, about prayer, meditation, spiritual practices, and especially about how spiritualities address the problems of the world. Toward the end of the conversation I asked, "Can you give me a short statement, a one-liner that captures your understanding of spirituality?"

"Sure," he said. And without a moment's hesitation he continued, "We are all part of the problem, and we are all part of the solution."

I really appreciated his brief statement because it captured in a few words the philosophy of most Eastern religions. As we discussed the basis of his one-liner it became clear that Eastern spirituality is grounded in the notion that the human spirit is trapped in a material cycle of birth and death followed by a reincarnation into another form of material life. In this system of thought, the goal of spirituality is to be released from this life-and-death cycle of materiality, ultimately uniting with the invisible spiritual reality that lies beyond the physical known world.

Thus the goal of this life is to enter the state of Nirvana (the word literally means "the act of extinction" and comes from a combination of Sanskrit words that mean "to blow out"). In Nirvana one achieves the extinction of desire and individual consciousness. Because Eastern spirituality defines the problem of human existence as an imprisonment to material existence, the solution is to extinguish the human imprisonment to material awareness and enter Nirvana, where physical existence means nothing. Nirvana may be achieved through the eightfold path of a right understanding, right purpose, right speech, right conduct, right livelihood, right effort, right alertness, and right concentration. Failure to achieve Nirvana consigns a person to another cycle of material being where there is yet another opportunity to achieve Nirvana as well as another chance to fail and thereby repeat the process. And so it goes in what may be an endless cycle.

As we were approaching the Los Angeles airport I asked, "Would you like me to give you a one-liner that captures the Christian vision of reality?" He was willing to hear the underlying story of Christian spirituality. So I began, "We are all part of the problem." These words captured his attention because that is where he started. But I pointed out that the problem from the Christian perspective was not that of being imprisoned by material existence but that of sin and rebellion against God, a choice made to live without reference to God and to his will for our lives. Then I added, "But only one man is the solution, and his name is Jesus." I do not know if he got my point or not, but I made it clear that we cannot be the source of our solution, that we cannot get ourselves out of our fix. Also, I made it clear that the problem from a Christian perspective is not material existence but sinful and willful rebellion against communing with God and living in relationship with him. I commented on our relationship to the first man, Adam, and that we, like him, rebel against God, and there is nothing we can do to stop us from sinning and rebelling—no work, no ascetic practice, no self-discipline, no religious practice that can restore communion with God. One man, Jesus, the second Adam, God incarnate, does for us, however, what we cannot do for ourselves. In the flesh, God reverses Adam's rebellion and establishes a relationship with God by being our sacrifice for sin, by overcoming evil, and by being a model by which we are to live. There is, of course, much more to the Christian story than that, but I at least gave him the framework of Christian thinking, the context out of which Christian spirituality arises. One can see from this conversation that to say, "I am spiritual," does not mean a great deal. To say, "I am spiritual in an Eastern way," or, "I am spiritual in a Christian way," is more meaningful because it identifies the story that frames the spiritual life.

Let the point stand here—*spirituality* is a common term, but that does not mean all spiritualities are alike. Spiritualities on the surface may look similar, but they are rooted in vastly different understandings of the nature of reality and truth.

The Story behind the New Spirituality

It would take another book to examine all the philosophical and theological assumptions that lie within the story of the new spirituality. Space does not permit that. However, a brief insight into the contours of the new spirituality will at least allow us to gain a glimpse of the differences it holds with the historic Christian story and its spirituality.

First, the story of the new spirituality presents a particular view of God and the world. It is an interesting fact that this new story and its spirituality is rooted in what has been termed the *new science*. In the modern worldview scientists treated the world of nature as an object to be analyzed, dissected, and categorized. But new scientific studies have led into a view of nature as a living, interconnected ecosystem. Nature is alive with the sacred. Nature is a mystery. Nature has godlike qualities. What has been discovered through quantum physics is a nondefinable energy that permeates the whole universe. The world is not a machine that works like a clock, as proclaimed by Enlightenment science, but an organism that is full of life. Scientists who once proclaimed the absence of God became "outspoken advocates and devotees of new spiritual systems, while at the same time science has increasingly been employed to prove theological and spiritual propositions."[9]

The new science is combined with a very old view known as *pantheism*. This word is a combination of the Greek word *pan*, which means "all," and *theism* from *theos*, which means "god." By putting the two words together, *pantheism* means "all is God." In this view God has no existence apart from the world, and the world has no existence apart from God. The world is God, and God is the world. Everything is God—nature, people, plants, and animals.

Second, the story of the new spirituality introduces a new idea of the self. Pantheism results in a very different view of the human person. Pantheism has no real doctrine of God, nor does it have a doctrine of creation. What is God? Everything is God. Everything is *one*. God, who has no personal or infinite reality beyond the material world we see, is the impersonal reality of all that there is. Therefore I am God. Shirley MacLaine, a movie actress and New Age guru, puts it rather well when she writes, "If everyone was taught one basic spiritual law, your world would be a happier, healthier place and that law is 'everyone is God, everyone.'"

The pantheistic view of God, central to the new spirituality, has its own view of sin and redemption. Sin refers to the refusal to live at one with the universe. This can be seen, for example, in the Shirley Mac-Laine statement that this world would be a "happier, healthier place" if only we would rediscover the fundamental law that "everyone is God." She acknowledges the disorder, dislocation, and disarray of humanity. Redemption will come when we begin to live with the realization that "all is God."

It is here that the new psychology helps the individual to achieve redemption. The psychology of the self calls for self-actualization. It tells you to release the God-consciousness that lies deep within you so that you may become one with the universe.

The *message* of the New Age spirituality is very clear: "You are god, but you are not living like god. Choose to be the god you are and you will achieve a better, healthier, and happier life." Go back several pages and read again the quote from *Awakening to the Sacred* and note its evangelistic appeal based on a pantheistic view of the world and of the self. If all is God and God is all, then we must seek the mystery that lies at the very ground of nature and being. We must affirm all of nature and actualize the God who lies within the self. It goes something like this: You are just living a material life taking care of your material needs—food, clothing, housing, material enjoyment. That's not the real you. The real you is the spiritual consciousness that lies hidden and buried in the material appearance. Go deep into yourself. Find the mystery that is beneath you. Allow this mystery to put you in touch with the sacred reality of the *one* so that you may be released into your spiritual self, the real you. You will then be free from the material attachments of life and find meaning in a transcendent communion with God, the sacred underlying energy of the self.

Consequently, and this is the third distinction, *the spiritual goal for each person in the new spirituality is an ultimate release from material existence into a pure state of spiritual oneness with the* one. For example, a woman dining in our home said to me, "What you see sitting before you is not the real me. It is only a material manifestation of the real me, which is the energy that underlies what you see. I believe that after the death of my body my energy will keep coming back as another person, an animal, or even a plant until I am released from my physical manifestation."

"But Irene," I said, "if the real you is not what I see, then you have no real meaning. You are not a person. You are simply a manifestation of an evolving energy. Consider the Christian view of the person. You are really somebody, a unique spiritual/material being made in God's image and destined to live forever in the Irene who sits at my table and eats." She had no answer.

Fourth, the new spirituality is essentially the recovery of ancient Gnosticism. (The word means "knowledge." Gnostics claimed to know the secrets of the universe and argued that if you know these secrets, you will be set free.) Gnosticism was a major threat to Christianity in the first and especially the second century. There are many variations of this sect. They all held in common, however, that *the spirit has been taken captive by the material*. Thus, the spirit is, so to speak, entwined with the material, and the goal of the individual is to connect with the spirit and find release of the spirit from its physical imprisonment through enlightenment.

Like ancient Gnosticism, current spirituality is a matter of knowing self. Because the inner self is God, the path to godness, to a fulfilled spiritual life, is within the self and found by moving from an unconscious life to a conscious awareness of our unity with the *one*. We are to tap into its potential and to actualize the spiritual nature that we share with the cosmos. This is salvation in the new spirituality.

Sin, for the Gnostics, is the refusal to get in touch with our divine unconsciousness and acknowledge the *oneness* of all things. They see sin as the separation of life into pieces, into opposites that are antagonistic, one against another. Gnostics believe this refusal to accept the oneness of all things and the life force that lies behind everything produces anxiety, hate, greed, lust, violence, and all that tears life apart.

Salvation from all this strife is the result of turning one's life back to the *one*, to the unity of all things, to the energy and life force that animates reality. Having transcended all opposites, those with this belief system fuse with the divine and find peace in union with the *one*.

Spirituality is the name of the process. The spiritual disciplines of prayer, meditation, and openness to the energies about us embraced by the Gnostic followers brings them to this mystical experience of the *other*. Therefore, the goal for the ancient Gnostics as well as for those followers of the Neo-Gnosticism of today, such as Shirley MacLaine, is to achieve the dissolution of material existence, to end material reality so that ultimately all disappears into the energy, the life force that underlies all of our perceptions of materiality.

CHRISTIAN SPIRITUALITY IN A NEW AGE WORLD

One can easily see that the worldview of popular spirituality is diametrically different from the historic Christian story. The Christian understanding of God, creation, sin, redemption, the church, a life of faith and obedience, the new heavens and the new earth constitute a different story.

But herein lies a problem—a deep and very difficult issue that we as Christians must admit and then deal with: *the new spirituality is very popular*. It has gained numerous converts and has spread widely through its enthusiastic and passionate adherents. Perhaps it is because we live in the culture of narcissism where the appeal to the self as God and to the discovery and actualization of the self as spirituality simply connects with the psyche formed by the spirit of the narcissistic culture.

Then, too, popular spirituality fits the spirit of postmodern relativism. In popular spirituality there are *no beliefs to which you must adhere* because there are no absolutes. Anyone can create their own set of beliefs on their own conjecture, their own dreams, or even their claim to personal illumination.

There is also *no particular community to which you belong* in popular spirituality. Community with the self and with the whole creation feels very freeing. Getting in touch with the life force of nature is a very individual thing, and there is no need to do that together in community with other people, where there may be an accountability or an expectation of belonging.

Then, too, the new spirituality makes *no demands on moral behavior*. In popular spirituality one only needs to be consistent with self and accountable to the self, so a freedom to go beyond all the strictures of Christian moral codes allows for greater self-expression in sexual behavior and lifestyle while still being very spiritual because you are in tune with the self.

On the other hand, Christian spirituality is characterized by a clear set of beliefs, it requires accountability in a community of belonging, and it teaches one how to behave as one who is in union with Jesus Christ. Why, in this culture, would someone submit to belief, belonging, and behaving when popular spirituality offers freedom from all systems of belief, all communities of accountability, and all strictures of sexual behavior?

Is it possible to retrieve ancient spirituality today, and if so, who will be able to do this? As I see it there are three approaches: resist, adapt, transform.

Resist: Intellectual Spirituality Defended

There are many Christians who have been shaped by the modern worldview of rationalism. In this mindset, ministry has been characterized by a defense of Christianity against the secularization of culture. Because Christians have so thoroughly integrated Christianity and modernity, however, their attitude toward a new culture of spirituality is to resist it by calling on the church to stay with a modern form of Christianity defended by reason and science. Our pulpits, Sunday school, and Christian education of children at home speak often from a defensive Christian posture toward our secular society. Francis Schaeffer's apologetic, mentioned earlier, falls into this category. He insisted on factual, propositional truth and the defense of truth through philosophy, logic, and scientific evidence. Schaeffer's approach is the modern way of presenting historic Christianity, and as a result many embrace an intellectual spirituality based on reason as the way into the future.

Adapt: Experiential Spirituality Defended

Another group of Christians are those men and women who have been shaped by the post-sixties revolution and have ministered in the period of history during which the culture of the new spirituality has emerged. These folks are the pragmatists, and as such, they are very much in tune with the changes taking place in communication, business, marketing, and advertising and have been influenced strongly by the therapeutic emphasis of psychology. While they have maintained the basic doctrines of historic Christianity, they have simplified Christian commitment to the very basic emphasis of an experience of Christ. Because they have cast the Christian net toward human need, the ministry emphasis is characterized by what Jesus can do for *you*.

Remember the generation of the eighties? Their thinking took root in popular culture and, unfortunately, found expression in the new Christian culture of that period and continues to this day. This emphasis has resulted in a me-oriented Christianity and spirituality. Preaching, worship music, retreats, and many of the more popular books reflect the therapeutic, narcissistic culture. God is primarily there for *me*, to give *me* salvation, to heal *my* broken life, to give meaning to *my* existence, to make *me* successful as a person in all *my* relationships. While Christianity does have a subjective dimension, the pragmatic emphasis on subjectivity seems to miss the larger scope of Christianity as the story of the world and of human existence. Therefore it reduces the faith to an existential personalism that fails to adequately distinguish itself from the narcissism of popular spirituality. It generates a preoccupation with a journey into self, a focus on personal experience much like that of the medieval mysticism we looked at previously.

Both the resisters and the adapters are Christian. I do not question their commitment. They are trinitarian and committed to Jesus as Lord, and they call people to faith and to a spiritual walk with God. My concern is that the resistors are too committed to a modern culture and the adapters have taken on too much of the postmodern culture. The resistors have wed the faith to modern rationalism and science and continue to defend the faith on arguments that people simply don't care about anymore. On the other hand, the adaptors' faith bears such a likeness to popular culture that it appears indistinguishable from it.

So the question is this: As we reflect together on Christian spirituality in the twenty-first century, can we do so in a way that is not dependent on modern reason and science as the resistors who posit an intellectual spirituality and the adaptors who posit a spirituality of the self? Is it possible to recover a Christian spirituality that is based on truth yet engenders a passionate response? Can we have both spiritual truth and spiritual passion without attaching spirituality to the modern worldview or the postmodern vision of reality?

I think so. However, we will have to think very differently in order to accomplish this task of recapturing the true Christian narrative from the predominant grip of the modern worldview on the one hand and the influence of narcissism on the other.

The Ancient-Future Option: Truth and Passion

In this book I present a third option: the return to an ancient spirituality in which spirituality and the spiritual life are situated not in a modern, rational worldview, nor in a postmodern, narcissistic worldview, but in God's story as a comprehensive vision of the world, its history, and the meaning of human existence.

So how can this ancient-future option speak an effective spirituality into the current culture of spirituality? First, it can do so by affirming that an ancient spirituality is not rooted in modern assumptions. Ancient spirituality is not attached to the modern worldview that privileges reason and science. There is no need to prove the Christian faith with rational arguments. There is no need to attach Christianity to the old Newtonian science. Second, it can do so by affirming that ancient spirituality is not indebted to the new spirituality. It does not embrace the *consciousness revolution* rooted in a pantheistic view of God, nor does it bow to therapeutic culture rooted in the narcissistic preoccupation with the self or psychologies that call for self-actualization as the source for meaning. It springs, instead, from the divine embrace, from God's own solution to the human condition of separation from God.

Ancient-future spirituality goes back in order to go forward. It goes behind John Wesley, behind the Reformers, to the early church and the sources of Scripture. But it is not a new biblicism. It holds to the final authority of Scripture but recognizes that Scripture was written, canonized, and interpreted within the community of the early church over several centuries of development.

Therefore, ancient spirituality looks with great interest on the earliest interpretation of the Christian faith, forged out by Christians while the pagan society surrounded them. It has a deep regard for the early Christian creeds—the Apostles' Creed, the Nicene Creed, the Chalcedon Creed—as summaries of Christian faith that have preserved the biblical teaching of an incarnate Christianity, and it holds these creeds in high regard. It is here in the recovery of the ancient narrative of faith hammered out against the pantheism, Gnosticism, and paganism of the Roman world and Greek culture in which Christianity originated that we find a spirituality rooted in Scripture and articulated by the early church fathers that offers a viable alternative to today's New Age spiritualities.

As a way to illustrate the point of this chapter I asked one of my friends, George Koch, the pastor of the Episcopal Church of the Resurrection in West Chicago, to tell me the story of his journey in New Age and Eastern Religions and ultimate embrace of Christian spirituality. George left the church and stopped being a Christian after the revolution of the sixties and the failure of his church to address the changing cultural situation and dismissing everything outside its small orbit. He then "entered deeply into yoga and meditation and Eastern religions." He ultimately became the president of the Theosophical Society in Los Angeles and contributed significantly to New Age's spirituality through speaking and writing. Eventually George became disillusioned because those "who had dedicated themselves to seeking holiness and enlightenment, didn't seem to accomplish either." His own striving "seemed to have little good result." So, he "disengaged" and turned away from all religion and spirituality.

Later, however, when George was married and children came into their life, George and his wife chose a church to attend so that the children might receive "moral teaching." But they "didn't want to believe in any of that stuff." During the processions, however, seeing the cross process by, both George and his wife were struck by the meaning of the cross and realized, "God loves us so much that his only begotten son *had become one of us*, offered forgiveness freely and provided the means for us all to be reconciled to the Father." George said, "We needed forgiveness not enlightenment or powers or spiritual self-aggrandizement." He saw that in his journey into New Age he had been "striving for godlike enlightenment, the acquisition of spiritual powers." He realized we are not "little gods learning to be more powerful gods" for "we do not need to strive to be accepted and reconciled to God . . . it is a gift . . . and it is really good news!"[10]

Conclusion

In this chapter on Christian spirituality in a New Age world, I have attempted to help us understand the current culture of secularism and the new spirituality. I have emphasized first that the rise of secularism, the movement away from the historic worldview of the Christian West, has been replaced by the secular conviction that there is no god who has created, who has revealed himself, and has redeemed the world. This secular narrative, the product of chance evolution, says that we must make our own way in the world determining what is right and wrong, guided by reason. Secularism continues on to say, "Become the person common sense and reason calls us to be" and "make a new world of peace and prosperity through reason and science."

In the midst of this secular narrative, however, a new religious story has emerged. This new spiritual story is rooted in a pantheistic view of God and the material world. God is the impersonal energy of nature, the Spirit of the material order. Spirituality is about tapping into this life force. It says, "Find oneness with the God of nature. Discover your God-consciousness. Join the energy forces of the world as the world progresses toward its own perfection."

We live in a world where these two philosophies want to narrate the world. The secularist still wants to shape the world by humanism, through reason and science that will propel the world through progress to a brighter future. The New Age spiritualist wants to narrate the world through a pantheistic process of discovering the god within nature and ourselves and move, with the evolving world, toward the end of materiality into an eternal spiritual state of bliss.

Given the world in which we live, how do we narrate what God has created us to be? How do we narrate the world to become the world God intended it to be? We dare not join the secularist agenda and adapt our faith to reason, science, and progress. We dare not join the New Age and adapt our faith to a focus on self-discovery or to pantheistic evolution toward the nonmaterial. I suggest a rediscovery of ancient spirituality. Consider three reasons why it is important for us to listen to God's ancient voice of spirituality.

First, and I think most importantly, what I present as ancient spirituality is *biblical truth*. We live in the Western culture in the postmodern era where a claim to have truth is not popular. I am fully aware of the unpopularity of asserting truth in the area of spirituality, because spirituality, as it is currently presented and discussed, is highly subjectivistic. Everyone wants to speak of "my" spirituality and claim an ownership to something that is uniquely individual and personal. Ancient Christian spirituality rejects subjectivistic and innovative approaches to spirituality rooted in personal preference or in the discipline of psychology. Ancient spirituality is, instead, based on creation, incarnation, and re-creation—the biblical insights that inform and shape a true spirituality. This Christian spirituality that arises from the major themes of biblical thought has been a recurring theme throughout history. It now speaks to the crisis of twenty-first-century spirituality as the church transitions into the postmodern world with its pressures toward the revival of ancient Gnostic spiritualities.

Second, ancient spirituality, as I will show, *has been unfortunately lost in the church today*. During the first seventy years of the twentieth century the discipline of spirituality was rarely addressed. One can look at the books published by the major evangelical publishing houses and find very little on spirituality. One can also look at the curriculum of various evangelical seminaries and find that in those years almost no attention was given to the subject of spirituality. Evangelical Christianity, its publishing houses, its seminaries, and many of its churches were either oriented toward the intellectual defense of Christianity or toward a revivalistic approach to the faith. It was the rise of the New Age movement in the seventies and eighties that stimulated an interest among evangelicals in the subject of spirituality. The focus on the recovery of ancient disciplines has had a positive effect on the recovery of spirituality among evangelicals. However, in recent years too much emphasis has been placed on psychology as a source for understanding spirituality. This emphasis has resulted in an unfortunate focus on the self and an approach to spirituality that ignores the biblical roots and historical development of a spirituality that is specifically Christian.

Third, ancient spirituality *speaks a prophetic word* into the crisis of the church in our time. Ancient spirituality is deeply rooted in the message of grace, a message that pertains to the meaning and function of the church, its worship, its use of Scripture, its grasp of the Eucharist, its encouragement in prayer, the place of the disciplines, and matters pertaining to justice. Unfortunately, spirituality has been separated from the life of the church and its ministry to the world and turned into a private matter of the heart. While spirituality certainly has to do with the heart, it pertains to all of life, to world history, and to the meaning of human existence; spirituality is not a matter that stands alone apart from the full life of the church. Consequently, I intend to apply spirituality to the whole life of the church and to the whole life of the world and not follow the current reductionistic pattern of making spirituality merely a function of a privatistic relationship to God. Spirituality is a personal relationship to God that pertains to all of life.

Given the challenge of the new spirituality, it is reasonable to ask whether or not it is possible to recover an ancient spirituality in our culture. Is it possible to narrate once again the world through a God who creates, becomes involved with creation, and restores creation and creatures to himself? Is it possible to proclaim and live out a spirituality based on this story as truth and do so with passion, zeal, and freedom? Is it possible to call people into a mystical union with God through Jesus Christ by the Holy Spirit? Will this message be heard in a culture bathed in the new and competing spirituality?

The answer is resoundingly "yes." But to do so, we must learn once again God's vision of the world and our place in it. This is the challenge to which we turn in part 2.

A Summary for Reflection and Conversation

Summary	Reflection
The Christian narrative has been undermined.	Secularism is "the movement away from historic religious sensibilities to a new condition of life."
A new narrative now challenges the Christian narrative.	New Age and Eastern religions seek to replace the Christian narrative of creation, incarnation, and re-creation.
We must examine the *story* behind all spiritual practices.	New Age and Eastern religions are grounded in the story of pantheism in which God is the world and the world is God. Spirituality is the recovery of our *oneness* with all that is. We must actualize our own spiritual self.
Will ancient-future spirituality once again narrate the world?	God's passionate embrace of us; our passionate embrace of God. *We believe, we belong, we behave.*

THE CHALLENGE

Returning Spirituality to the Divine Embrace

THE CHALLENGE: RETURNING SPIRITUALITY TO THE DIVINE EMBRACE

Chapter 6   *Christian spirituality is situated in God's story of the world— the story of God creating and becoming incarnate to reconcile the world to himself. The divine embrace, the story of God's incarnation, death, and resurrection, is told in the typologies of creation/re-creation, first Adam/second Adam, Exodus event/ Christ event. In the divine embrace God was united to humanity so that we might be united to God. Christ by the Spirit recapitulates the world and returns it to the Father.*

Chapter 7   Baptism into union with Jesus is the sign of our new spiritual identity with the Triune God and with each other in the church. In baptism Christians embrace the new life that is the gift of God's grace through Jesus Christ by the Spirit.

Chapter 8   The spiritual life is a living into our baptism—dying to all that is sin and death, rising through the new birth into the new life modeled by Jesus, the one who images humanity completely united to God's original purposes for creation. The spiritual life contemplates the mystery of God revealed in Jesus Christ and participates in the purposes of God for humanity.

Chapter 9   The spiritual life is disciplined by the rule of steadfastness, fidelity, and obedience; it attends to prayer, study, and work; it meets God in daily life, in material things, and in people.

Chapter 10 The spiritual life is nourished by the church, which is the continued presence of the incarnate Jesus in and to the world. The spiritual life is nurtured by worship that sings, prays, preaches, and enacts the divine embrace in its daily prayer, weekly celebration, and yearly attention to God's saving embrace in the services of the Christian Year.

6

GOD'S STORY

*He Stretched Out His Arms of Love
on the Hard Wood of the Cross*

When I fly in an airplane and the person next to me is reading a book, I usually take a peek to see what is being read. Recently, on a trip to Chicago from Oakland, California, the person next to me was reading a rather large book titled, *A Brief History of Everything*.[1] I remembered that I had bought the book several years ago because of its interesting title, had put it on my shelf for future reading, and had neglected it. But now my interest was revived. I wondered what this writer could possibly say about the history of everything. Upon arriving home I took the book off my shelf, dusted it off, and read it.

The book's author, Ken Wilbur, makes quite a claim. He promises to answer: "What drove chaos to order? . . . How did matter give rise to life? . . . Is there a spirit of ecology? . . . Are the same currents at work in human evolution as in the cosmic game at large?" Then, regarding the Divine Domain (his words for God), he looks at "how it might indeed be related to the creative currents in matter, life and mind. How and why did religion give way to psychology?" And he asks that all important question: "To whom do we turn for answers? . . . Where do we finally place our ultimate trust for the really important questions?"[2]

Wilbur asks the right questions. Where did what exists come from? Is there any meaning to what is? Does something or someone lie beyond the realm of the material? Is material real or merely an appearance of some deeper spiritual reality? Is there any meaning to all of this? Are life and history moving to some destiny?

Every religion and philosophy in the world addresses these questions. Whether you embrace Hinduism, Buddhism, Islam, Judaism, the Christian faith, or one of the many other world religions, the question, "What is spirituality?" will always arise out of the fundamental story or vision of that particular religion or philosophy and be answered within that paradigm. So *it is crucial to understand the vision behind the spirituality you embrace.*

Most of the religions of the world are set within dualistic visions of the world. Dualism sets the spirit against matter and teaches that spirituality is attained when a person transcends matter and dwells in the realm of the spirit. But the Christian story, radically different from all the other stories of the world, brings spirit and matter together. God creates and becomes incarnate in the history of the material world to redeem it from the power of evil and to restore creation to himself through Jesus Christ and the Spirit. Therefore Christian spirituality is not an escape from this world, rather it is the discovery and the experience of spiritual purpose in this world. To understand this kind of spirituality, we turn to the Christian vision of God and the world.

THE OUTLINE OF GOD'S EMBRACE

This entire book concerns God's embrace, how we understand it, enter it, contemplate it, and live in it. Let's start then, not with the details, but with a general outline setting forth the biblical and ancient understanding of what constitutes true spirituality. The contours of God's divine embrace are captured in a few words: *God, creation, fall, incarnation, death and resurrection, re-creation, new heavens and new earth.*[3]

We began this book with this same story I told my dinner guests. It is very simple. God created the world as a place of dwelling and created human beings to be in union with him, to enjoy his creation, to live in it, work in it, play in it, and make it the theater of God's glory. But God's creatures rebelled against God's purposes, went their own way, and developed an anti-God culture full of violence, hate, and greed. So out of the Father's all-encompassing love for his creation, God became one of us, "dwelt among us" in the incarnational embrace, and in union with us in Jesus, God restored the union of humanity with himself and modeled the purpose of life. True biblical spirituality claims our union with

God and the spiritual life that comes forth as a spring of living water from that union is a life that embraces the original purposes of God for creation and creatures. When I told this story to my dinner guests, the responses I heard were gratifying: "I got it! I got it! I got it!" "I've never heard spirituality expressed that way before," and, "That's a good story. What are we to do?"

Christian spirituality and the spiritual life that we live in God's creation is situated in this narrative, the story of God's world. This is the embrace that reads the whole world and reads us individually. When we allow ourselves to be read and to be described by this embrace, we have come onto the path of Christian spirituality; we have started the Christian journey. Christian spirituality is not a journey into self as if spirituality is found in the deep recesses of our nature, hidden inside of us, waiting for release. No, true Christian spirituality is the embrace of Jesus, who, united to God, restores our union with God that we lost because of sin. This is how the ancient church understood God's embrace.

READING THE STORY OF GOD'S EMBRACE THROUGH PICTURE LANGUAGE

If it is true that the Bible tells the story of the world and of the purpose of human existence, we must ask, "How does the Bible tell its own story?" It does so in a compelling figural language of typology.[4] The word *typology* comes from the Latin word *typus* and means "image or impression as the result of a blow." In Scripture the word is used as a foreshadowing of a reality in which its fulfillment is found. Therefore, a type with its fulfillment forms a picture that gives insight and understanding. Instead of reading the Bible to find the author's intent through a systematic analysis of its historical setting and grammatical precision, the typological reading of the Bible is a more imaginative and poetic reading. For those of us who have been taught to read the Bible with detailed attention to the grammatical structure of every sentence and to a careful study of every word, this typological approach to reading the Bible will be new. A shift in thinking will have to be made. Let me put this shift into a personal perspective.

When I attended seminary during the 1950s, this ancient typological interpretation of Scripture was ignored in favor of a rational study of the Bible. We were taught to approach the Bible as an object to be analyzed and dissected through the study of its language (meaning of the words), analysis of its cultural setting, and evaluation of its theological ideas. Consequently, classes focused primarily on the use of tools that extracted truth from the text through the study of the biblical language, the life situation of every text, and a view in conformity to the common theology of the church. I was told by my professors, "You can discover the *one* interpretation of every text and understand the author's intention."

This method of reading Scripture, however, resulted in a dry and intellectual view of the faith. The more I employed *only* the biblical, historical, and theological method, the more remote God became for me. Falling into what has been traditionally known as the "God in the box" syndrome, I became increasingly dead to Scriptures and found my study led to lifeless propositions that I could easily defend. Something was missing.

What was missing was the very heart of the Bible—the embrace of God expressed in the images that connected the two Testaments and envisioned God restoring the world. I had exchanged the divine embrace for a list of propositions. The story had become lost to me. The faith became merely an intellectual construct.

So, I invite you to read the Bible, not for bits and pieces of dry informa-tion, but as the story of God's embrace of the world told in poetic images and types. This visionary way of reading the Bible whole was the way the Bible was approached by the New Testament writers and by the early church fathers, and it was highly valued until the advent of modern biblical criticism. Today the visionary way of reading the Bible is being recovered because we live in a culture of images and types (these two words may be used interchangeably). The typological reading of the Bible discloses the story of God's embrace in a pictorial way and invites us to see God not as an object of study but as the subject who acts in the world and in us to redeem and restore both.

This idea of communicating through picture language is very old. It goes back to ancient cultures, before the invention of writing when people drew pictures and told stories as means of keeping alive what only later generations would write down. In biblical times, in ancient Rome, and during the medieval era picture language was very much part of culture and of everyday experience. But in the modern world (1750–1960) the image was suppressed by the dominance of the rational word. Now, at the beginning of the twenty-first century, communica-tion theory has gone full cycle and we are critiquing the dominance of rational words as we rediscover the human heart's languages of pictures, signs, symbols, types, and imagery as old forms of communication come alive again.

Words, when used only as rational propositions, tend to foster intel-lectual notions, remote abstractions, exactness, and strict precision. While analysis of detail may produce clarity to which there is a great deal of value, the downside of clarity is that it fails to evoke imagination. Clarity tends to conclude, to bring to an end, to shut down. Clarity of thought is generally linear and driven by firm and undeniable conclusion. Certainly there is a vital place for verbal, linear, and logical thinking. But in spite of all the contributions of print, cognition, and clarity, these forms of communication have not been enough to sustain the spirit of being human. Humans need to see, to dream, to imagine in ways that go beyond the strictures of words used as rational and scientific facts. Now, once again, in a postcritical period of history, typology holds the promise to be a significant way of reading the biblical story of God's embrace.

When the cognitive aspect of the person dominates the symbolic side, a vital part of humanity is neglected and the human spirit is squelched. That is what happened during the Enlightenment. We lost the capacity to envision. In recent years the symbolic side of human beings has been revived. We now know that knowledge is not only communicated by words, it is communicated also by body language, immersion in community, historical tradition, rituals, images, symbols and pictures, experience, atmosphere of sight and sound, vibrations of the voice, space and environment, perception, art, indications, analogies, types, metaphors, stories, parables, and the like.

Reading the Bible as God's embrace of us may be a problem for some because the Enlightenment emphasis on cognitive understanding and learning through words has thoroughly shaped the modern approach to ministry. Only a few pastors and congregations pay attention to communication through space, environment, sensual, and visual forms of language. But that is changing. Younger leaders in particular recognize that we live in a world where the image, the symbol, and the metaphor are extremely important to keeping alive and passing down the faith and its mission in a postmodern world. These leaders help us see and experience God's divine embrace.

Some Christian men and women argue that we must create new images, symbols, and metaphors within the church. I do not agree. Biblical images need to be rediscovered. For some these images are dead. But they are dead not because they are useless but because their real meaning has been lost.

Therefore, in this chapter I will unpack God's embrace of the world using the primary images from Scripture as Christians did in the ancient church. By allowing the original meaning of these images to grasp us, as they have in various periods of history, we will be free once again to envision spirituality in a very biblical and ancient way. Our concentrating on images, however, should not be seen as a rejection of words. For example, in the 1990s book *The Rise of the*

Image, the Fall of the Word, the author asks us to think through the vast communication change taking place in our society as culture shifts from a word-centered society into an image-driven world. The author does not argue that words have become obsolete. He affirms the invention of writing as "a recipe for wisdom" and acknowledges that writing made possible "most of our cultures."[5] The burden of his book, though, is to show that "images use our senses more effectively than do black lines of type stacked on white pages."[6] We learn especially through word pictures, images, and types. And so that is how I will present God's embrace—through three powerful typologies that paint a picture of God embracing creatures and creation, reestablishing union with himself.

THREE COMPELLING TYPOLOGIES

When the ancient church fathers read God's story of his divine embrace of creation using the picture language of typologies, they did not read it as if it were fiction or myth. They read the Bible as the true account of God's activity in history culminating in a real, historical incarnation, death, and resurrection and anticipating a real end to history as we know it in the new heavens and new earth. God's story, unlike the Greek mythologies, takes place in real time, real space, and real history.

The Bible tells the story of God's embrace not only in words but also in signs, symbols, images, and types that participate in the reality they represent. These types are far too numerous to recount here, so let it be sufficient to explore three major types—creation/re-creation, the first Adam/second Adam, and the Exodus event/Christ event. These types are not only a significant way for us to read the Bible, but, as importantly, these types read the world, its history, and our place in the cosmic drama of God. We read God's embrace. God's embrace reads us. God's embrace tells us of our origins, of our failings, and of our redemption.

The God Who Creates, Re-Creates, and Makes All Things New

I think everyone who has seen Mel Gibson's movie *The Passion of the Christ* has a favorite line from the film. My favorite words were spoken when Jesus's mother came to him while he was carrying the cross. Looking at her with compassion he said, "I make all things new."[7]

In these words there is an embrace of the world that sets our imaginations free to see the world as God's restored world, the theater of his glory. But does God's story *really* say that God is at work to make all things new? Let's look more closely at the story.

Here is what Paul, the first interpreter of Jesus, said:

> The creation waits in eager expectation for the sons of God to be revealed. For the creation was subjected to frustration, not by its own choice, but by the will of the one who subjected it, in hope that *the creation itself will be liberated from its bondage to decay and brought into the glorious freedom of the children of God. We know that the whole creation has been groaning* as in the pains of childbirth right up to the present time.
>
> Romans 8:19–21, italics mine

Paul's vision of a restored world through the divine embrace is expressed also in an ancient hymn sung at Colossae:

> For by him all things were created; things in heaven and on earth, visible and invisible whether thrones or powers or rulers or authorities; all things were created by him and for him . . . through him *to reconcile to himself all things; whether things on earth or things in heaven,* by making peace through his blood, shed on the cross.
>
> Colossians 1:16, 20, italics mine

But, how are we to interpret this vision of a restored world? What difference does it make in our personal, family, or work life?

In our Western mind we carry a static view of creation. *We need to exchange a static view of creation for a dynamic one. Creation is ongoing in the sense that God is involved in creation with his own two hands—incarnate Word and Spirit—embracing the world to bring it into its final destination, the new heavens and the new earth.* Christ has conquered sin and death by his death and resurrection, and in his return, he will put evil away forever, and heaven and earth and all that is within them will be united to God, fulfilling God's eternal purpose for creation. The vision is: paradise lost; paradise regained.

A few years ago while I was teaching at Wheaton College on how God makes all things new through the divine embrace, a student became visibly upset. "What you are teaching is wrong," he cried.

After some discussion I threw a quarter to him. "Matt, as soon as this class is over I want you to use this money to call your dad. I know your dad, and I'm sure he has Calvin's commentary in his office." (John Calvin, one of the major framers of Protestant Christianity, drew from the ancient fathers of the church.) "Ask him to look up Calvin's comment on Romans 8:18–27 and come back to the next class and tell me what your dad read to you." (Matt's favorite Reformer was John Calvin. That is why I asked him to have his dad read Calvin to him.)

Matt did just what I asked. And this is what his dad read to him from Calvin's commentary: "I understand it in this sense: 'There is no element and no part of the world which, touched with the knowledge of its present misery, is not intent on the hope of the resurrection.' . . . God will restore the present fallen world to perfect condition at the same time as the human race."[8] Calvin, like the ancient church fathers, taught that creation would be restored at the second coming of Christ. Matt, however, having been influenced by a popular Gnostic rejection of creation, assumed that matter was intrinsically evil and would be destroyed by God at the end of history. But God's story teaches that creation is not evil but good.

So God "makes all things new" not by destroying creation and starting all over again but by destroying the evil that puts God's good creation under what Paul calls "the bondage to decay" (Rom. 8:21). To understand this tension between a good creation and the power of evil working in God's creation, a power that will be destroyed in the end of history, we must understand the biblical picture of evil.

God's story from Genesis through Revelation shows in illustration after illustration that there is something wrong, very wrong, in the world. The problem is evil. Evil is not the substance of matter. Evil is rebellion against God and God's purposes for creation. This rebellion proceeds from people who are free to live their lives in an embrace of God or to direct their lives away from God in an embrace of self.[9]

For example, Paul, in his letter to the Romans, describes people as "godless and wicked." He claims that they suppress the truth by their wickedness. They refuse to give thanks to God. "Their thinking became futile and their foolish hearts were darkened." They think of themselves as wise, but they have become "fools" going so far as to exchange the "glory of the immortal God for images made to look like mortal man and birds and animals and reptiles" (Rom. 1:18–23). In other words, God's creatures turn in on themselves and fall into a love of self; they assert the self and organize everything around the self. "It's all about *ME!*" cries the popular slogan.

So, we ask, "If this sinful condition is not intrinsic to the very stuff of creation, where does it come from?" The biblical perspective, as I've already suggested, is that sin is not a material substance but a rebellion against God. Biblical history as well as all the histories of the world show that humanity has united against God's purposes again and again to embrace war, not peace; hate, not love; power, not servanthood; selfishness, not selflessness; greed, not sharing. God's vision for humanity is to care for the earth and to live in the world doing God's will "on earth as it is in heaven." But human rebellion against God and God's purposes for the world has resulted in subjecting God's good creation to human dysfunction. So human rebellion has wounded nature so that it is in "bondage to decay" (Rom. 8:21).

The source of this great evil is not within God or in what God has made. It lies within freedom that God gave to his creatures. God took a risk in creating men and women. Humanity was originally created in union with God and God's vision for the world. However, Adam and Eve were free to reject continuation in this union, and they did. And in doing so they embraced the rebel of heaven itself, the fallen angel Lucifer, who, wanting to be like God, rebelled against God and set himself up as anti-God. (The rebellion of Lucifer in the heavens is described in Isaiah 14. Though this passage refers to the fall of the earthly Babylonian king, it is viewed also as a reference of the fall that took place in the heavens, especially v. 12, "How you have fallen from heaven.") It was Lucifer, in the form of a snake, who tempted Adam and Eve, leading to the human fall and sinful rebellion against God that initiated the devastating chain of events which followed. Consequently,

> The earth was corrupt in God's sight and was full of violence. God saw how corrupt the earth had become, for all the people on earth had corrupted their way. So God said to Noah, "I am going to put an end to all people, for the earth is filled with violence because of them. I am surely going to destroy both them and the earth."
>
> Genesis 6:11–13

Notice that the punishment is the result of human evil, not because God created an intrinsically evil world.

The ensuing flood is seen as a type of God's judgment that will come against all evil at the end of history: "Just as it was in the days of Noah, so also will it be in the days of the Son of Man" (Luke 17:26). The judgment in the time of Noah was not a judgment against God's material creation but a judgment against evil, a judgment on the rebellion against God that has influenced the unfolding of culture and civilization away from the purposes of God.

The opposite of rebellion against God is doing God's purposes in creation. The spiritual life embraces God's creation and wholeheartedly loves it—its beauty; its rhythms of day and night, week to week, year to year; its inhabitants; the life-ordering structures that govern it, work that cares for it, pleasures that enjoy it. For creation is the speech of God declaring "the glory of God" and "the work of his hands" (Ps. 19:1) and revealing "his eternal power and divine nature" (Rom. 1:20).

Creation itself is not only a picture language of God's creative act, it is the very place where a spiritual union with God is lived out. Christian spirituality knows that evil does not reside in materiality but in the willful disobedience of humanity against God. In its calculated embrace of evil, humanity has extended its fallen nature into culture-making—thus society reflects the fallen state. In every area of life rebellious, sinful humanity has left its mark—in politics, economics, institutions, ideologies, marriage, families, and personal relationships—all are out of sync with God's intentions for the human family. And this sorry state of the current situation, this painful tearing at the very fabric of human existence, this anti-God state of affairs is due solely to humanity's prideful, arrogant self-esteem in which union with God has been discarded and treated with disdain.

Is there any hope? Certainly not in fallen humanity. We are not able to repair our relation to God and achieve union with him again. We are the problem. Hope for the restoration of this world and for humanity must come from God. Only God can restore his own handiwork. For this reason God became one of us and embraced our sinful condition in his incarnate union with Jesus. God united to man in Jesus by the Spirit, reversed the sin of the first Adam, so that all things could be made new.

Here, then, in this typology of creation and re-creation, God's story of restoring his creation gone astray is pictured. The material world is good, but human rebellion against God's purposes in creation has wounded all the structures that order and organize our personal and collective lives. But this creation will be made new. How? God embraced us, became the second Adam, and reversed the effect of the first Adam on creation.

The Second Adam Reverses the Sin of the First Adam

God's embrace of us in Jesus is captured by Paul in these words:

> So it is written: "The first man Adam became a living being"; the last Adam, a life-giving spirit. The spiritual did not come first, but the natural, and after that the spiritual. The first man was of the dust of the earth, the second man from heaven. As was the earthly man, so are those who are of the earth; and as is the man from heaven, so also are those who are of heaven. And *just as we have borne the likeness of the earthly man, so shall we bear the likeness of the man from heaven.*
>
> 1 Corinthians 15:45–49, italics mine

In another passage Paul compares the first Adam with the second Adam:

Just as the result of one trespass was condemnation for all men, so also the result of one act of righteousness was justification that brings life for all men. For just as through the disobedience of the one man the many were made sinners, so also through the obedience of the one man the many will be made righteous.

Romans 5:18–19 (see the larger context of verses 12–21)

The contrast is clear. The first Adam brought sin, death, and condemnation. We are all fallen in him and unable to live in God's embrace even if we want to do so, for while dead to sin in the first Adam, we cannot choose our way out of sin to God. Choosing on our own is not going to free us from the law of sin and death, for what is going on is a spiritual battle of gargantuan proportions, and no degree of journey into self or becoming "one" with the universe is going to change that basic fact. But the second Adam, the one from heaven, did for us what we cannot do for ourselves. Through his life, death, and resurrection he has restored us. In and through him we may live in the embrace of God.

That the second Adam will make all things new is traced back to a prophecy in Genesis. Here the writer introduces us to the curse that rests over creation because of sin. But in these words there is also a glimpse at the promise of Christ through whom reconciliation with God is made possible. "I will put enmity between you and the woman, and between your offspring and hers; he will crush your head, and you will strike his heel" (Gen. 3:15).

In brief this prophecy speaks to the conflict between good and evil and points to the outcome of the conflict. The powers of evil will strike at the heel of the seed of woman, Jesus being that seed, which is interpreted as the blow delivered to Christ on the cross. But the blow delivered to the power of evil is the fatal crushing of the serpent's head. From God's perspective, the entire history of the world is the conflict with Satan and the powers of evil. God's mission is to recover the world that was stolen from him by Lucifer and his fallen angels. The crushing blow to all evil is found on the hard wood of the cross and in Christ's resurrection from the dead. Here God enters into the suffering of the world, literally, embraces the sin and suffering of the whole world, taking it into himself on the cross and destroying its power over us in his resurrection.

Jesus Christ alone provides the solution for which the whole world groans. God defeats evil on the cross for us. He wins a great victory over evil for us. In his resurrection he conquered the results of sin—which is death—so that death is not the last word written over our life. "'Death, has been swallowed up in victory.' 'Where, O death, is your victory? Where, O death, is your sting?' The sting of death is sin, and the power of sin is the law. But thanks be to God! He gives us the victory through our Lord Jesus Christ" (1 Cor. 15:54–57).

The point of the image of the second Adam is this: *the very essence of the Triune God became incarnate in Jesus. Jesus, the God-man in our humanity, took into himself our sin and death and overcame it on the cross and by the empty tomb, reestablishing our union with God. Spirituality springs forth and is lived out of God's embrace of us and is the gift of God received in faith and lived out with Christ, who now dwells in us by the Spirit.*[10]

The Exodus Event of Israel Is a Type of the Christ Event

The two types we have looked at so far—creation/new creation, first Adam /second Adam—are complimented by the third typology, the Exodus event/Christ event. *The ultimate restoration of the whole world is pictured in the Exodus event. This divine embrace of Israel is a type of God's embrace of the whole cosmos in the Christ event to be fulfilled in the new heavens and the new earth.* Space does not permit an exploration of the rich plentitude of all the types foreshadowed in the Exodus event, but a few of the more prominent types will allow us to peer into the deep realities of God's pictorial language.[11]

Compare some of the many images of the Exodus event with the Christ event:

Moses as the central figure of the Exodus, and Christ as the focus of the New Testament

the narratives surrounding the birth of Moses and the birth of Jesus

Moses's confrontations with Pharaoh, and the temptation of Jesus by Satan

the miracles of Moses and those of Jesus

the Passover of the Jews on the night before the Exodus, and the Passover supper of the Lord on the night before his arrest and crucifixion

the sacrifice of the lamb for Passover, and Christ as the Lamb who takes away the sins of the world

the blood smeared on the doorposts of the Jewish homes so that the angel of death would pass over that home and not bring death to the firstborn, and the blood of Christ that cleanses us from sin the deliverance of Israel from their bondage to Pharaoh, and the freedom Jesus brings from the power of evil

the salvation of the Jews through the waters of the Red Sea, and the waters of baptism that immerse us into the salvation of the death of Jesus (our pathway to safety and a new life)

the new life to which the Jews are brought on the other side of the Red Sea, and the new life we have through the resurrection of Jesus

the formation of Israel as the people of God, and the calling of the church to be God's new people

the covenant made with Israel to be the people of God, and the new covenant made in Jesus

the calling of Israel to worship God, and the calling of the church to be a people of worship

the tabernacle of Israel as a place of God's dwelling, and Jesus, God made flesh to tabernacle (dwell) among the people of the earth

the sacrifices instituted by God within Israel to point the way to God, and Jesus, the ultimate sacrifice who opens the way to heaven

the high priest of Israel, who makes atonement for the people, and Jesus, our High Priest, who makes the one true atonement for us all

the Law, given to show the way of holiness, and Jesus, who fulfills the Law for us

the Sabbath that remembers and pays reverence to God the Creator, and Christ, our Sabbath, who re-creates

the Promised Land, the future hope of Israel, compared to the new heavens and the new earth, the hope of all the earth

There is virtually a sunburst of images, signs, and symbols surrounding the redemption of Israel out of Egypt and the redemption of the world through Jesus. This method of proclaiming God's embrace of the world ties both Old and New Testaments together and demonstrates God's way of communicating the meaning of world history and of human existence through the picture language of typology (for these and other types, see Heb. 6:13–10:18).

So what do these three types tell us about God and God's embrace of the world? God is doing a new thing. It is complex, and yet it can be summarized in a single word. The ancient church called it *recapitulation*. The word means "to do over again." In Jesus Christ, God does creation "over again." Jesus Christ is the second creation, the new beginning of creation and creatures.

THE THEOLOGY OF RECAPITULATION

God's embrace of us in Jesus recapitulates the human situation. He is the second Adam who reverses, renews, and restores union with God. This vision of recapitulation is found in Paul's letter to the Ephesians where Paul writes: "And he made known to us the mystery of his will according to his good pleasure, which he purposed in Christ, to be put into effect when the times will have reached their fulfillment—to bring all things in heaven and on earth together [recapitulate] under one head, even Christ" (Eph. 1:9–10). The mystery of God to restore his original purpose for creation and humanity has now been revealed in Jesus Christ, the one who restores God's vision by the spirit. He *alone* recapitulates, renews, restores God's vision.

To depict how dominant this view was in the early church, let us consider Irenaeus's thoughts on recapitulation in *Against Heresies* (AD 180). By the middle of the second century the heresy of Gnosticism had become prevalent throughout the Roman Empire. Irenaeus, the most significant Christian thinker and most influential theologian of the same period, wrote *Against Heresies* to refute the heretical notion that material order was evil and that Jesus was a phantom. He writes in his preface, "As well as I can, then, I will briefly and clearly describe the position of the present false teachers. . . . I will further provide, as far as my modest ability extends, the means of overthrowing it, showing how absurd and foreign to the truth are the things they say."[12]

Irenaeus's comments on recapitulation state how the *early church's convictions were rooted in the divine embrace.* The themes I have developed (the three typologies) summarize the faith and defend God as the one who not only creates but re-creates. I encourage you to reflect upon the many images involved by Irenaeus to capture this recapitulation.

So the Lord now manifestly came to his own, and, born by his own created order which he himself bears, he by his obedience on the tree renewed [and reversed] what was done by disobedience in [connection with] a tree; and [the power of] that seduction by which the virgin Eve, already betrothed to a man, had been wickedly seduced was broken when the angel in truth brought good tidings to the Virgin Mary, who already [by her betrothal] belonged to a man. For as Eve was seduced by the word of an angel to flee from God, having rebelled against his Word, so Mary by the word of an angel received the glad tidings that she would bear God by obeying his Word. The former was seduced to disobey God [and so fell], but the latter was persuaded to obey God, so that the Virgin Mary might become the advocate of the virgin Eve. As the human race was subjected to death through [the act of] a virgin, so was it saved by a virgin, and thus the disobedience of one virgin was precisely balanced by the obedience of another. Then indeed the sin of the first-formed man was amended by the chastisement of the First-begotten, the wisdom of the serpent was conquered by the simplicity of the dove, and the chains were broken by which we were in bondage to death.[13]

Note how Irenaeus draws a parallel between the events that occurred in the Garden of Eden and the garden of Christ's crucifixion to express the divine embrace through which the whole world is recapitulated by the arms of God—Jesus and the Spirit.

> The "disobedience in [connection with] a tree" was reversed by "his obedience on the tree."
>
> The seduction of Eve was reversed by the good tidings given to Mary.
>
> Eve betrothed to a man was reversed in the betrothal of a man to Mary.
>
> Eve seduced by the word of an angel to flee from God, having rebelled against his word, was reversed by Mary when from the word of an angel she received glad tidings that she would bear God by obeying his word.
>
> Eve disobeyed God and so fell, but Mary obeyed God, reversing the disobedience of Eve.
>
> The human race was subject to death by the act of a virgin, so the human race was saved by the act of another. (This is a poetic parallelism and not to be taken that Mary is a coredeemer, as the next paragraph will clearly state. Mary is honored as a crucial link in the plight of humanity, however, for she willingly gives her womb as the birthing place for the Savior of the world.)
>
> Mary therefore reverses disobedience by her obedience.
>
> The fruit of Mary's womb reverses the sin of the first-formed man through the chastisement of the first begotten, thus the wisdom of the serpent was conquered by the dove.

The result of all these reversals was that the chains were broken (an allusion to the bondage of sin) by which we were in bondage to death.

"Therefore, he renews these things in himself, united man to the Spirit; and placing the Spirit in man, he himself is made the head of the Spirit, and gives the spirit to be the head of man, for by him we see and hear and speak."[14] These words clearly point to Jesus Christ as God's embrace, whose work of recapitulating the world was accomplished by the Spirit. Here is the ancient theological understanding: When Adam was created, he was given the Spirit. The Spirit united him to God and established the communion and fellowship he and Eve experienced with God in the place of God's habitation, the Garden. When Adam and Eve fell, they lost the Spirit who united them in the fellowship of the Godhead. However, in the embrace of God and man in Jesus Christ (accomplished by the Spirit), humanity is united once again to God and God's vision for the world. The next paragraph from Irenaeus focuses on the *how*—how Jesus, by his life, death, and resurrection, accomplished our union with God's vision.

> He, therefore, completely renewed all things, both taking up the battle against our enemy, and crushing him who at the beginning had led us captive in Adam, tramping on his head, as you find in Genesis that God said to the serpent, "And I will put enmity between you and the woman, and between your seed and her seed; he will be on the watch for your head, and you will be on the watch for his heel." From then on it was proclaimed that he who was to be born of a virgin, after the likeness of Adam, would be on the watch for the serpent's head—this is the seed of which the apostle says in the Letter to the Galatians, "The law of works was established until the seed should come to whom the promise was made." He shows this still more clearly in the same Epistle when he says, "But when the fullness of time was come, God sent his Son, made of a woman." The enemy would not have been justly conquered unless it had been a man [made] of woman who conquered him. For it was by a woman that had the power over man from the beginning, setting himself up in opposition to man. Because of this the Lord also declares himself to be the Son of Man, so renewing in himself that primal man from whom the formation [of man] by woman began, that as our race went down to death by a man who was conquered we might ascend again to life by a man who overcame; and as death won the palm of victory over us by a man, so we might by a man receive the palm of victory over death.[15]

The theme is that God's embrace by way of Christ's incarnation, death, and resurrection renewed all things. He renewed all things because he won a decisive battle against the powers of evil. The power that had led us captive in Adam was now crushed and trampled on in fulfillment of the promise of God that the battle with evil would be won through the seed of the woman in the fullness of time. This reversing event was accomplished by a man united to God, so that "as our race went down to death by a man who was conquered we might ascend to life by a man who overcame. Even as death is the consequence of the first man, so life over death is the victory of the second man."[16]

Finally, Irenaeus relates this divine embrace to the matter of our spirituality. He emphasizes the powers by which God, in union with our humanity in Jesus, accomplished the recapitulation and united us all to God again.

So, then, since the Lord redeemed us by his own blood, and gave his soul for our souls, and his flesh for our bodies, and poured out the Spirit of the Father to bring about the union and communion of God and man—bringing God down to men by [the working of] the Spirit, and again raising man to God by his incarnation—and by his coming firmly and truly giving us incorruption, by our communion with God, all the teachings of heretics are destroyed. . . . He would not have had real flesh and blood, by which he paid the price [of our salvation], unless he had indeed *recapitulated* in himself the ancient making of Adam. Vain therefore are the Valentinians [Gnostics] who reject the [new] life of the flesh and scorn what God has made.[17]

Achieving Union with God and God's Vision for the World Again

God's embrace of the world and its recapitulation was at great cost to God's Son. It was accomplished by his own blood, the giving of his soul for our soul, his flesh for our flesh, and the pouring out of his Spirit in order for us to embrace God. This was done in the flesh. Irenaeus is here debating the Gnostics, who believe in the eternal dualism of flesh and spirit. The Gnostics believe that salvation and spirituality is to be saved from this world that was created by the evil God. To this thinking Irenaeus is saying, "No." God created a world as a habitation for himself and creatures as his family. Just as the fall was a real, embodied experience that occurred in the flesh and blood of Adam and Eve in a physical place called the Garden of Eden, so the reversal of their sin, the redemption of all creation, is accomplished by God made flesh in Jesus. He reversed the fall in his suffering on the cross and resurrection from the tomb. He reversed the sin that separates us from God, and he has united us to God again by the Spirit. He has won back the world and its creatures and made them new again.

This story is characterized by all the elements of a good drama. It takes place in a particular setting (the world). The script has a protagonist (God the Father, Son, and Holy Spirit) and an antagonist (Satan and all the powers of evil). Consequently there is a conflict that runs through the whole story. The story is the struggle to rule creation. The struggle involves a cast, primarily the people of Israel and the people of the church. The cast is full of significant players—some good, others evil, and all subject to the law of sin and death.

As the drama unfolds first in the people of Israel, we are introduced to numerous types, signs, and symbols that point to the primary way in which the hero of the story (Jesus) overcomes the powers of evil. The victory has been won as was the case when the allies took the beaches at Normandy in World War II, but the fighting is not over yet. The struggle continues in a new people, the church, the people of God. Individuals and the whole corporate church, Christ's body, continue to struggle with evil even though the outcome of the struggle is certain. Assurances of victory over evil appear in signs that have been given to God's people to point to his ultimate victory over the powers of evil and his reclamation of lordship over the entire creation.[18]

CONCLUSION

In summary, recalling the book I mentioned at the beginning of this chapter, *A Brief History of Everything*, I argue God's story is the brief interpretation of everything. It tells us where humanity originated from, why this world is full of suffering and evil, how union with God and God's vision has been restored. It is a picture, a true picture of the world and our place in it. And through this picture we hear the voice of God who says, "I did for you what you simply could not do for yourself. I became one of you. I took your rebellion into myself. I died to overcome the power of sin that has led to this awful separation between us. And I rose victorious over death, breaking the power of all that is death in the world and the grip in which it holds you. I overcame death and began a new creation; I opened the way for you to live in my embrace of you and the world. Through my Son Jesus and by my Spirit I have embraced you so that now, united with me, you may embrace me as a child learns to embrace a mother because the mother first embraced the child. Now go and live the spiritual life, embrace me and my purpose in creating you and putting you in this world to be the priests of my creation. Make your life and this world the theater of my glory."

Here then is Christian spirituality: *We are spiritual because of God's divine embrace of humanity and all creation.* By his own two hands—the incarnate Word and the Spirit—God's divine embrace has restored our union with himself for us. He has done for us what we cannot do for ourselves—re-establish the connection with God that we ourselves broke in our rebellion. How we enter this vision and become passionate about it is the subject of the next chapter.

A SUMMARY FOR REFLECTION AND CONVERSATION

Summary	Reflection
The story of God's embrace	The contours of the story of God's embrace are captured in a few words: God, creation, fall, incarnation, death and resurrection, re-creation, new heavens and new earth.
Reading God's embrace through picture language	Rediscovering typology
Creation/re-creation	Rom. 8:19–21; Col. 1:15–21
First Adam/second Adam	1 Cor. 15:45–49; Rom. 5:12–21
Exodus event/Christ event	Exodus 12; Heb. 6:13–10:18
Recapitulation	"To do over again"

THE CHALLENGE: RETURNING SPIRITUALITY TO THE DIVINE EMBRACE

Chapter 6   Christian spirituality is situated in God's story of the world— the story of God creating and becoming incarnate to reconcile the world to himself. The divine embrace, the story of God's incarnation, death, and resurrection, is told in the typologies of creation/re-creation, first Adam/second Adam, Exodus event/ Christ event. In the divine embrace God was united to humanity so that we might be united to God. Christ by the Spirit recapitulates the world and returns it to the Father.

Chapter 7   *Baptism into union with Jesus is the sign of our new spiritual identity with the Triune God and with each other in the church. In baptism Christians embrace the new life that is the gift of God's grace through Jesus Christ by the Spirit.*

Chapter 8   The spiritual life is a living into our baptism—dying to all that is sin and death, rising through the new birth into the new life modeled by Jesus, the one who images humanity completely united to God's original purposes for creation. The spiritual life contemplates the mystery of God revealed in Jesus Christ and participates in the purposes of God for humanity.

Chapter 9   The spiritual life is disciplined by the rule of steadfastness, fidelity, and obedience; it attends to prayer, study, and work; it meets God in daily life, in material things, and in people.

Chapter 10   The spiritual life is nourished by the church, which is the continued presence of the incarnate Jesus in and to the world. The spiritual life is nurtured by worship that sings, prays, preaches, and enacts the divine embrace in its daily prayer, weekly celebration, and yearly attention to God's saving embrace in the services of the Christian Year.

7

My Story

Coming within the Reach of His Saving Embrace

Now that we have a glimpse of God's embrace of creation, incarnation, and re-creation, we ask, "How do his people respond to God's embrace?" To reflect on this question we will go to the sacred text of Acts, to a story that tells us what happened in the days after the resurrection of Jesus, and especially what occurred only a few days after Jesus ascended into heaven, on the day of Pentecost.

Pentecost, an annual Jewish festival celebrating the harvest, occurs fifty days after Passover. So fifty days after the death and resurrection of Jesus (at Passover), numerous Jews from all over the Roman Empire are gathered in Jerusalem to celebrate the annual Feast of Firstfruits. On that particular day of celebration for that year strange things began to occur. Luke, a disciple of Jesus and the writer of the book of the Acts of the Apostles records the following:

> When the day of Pentecost came, they were all together in one place. Suddenly a sound like the blowing of a violent wind came from heaven and filled the whole house where they were sitting. They saw what seemed to be tongues of fire that separated and came to rest on each of them. All of them were filled with the Holy Spirit and began to speak in other tongues as the Spirit enabled them.

Acts 2:1–4

145

These signs and wonders in the upper room where the disciples were all gathered together created a great deal of confusion. "What is going on here?" they asked. According to Luke, Peter stepped into the situation and preached the first recorded Christian sermon. Read the sermon below and you will see that it tells the story of God's embrace, summarizing how God worked in his people Israel foreshadowing the coming of Christ. The concluding words, which I have put in italics, make an incredible claim:

> Then Peter stepped forward with the eleven apostles, and shouted to the crowd, "Listen, all of you, visitors and residents of Jerusalem alike! Some of you are saying these men are drunk! It isn't true! It's much too early for that! People don't get drunk by 9 A.M.! No! What you see this morning was predicted centuries ago by the prophet Joel—'In the last days,' God said, 'I will pour out my Holy Spirit upon all mankind, and your sons and daughters shall prophesy, and your young men shall see visions, and your old men dream dreams. Yes, the Holy Spirit shall come upon all my servants, men and women alike, and they shall prophesy. And I will cause strange demonstrations in the heavens and on the earth—blood and fire and clouds of smoke; the sun shall turn black and the moon blood-red before that awesome Day of the Lord arrives. But anyone who asks for mercy from the Lord shall have it and shall be saved.'
>
> "O men of Israel, listen! God publicly endorsed Jesus of Nazareth by doing tremendous miracles through him, as you well know. But God, following his prearranged plan, let you use the Roman government to nail him to the cross and murder him. Then God released him from the horrors of death and brought him back to life again, for death could not keep this man within its grip.
>
> "King David quoted Jesus as saying:
>> 'I know the Lord is always with me. He is helping me. God's mighty power supports me.
>> 'No wonder my heart is filled with joy and my tongue shouts his praises! For I know all will be well with me in death—
>> 'You will not leave my soul in hell or let the body of your Holy Son decay.
>> 'You will give me back my life, and give me wonderful joy in your presence.'
>
> "Dear brothers, think! David wasn't referring to himself when he spoke these words I have quoted, for he died and was buried, and his tomb is still here among us. But he was a prophet, and knew God had promised with an unbreakable oath that one of David's own descendants would [be the Messiah and] sit on David's throne. David was looking far into the future and predicting the Messiah's resurrection, and saying that the Messiah's soul would not be left in hell and his body would not decay. He was speaking of Jesus, and we all are witnesses that Jesus rose from the dead.

"And now he sits on the throne of highest honor in heaven, next to God. And just as promised, the Father gave him the authority to send the Holy Spirit—with the results you are seeing and hearing today.

"[No, David was not speaking of himself in these words of his I have quoted], for he never ascended into the skies. Moreover, he further stated, 'God spoke to my Lord, the Messiah, and said to him, Sit here in honor beside me until I bring your enemies into complete subjection.'

"Therefore I clearly state to everyone in Israel that God has made this Jesus you crucified to be the Lord, the Messiah!"

Acts 2:14–36 TLB, italics mine

The message is that God's vision for humanity and for all creation is now fulfilled in Jesus Christ. He is the fulfillment of all the types, shadows, and prophecies of Israel's history. Therefore he is the Messiah (God's anointed one), the Lord (the ruler over all creation). The recitation of this story struck at the heart of many listeners so that "when the people heard this, they were cut to the heart and said to Peter and the other apostles *'Brothers, what shall we do?'"* (Acts 2:37, italics mine).

God's embrace for the world revealed in Jesus Christ, simple, yet profound, strikes a listener by the power of the Holy Spirit with such force that the appropriate response is not, "Prove it," but, "What should I do?" Isabel, who sat at my right that night at dinner, experienced the same impact to the story as did its first hearers. Her response was "That's a good story! What are we to do?"

The answer today is the same as it was in the early church: "Peter replied, 'Repent and be baptized, every one of you, in the name of Jesus Christ for the forgiveness of your sins. And you will receive the gift of the Holy Spirit'" (Acts 2:38).

Peter sets forth the three steps it takes to consciously receive God's embrace: (1) *repent,* (2) *be baptized for the forgiveness of sins,* and (3) *receive the gift of the Holy Spirit.* Here, then, is how a person responds to the passionate embrace of God.

REPENT: A REVERSAL OF IDENTITY

God's vision for us is a *reversal of our present identity*—we are called to turn away from the "power of the air" (Eph. 2:2 RSV), which is the systems of the world. We are to turn from our identity with the cosmic rebellion against God to become what God created us to be and to participate in God's vision for the world, making the world a place of his visible presence. Paul writes, "Therefore, if anyone is in Christ, he is a new creation; the old has gone; the new has come!" (2 Cor. 5:17).

The point is clear: Our spiritual identity is no longer with Adam but with Jesus. Due to our identity with Jesus, a new creation comes into being from the very day that a person is cut to the heart, and an about-face begins to take place. This *metanoia* is not a one-time act but a *continuous* turning away from the old life in union with Adam.[1] Thus, repentance is a process, a daily, even momentary, entering into the cross, bringing to the cross our rebellious self-centered turning away from God and his purposes for our life, so that all those ways in which we repeatedly fail to be what God has created us to be are nailed with him on the cross and carried to the grave, so that in union with him we may also continuously rise with him in the resurrection to the new life.

That there can be no resurrection to the new life without repentance of the old life is dramatically portrayed in the new believers' renunciation of Satan that took place as they were to be baptized into God's embrace. These new converts *literally and physically renounced their former embrace of Satan and all his ways.* Cyril of Jerusalem in a sermon on 1 Peter 5:8, "Your enemy the devil prowls around like a roaring lion looking for someone to devour," provides us with a dramatic picture of their renunciation:

> You [were] told to stretch out your hand, and to address the devil as if he were before you: *I renounce you, Satan. . . .*
>
> So what each of you said as you stood there was: "I renounce you, Satan, you wicked and most cruel tyrant", and your meaning was "I no longer fear your power." For Christ has dissolved that power by sharing with me in blood and flesh, so that he might annihilate death by death and save me from subjection to eternal slavery. I renounce you, you cunning and most vicious serpent. I renounce you, you plotter, who under the guise of friendship have worked all manner of wrong and caused your first parents to secede from God. I renounce you, Satan, author and associate in every evil.[2]

In today's world of self-focused spirituality, there seems to be little sense that coming into the embrace of God means taking up arms against our old embrace of evil. Martin Luther, the great Protestant Reformer, understood the radical battle of continuous repentance in his famous hymn "A Mighty Fortress Is Our God." I have sung this hymn many times, but I remember with particular fondness singing this hymn in a Catholic church on the first Sunday when the Latin Mass was changed to English. I joined my Catholic brothers and sisters on that day in the cathedral in Chattanooga and stood with them to sing Luther's hymn for the procession, joining with them in those telling words of the third verse:

And though this world, with devils filled,
Should threaten to undo us,
We will not fear, for God hath willed
His truth to triumph through us:

The Prince of Darkness grim,
We tremble not for him;
His rage we can endure,
For lo, his doom is sure;
One little word shall fell him.[3]

While men and women in Luther's day as well as people in the early church had been taught taking up life in Christ meant renouncing Satan and all his works, there seems to be little sense in today's world of self-focused spirituality that coming into the embrace of God means taking up arms against our old embrace of evil. This repentance, this turning away from evil can have a dramatic beginning or can come as a result of a process over time. But in either case, repentance is continuous.

As an example of an immediate repentance, I know a man who was living a highly self-centered, rebellious life, looking for fulfillment in the wild life, especially women and booze. He was persuaded by a friend to attend a service at Park Street Church in Boston. God's story was proclaimed. The man was struck by its truth and felt the embrace of God. He immediately turned away from his rebellious, self-centered life and, even though he was in his early thirties, promptly enrolled as a student at a Christian college. He finished college in three years, went on to seminary, and served Jesus tirelessly as a missionary in India. He never turned away from the *metanoia* that changed the direction of his life when he first heard God's story. His *metanoia* was dramatic and occurred in an instant and remained continuous.

I love a story like this. We all do. It seems, though, that this kind of dramatic change of direction is associated more with first-generation Christians, those who are first in their family's recent past to renounce Satan and all his ways and to pick up their cross daily as they turned to serve Christ.

This was true in my dad's family. He was the first to become a Christian, then his parents, his brother and sister, and then many of the children and children's children. We inherited a Christian culture, a Christian habit of life. So the first person, like my dad, who experiences an immediate *metanoia* can say, "Once I lived like that . . . now I live like this." In this instance, the drama of a life going in the wrong direction that is then redirected to a new and changed way is so clear, so obvious, so meaningful that there is no missing the point.

But what about those of us who are second-, third-, or fourth-generation Christians? We grew up in a Christian family, were in an active youth group, maybe went to a Christian school, and married in the faith. Where is that life-changing identity for us?

I am one of those second-generation Christians. I grew up on the mission field. During my teens, my dad was a pastor in the States. I went to Christian schools and palled around with Christian friends from my youth group. The boundaries of home, church, and school were very tight. I was high-spirited, but like many others in my situation, I never fell into the wild crowd. From all external appearances, I looked and acted like all the other Christian young people with whom I associated.

So where was repentance and turning the other way for me? *Metanoia* was a clear moment in time for my Boston friend and for my father, but what about me? What about all who grow up Christian? Where is our respective *metanoia* experience? To answer this question, let us return to the text and see what actually happened on the day of Pentecost.

Turning Away from the Old Identity

The key to understanding our *metanoia* is expressed in the words following the Pentecost event: "With many other words he warned them; and he pleaded with them, 'Save yourselves from this corrupt generation.' Those who accepted his message were baptized, and about three thousand were added to their number that day" (Acts 2:40).

What do these "many other words" tell us about repentance? They deal with the matter of identity. Once we were identified with Adam as rebels against God. Now we are identified with Jesus.[4] The old identity expressed itself with a focus on the first Adam. The old identity, like Adam, turns in on the self, worships and adores the self, preserves the self, lives out of the self. The new identity with Jesus is an identity with the second Adam. Now it is Jesus who shapes our self-understanding and action. The new self is called through the image of baptism to "be like Jesus," to be transformed in the image of Jesus, the one person who truly images what authentic humanity looks like. Jesus is not only our Savior, he is also the image of perfect humanity. He models what we were originally created to be, and now, in our new creation, we are to imitate him in his humanity.

The issue of *metanoia* is an issue of continuous identity. Who shapes the very nature of your being from day to day? St. Paul clearly teaches these two identities—one with Adam, the other with Jesus—in his letter to the Roman Christians: "Sin entered the world through one man, and death through sin, and in this way death came to all men, because all sinned" (Rom. 5:12). Paul's point is that we are in solidarity with Adam.

We belong to him. We do what Adam did. We continuously rebel against God and unfold life in the wrong direction. Like Adam, we listen to the wrong voice. The voice says, "Find yourself," "Be yourself," "You are the independent master of yourself," "Truth lies within you," "Be true to self."

The question here is not primarily that of *doing bad things*. The real issue is *with whom do you identify?* Are you committed to follow the nature of rebellion against God's purposes for life inherited from Adam, or are you willing to say, "I need to have my nature formed by the second Adam, the one who is in full union with the purpose God has for his creatures and the world"? The question is "With whom do you identify—Adam or Jesus?" To enter God's embrace means a continuous turning from Adam-identity to Jesus-identity.

Identifying with Adam will ultimately result in a person seeing self as though the self is the ultimate being. In our time the ill effect of following Adam is the view that the self is ultimate. This finds expression in a form of relativism that emphasizes the "do what you want" philosophy because ultimately "you are the only one to whom you are accountable." Christian spirituality, on the other hand, begins with day-by-day repentance, a continuous change that takes place in the mind, the heart, and the will.

Repentance is to hear God's story and to be struck by its truth, in the heart—in the innermost chamber of our being—every day. Repentance is the desire to leave behind our old identity with the first Adam and continually turn toward a new identity in Jesus. In some cases this reorientation of direction may have a dramatic origin. In other cases, as in those from a Christian upbringing, a person's new identity may come from a gradual, almost imperceptible process of awareness of their spiritual identity. But for both, whether immediate or gradual, there is a dramatic ritual that marks our embrace of Jesus. We find that ritual expressed on the day of Pentecost in the rite of baptism, the second act of entering God's embrace.

BAPTISM: THE MARK OF OUR NEW SPIRITUAL IDENTITY

God's vision for us is that our lives be immersed with Jesus, passionately. Acts 2:40 tells us that those who had been cut to the heart heard "the many other words" of Peter telling them to "save yourselves from this corrupt generation." They were called to turn away from their identity in Adam and turn to Jesus for a new identity. And their turning was expressed in a ritual that marked them as Christ's own. For as Scripture tells us, "Those who accepted his message were baptized" (Acts 2:41).

Baptism is the ritual that marks our new identity in Jesus. "We know," writes Paul, "that our old self was crucified with him" (Rom. 6:6) and that we are now "united with him in his resurrection" (Rom. 6:5). Baptism is a performative symbol.[5] When baptism is enacted in faith, the spirit of God performs, ascribes, and accomplishes the very meaning of baptism—a forgiveness of our old identity is made real, and a new identity with Jesus is actualized. Baptism in water in the name of the Father, the Son, and the Holy Spirit names the new identity we now have with Jesus and God's vision for our life in his world.

St. John Chrysostom, the fourth-century bishop of Constantinople, summarizes the transformation from one embrace to the other with these words: "He takes you down into the sacred waters, at the same time burying the old nature and raising 'the new creature, which is being renewed after the image of the creator.' . . . And another man comes up out of the font, one washed from all the stain of his sins, who has put off the old garment of sin and is clothed in the royal robe."[6] This new identity that comes from the grace of God's embrace is not accomplished through a form without intention. Faith accompanies baptism and trusts that Jesus indeed has been made our new identity.

Is Baptism Really That Important?

Still, there are some who are skeptical about the need to be baptized. For example, I once spoke to a small, evangelical Bible study group on baptism as the mark of Christian identity. A person in that group became visibly angry with what I was saying. While she was able to restrain her anger from an outburst, she nevertheless trembled with rage, and her face flushed as she said in a deeply controlled voice, "There is no need of baptism. I have never been baptized and never will because baptism is an *inner* reality." For her there was no value to a visible baptism in water in the name of the Father, Son, and Holy Spirit. I tried to explain that it was not an either/or but a both/and. Baptism is analogous to marriage, where both the inner commitment and outer ritual are necessary for marriage to be truly effective.

Perhaps this woman's rejection of baptism had grown from the knowledge of someone who had been baptized but never expressed an interior change. We all know people like that, who have been baptized but do not follow it in a baptized life. They are not involved in a church and seldom appear in worship except for Christmas and Easter. They may not exhibit much of a spiritual life, but if asked about their relationship to God they may say, "Well, I was baptized." This is a false hope because baptism, while it may occur in a moment of time, is a state of *continual being*. We are called to live daily in our baptism. Those who do not live in the divine embrace where their new identity has been established in baptism should not make a claim to have it. Baptism is a way of life.

But I am getting ahead of myself here. I will deal with the spirituality of the baptized life in the next chapter. Here I want to impress upon us the reality of our new identity in Jesus, the mark of which is baptism. How important is it for us to be marked by baptism? The answer is that it is crucial because baptism reveals we have been embraced by Jesus and share in God's vision for the world.

We all know people who have gone through an identity crisis. A genuine search for identity often occurs among those who have been adopted, while others experience a valid identity crisis when they discover they really do not belong in the vocation in which they find themselves. I frequently meet older students who left law, business, or medicine to enroll in seminary and pursue a calling into ministry. For those and others, "Who am I?" is by no means an idle question or one that can be easily dismissed.

But what is our Christian identity? Is not this also a valid question to ask? A clue to Christian identity is the command of Jesus to his followers to "make disciples of all nations, *baptizing* them in the name of the Father and the Son and the Holy Spirit" (Matt. 28:19, italics mine). To be baptized in water into the death and resurrection of Jesus and into the fellowship of the Godhead is a spiritual identity that we carry with us throughout our entire Christian life. This mystical union of God by faith in Christ is that very same union discussed at length earlier from which the true spiritual life springs; as the old hymn says, "Come, Thou Fount of Every Blessing." The hymn writer knew the Christian's union with God in Christ is where the source of the spiritual life in God's story resides. To contemplate baptism, then, is to focus on God's embrace. For baptism reveals God's embrace and a return to God's original purpose for life, to re-create all life.

Is Not Conversion My Identity?

Baptism is not always the answer given to the question, "What is your spiritual identity?" Many evangelicals, as pointed out previously, will associate their identity with their conversion, saying, "On such and such a date I received Jesus." I do not doubt the reality of a conversion, but I ask, "What is the divine mark of that conversion?" Is it *I* raised my hand, walked forward in a crusade, and received Jesus? Do we create our own mark of identity? Or does God do that?

From the beginning of the Christian church, baptism has been the mark of Christian identity, the image of God's embrace, and it remains so today. For example, as a professor in my early years at Wheaton College, I was asked to speak at a women's dormitory meeting and then lead the group in communion. I had already begun to read the early church fathers and was quite impressed with their teaching on baptism, so I spoke to these young women about baptism and the early church interpretation of its meaning. I made the point found in the *Didache*[7] that no one was to receive the bread and wine unless they had been baptized.

When communion was served, I noticed that one woman did not receive communion. When the service was finished she came to me and asked, "Did you notice that I did not take communion?"

"Yes, I did."

"Do you want to know why?"

"Sure," I said, "if you want to tell me."

She said, "I have not been baptized."

Knowing she was looking for some advice, I suggested she follow through with baptism in her local church. "I *want* to be baptized," she affirmed as I was gathering my materials to leave. But then, turning toward me with a sense of urgency she said, "I can't wait. I want to be baptized now!"

I realized that this was a matter of existential angst for her. Normally a person should be baptized into the community of a local church. However, because I sensed how urgent this was to her, I agreed to baptize her under several conditions. First, I asked her to gather a few people from her own immediate community (in this case her suitemates) to testify to her faith and good character. Second, I promised to write a letter affirming her baptism with water in the name of the Triune God to present to her pastor on the coming Sunday. (Baptism may be done by a Christian, at any time, and in any place. The church recognizes it as the one sacrament that belongs to all people of God. Nevertheless, baptism is ordinarily done in the local church by the pastor.) This woman quickly gathered her roommates, who testified on her behalf, and a brief baptismal service followed.

I have often reflected on this powerful experience—for her and for me. She was, like the Christians in Acts 10:44–48, baptized in the Spirit but not yet baptized in water. She did not yet wear the mark of her belonging to Jesus. And once she heard baptism was a divine mark that identified her with Jesus, she wanted it and wanted it now. Upon baptism, her identity was complete.

Throughout the history of the Christian church, baptism has always been the mark of Christian identity. It was so for the ancient fathers, the Reformers, the Puritans, and John Wesley, and because baptism as the mark of Christian identity has been lost in the contemporary Christian church, it is imperative that it be recovered. Some Christians say baptism is only an empty symbol. But there really is no such thing as an empty symbol or empty language. Language and symbols perform. They say, they do, they act, they communicate, they express the language of the heart. Think about the destruction of the twin towers in New York; think about the burning of the American flag or the symbol of toppling the giant effigy of Saddam Hussein in Baghdad. None of these symbols is empty. They are filled with meanings.

If you are skeptical about the power of symbols to mark your life, let me ask you to do something that no Christian would do. My example is *extreme* and only intends to make a point. So please read this example as I intend it. Here it is: get baptized in the name of Satan. Would you do it? Would you say, "Well, okay, it does not have any meaning, so I will go ahead and comply." Certainly not. "No way," you would say, "I do not want to identify with Satan, I do not want to be marked as Satan's own. I do not want to follow Satan." (A satanist, on the contrary, will be gladly baptized in the name of Satan, for satanist spirituality is a spirituality in union with Satan and his purposes in the world.)

So why is it that some well-meaning Christians regard baptism into Jesus so lightly so as to call it an empty symbol? If a person will not be baptized into Satan because it bears a symbolic meaning (I am using the world *symbolic* to mean "participates in the reality represented"), how much more is the significance of being baptized into union with Jesus and God's purposes in the world? Baptism says what it does, and it does what it says. It discloses our union with Jesus Christ, an embrace that establishes a new identity and opens the window on God's vision for our life in God's world.

When I lecture on baptism in class, I will sometimes point to a student and say, "Tell me your name." The student may say, "I am Steve." And I say, "Now I am going to give you your full identity: you are Steve, baptized into Jesus Christ." Christians have a new identity. Baptism into the name of Jesus is the sign, the symbol, the image of that new identity. Get up every day and say, "I am baptized into Jesus Christ. My life is to be lived in union with him." Paul puts it this way: "We were therefore buried with him through baptism into death in order that, just as Christ was raised from the dead through the glory of the Father, we too may live a new life" (Rom. 6:4).

Most people I talk to do not think of baptism as the mark of our spiritual union with Jesus. Pastor Ron Morrell, however, responds positively to the metaphor. He writes, "It ties our identity not with some movement or human person or teaching, but to Christ, himself. This is the big divide which separates us from the world. We are in this world as

Christians, but we do not get our identity from it but through being united to Christ."[8]

Ron is right. And unity, as he suggests, goes back to immersion. What are you immersed in? "I am immersed in postmodern culture." "I am immersed in rap." "I am immersed in pop music." We are in union with whatever we are immersed in. If you have been willingly baptized into Jesus, you have been immersed into the life of the Triune God through Jesus by the Spirit. But what is it about baptism in water that makes it the mark of our spirituality? How does baptism reveal God's divine embrace of his people?

Baptismal Water Reveals God's Re-Creative Action in Us and in the World

Why water; why this washing, this dunking, this sprinkling? Why take a substance of the earth—water that we drink, bathe in, swim in, play in—why take this liquid substance and go down into it and come up from it? The answer is this: Water is always associated with God's creative activity. Water is a metaphor for new life. The Spirit of God, the "giver of life" is always bringing something new out of the waters (creation, Red Sea, Jordan, baptism of Jesus). Therefore, the water of baptism is a metaphor that the Spirit of God is doing a new thing, so the waters of baptism constitute a divine mark, a mark of God's embrace.

Many of us, however, have been brought up to believe that baptism is not a mark of God's embrace, but *my* mark of *my* conversion. "*I* got converted, then *I* was baptized as a witness to *my* conversion" is the typical baptismal language of many evangelicals. And I understand why. This language is a reaction to the erroneous view that baptism *itself* saves. Some who hold to baptismal regeneration believe in a mechanical view of baptism: baptism *gives* salvation. In Scripture, however, baptism is not a means of salvation.

Also, the baptism act is not merely a testimony to salvation that occurred in a conversion experience. Baptism is instead the sign of God's embrace of us in the incarnation, death, and resurrection. Here, for example, is a prayer of thanksgiving over the waters, a prayer that represents the ancient emphasis on God's creative activity out of new waters:

> We thank you, Almighty God, for the gift of water. Over it the Holy Spirit moved in the beginning of creation. Through it you led the children of Israel out of bondage in Egypt into the land of promise. In it your Son received the baptism of John and was anointed by the Holy Spirit as the Messiah, the Christ, to lead us, through his death and resurrection, from the bondage of sin into everlasting life.

> We thank you, Father, for the water of baptism. In it we are buried with Christ in his death. By it we share in his resurrection. Through it we are reborn by the Holy Spirit. Therefore in joyful obedience to your Son, we bring into fellowship those who come to him in faith, baptizing them in the name of the Father, and of the Son, and of the Holy Spirit.[9]

These words clearly emphasize the creative activity of God associated with water. Baptism marks us with a new identity because water reveals the re-creative power of God's embrace.

For some the suggestion that baptism in *water* reveals the re-creative power of God's embrace may be troubling. So let me explain it by looking at the opposite opinion in ancient Gnosticism, a heretical Christian sect of the second century. The Gnostics regarded the material world as intrinsically evil. They rejected the use of water in their rites of initiation. "They say," writes Irenaeus, "that the mystery of the ineffable and invisible should not be performed by means of visible and corruptible things, and [that of] the inconceivable and incorporeal, by sensible and bodily; but the perfect redemption is the knowledge of the ineffable Greatness itself. . . . So the inner spiritual man is redeemed by knowledge, and they need nothing more than the knowledge of all things—and this is true redemption."[10]

Water is not used by the Gnostics because matter is regarded as evil. So instead of water baptism, the Gnostic pastor simply intones words over the new initiate. Irenaeus reports that a Gnostic pastor will say, "I do not divide the Spirit of Christ, the heart and the supercelestial power, the merciful; may I name your name, O Saviour of Truth." The new initiate responds with the words, "I am strengthened and redeemed, and I redeem my soul from this age, and from all things connected with it in the name of Iao, who redeemed his soul to full redemption in the living Christ." Then the whole Gnostic congregation says, "Peace to all on whom this name rests."[11] What we see here is a Gnostic identity that derives from a set of intoned words without any material sign.

By contrast to the Gnostics, God's embrace through which we receive a new identity is expressed in a material act. It uses water, a visible, tangible, material substance. But why use water? Why is it that words are not enough? Tertullian, the late second-century church father, Carthaginian philosopher, and theologian, wrote a treatise *On Baptism* in which he outlined the reasons for water baptism. His treatise was directed against the Gnostics, who "full well know how to kill the little fishes by taking them away from their water."[12]

Tertullian began his treatise on water by attacking the Gnostics who reject God's material creation. Their "first aim" he says is "to destroy baptism." He then summarizes the significance of water. He points to the creation of the heavens and the earth out of water (Gen. 1:2), to the "age of waters," and to the "dignity" of the waters in that they were the "seat of the Divine Spirit. . . . For the darkness was total thus far, shapeless, without the ornament of stars; and the abyss gloomy; and the earth unfurnished; and the heaven unwrought; water alone—always a perfect, gladsome, simple, material substance, put in itself—supplied a worthy vehicle to God."[13]

For Tertullian, the ultimate significance of water is the power of water to reveal God's creative action. "Water," he writes, "was the first to produce that which had life, that it might be no wonder in baptism if waters know how to give life."[14] He is not here saying that water alone apart from God gives life. Rather, the antecedent is the "Divine Spirit" who works through the material water, so that water *reveals the mystery of God's creative activity as it did in the origin of the universe, at the parting of the Red Sea, at Jesus's baptism, and at the birth of every child.*

Tertullian provides a second example of water as the image of God's creative power when he asks, "Was not the work of fashioning man himself also achieved with the aid of waters?" He concludes, "The material substance which governs terrestrial life acts as an agent likewise in the celestial." The water of baptism reveals that God's embrace is doing a *new* thing, fashioning and creating a new person out of the old. But like repentance, which is continuous, baptism is also a continual state of being, not an act done, left behind, and forgotten as a one-time act. For "we, little fishes, after the example of our ΙΧΘΥΣ, Jesus Christ, are born in water, nor have we safety in any other way than by permanently abiding in that water."[15]

We are to live day by day, moment by moment in the waters of baptism. Like fish who cannot live apart from water, we are to swim always in the water of our baptism into Jesus, for the baptismal water represents the creative action of God's hand, of the Spirit moving us to God's hand, and of the Word, both creating union with God and keeping us in God's embrace. For God embraces us with both arms—the incarnate Word and Spirit—and this embrace is symbolized by water, the seat of his creative power.

While the water of baptism discloses God's embrace, *the waters of baptism also reveal our returned embrace.* An ancient Egyptian monk by the name of Macarius reminds us that "grace hides its presence within the baptized, waiting for the soul's desire."[16]

There are several powerful biblical thoughts expressed in the saying of Macarius. First, this statement affirms that our spiritual condition is initiated by God and is not a consequence of our choice. God the Holy Spirit breathed life into our physical form at creation. This life was the presence of the Holy Spirit indwelling Adam and Eve. But we rejected the Spirit and went our own way. Now, as we repent and return to God, baptism is the symbol of receiving once again the Spirit that had been lost. In the waters of baptism God's divine action is not forced upon us or given to us apart from our will. Rather, God's Spirit is there, hovering over the waters, waiting to connect with that inner desire, the inner longing that Augustine spoke of when he said, "Our souls are restless until we find our rest in thee." Because baptism reveals our reunion with God, we are to remain in the waters of baptism where the divine initiative and the soul's desire meet in a continuous dynamic union in Jesus Christ.

Jack Boyd, a retired professor at Abilene Christian University, writes that the original meaning of *baptism* is "something on the order of 'to plunge, to dip, to immerse or wash.'"[17] Baptism is best expressed with lots of water, to a lavish use of it splashing and flying everywhere so there is no missing the point. For in baptism we are plunged and immersed into Jesus Christ, who restores God's creatures and creation as we stay in the waters bathed in God's perpetual grace.

I am told that in some African indigenous church many are baptized in the ocean. New converts are taken to the shoreline where four deacons pick them up by the hands and feet, swing them in the air, then throw them into a wave in the name of the Father. When they have rolled back on the shore the deacons pick them up and throw them into another wave in the name of the Son. And then again a third time in the name of the Spirit. I have it on good report that this is true. This ocean baptismal tradition is a great illustration of our being willingly plunged into the waters of baptism where God's creative power to restore us to himself by the work of his two hands is manifested in a material way.

The proper response is "Get me to that water; throw me in it; get me immersed in it. I want that water to rush all over me, around me, and through me. I want to be identified with Jesus, the one through whom I have been embraced by God."

In summary, baptism in water is the *physical, tangible sign of God's new and creating power to restore our spiritual relation lost at the fall and ultimately to restore the entire cosmos. It is the embrace in which we live.* So baptism is the mark of our spiritual embrace. It reveals our new union with Jesus Christ, through whom the forgiveness of our union with Adam is obtained, and a union with God through Jesus is begun by the Spirit.

THE HOLY SPIRIT: THE SEAL OF OUR NEW IDENTITY

There is a third response to those who were cut to the heart and asked, "What shall I do?" The answer was clear. First, repent. Second, be baptized for the forgiveness of sin.[18] Third, receive the gift of the Holy Spirit.[19] But what is this gift of the Holy Spirit? Paul, writing to the Ephesian Christians, says, "Having believed, you were marked in him with a *seal,* the promised Holy Spirit" (Eph. 1:13). Therefore, when we enter God's divine embrace we are not only marked by our baptism into Jesus and gain a new identity with Jesus, we are also sealed by God's other hand, the Spirit. By God's two hands we are made new.

So what does it mean to be sealed by the Holy Spirit? The Spirit seals the vision of God, the story into which by God's grace we have entered through repentance and baptism.

Baptism in the Spirit Seals (Guarantees) Communion with the Triune God

Paul tells the Christians at the church of Ephesus that the seal of the Holy Spirit is "a deposit guaranteeing our inheritance until the redemption of those who are God's possession—to the praise of his glory" (Eph. 1:14). Think of it! God's embrace of us in Jesus is a real and actual union in which God's Spirit now dwells within us. We become, as some ancient fathers like to say, "in-Goded." God's spirit takes up residence within us, and this results in our passionate embrace of God and of God's vision for the world.

To understand this receiving of God's Spirit, we must return to the picture of the Garden where the Holy Spirit was lost. The Garden story tells us that when God made Adam, God "breathed into his nostrils the breath of life, and the man became a living being" (Gen. 2:7). The ancient fathers interpret the "breath of life" to be the original union of humanity with the Spirit of God and God's vision for the world. This union, as we have seen, was broken by the rebellion of humanity against God. Therefore, when we turn away from our old identity and become united again with God through Jesus, God gives us once again his breath, his Spirit, to dwell in us.

In the ancient church, just before a person was baptized into Jesus, the bishop breathed into his face (the rite of *Ephreta*, the word means "breath") as a sign of receiving the spirit of God. So spirituality is our mystical union with God through Jesus by the Spirit that results in our participation in the life of the Triune God in the life of the world. In the ancient church this was signified by the seal of the Holy Spirit communicated by the imposition of oil on the forehead and often on the ear, nose, eyes, and collar bone to signify the Spirit's presence with the whole person.

Baptism in the Spirit Reveals That We Now Live in the Vision of God in the Life of the World

The mystical experience of living into the life of God's embrace in the life of the world has a very practical side to it. As I am writing these words I am preparing to deliver the homily at a family wedding. I am speaking on the texts chosen by the bride and groom. As I have reflected on these texts, I have become aware increasingly that these chosen Scriptures all refer to our participation in God.

First, marriage is in the name of the Father, the Son, and the Holy Spirit. I will remind this couple that to be married in the name of the Father, the Son, and the Holy Spirit is an invitation to bring marriage into the communal life of God. I will comment that God is not a *monad* (a single being) but a triune being. God has always dwelt in community. And when God created us, *God made us in his image to be like him and to live in community with him in the world of his dwelling.* Therefore, when Adam was alone, God said, "It is not good for the man to be alone" (Gen. 2:18). So God created woman not only for companionship but for completion. A man and a woman are joined, similar to the way the three persons of the Trinity live together, as beings in community.

Second, because this couple has chosen the text "Love the LORD your God with all your heart and with all your soul and with all your strength" (Deut. 6:5), I will remind them that the community of a man and a woman joined together in marriage is established under the community of God's love. The Triune God is not an absent object to marriage but very much a present power, a present reality in this new community, because in marriage we are to live in love toward each other in God even as the Father, Son, and Holy Spirit have lived toward us in love. This is the message of John 15:12–13: "Love each other as I have loved you," and, "Greater love has no one than this, that he lay down his life for his friends."

When Jesus commanded his disciples to love one another, a teaching now applied to marriage, the actualization of love is a participation in God. God's Spirit within us forms us by love in every community in which we live—in the community of singles, in the community of marriage, in the intergenerational communities of family, work, leisure, and in all of life. In other words, to participate in God means to live life as God intended life to be—in communion with him, with each other, with all people, doing the purposes of God in all of life motivated by the love between the Father, the Son, and the Spirit, a love in which we now participate because God's Spirit dwells within us. Marriage is lived out in God's vision for community, eternally grounded in the trinitarian relationship of love.

Marriage is not everyone's calling. But we are all called to be the church, where all the baptized participate in the triune love of God.

Baptism in the Spirit Reveals That Our New Life Is a Belonging in God's Community, the Church

Go back again to the Garden of Eden. God created a world to inhabit and a people for intimate communion and fellowship with himself. God's vision was a world full of his glory and a people passionately serving his vision. The rebellion of humanity against God resulted in the loss of God's family called to live out God's vision. Reluctantly, "the LORD God banished him from the Garden of Eden" (Gen. 3:23).

Despite this rebellion, throughout history God always has sought to create a community of people, his own family on earth to participate in his vision and to share his glory. He called Abraham and his kin to be his family; he rescued the Hebrew people from their bondage in Egypt and formed Israel to be his special people. Now through Jesus, God embraces a people, the church, Christ's body, to be his people on earth and to witness to his vision while doing his will on earth. When we are baptized into Jesus and through him into the community of the Triune God, we are baptized also into God's earthly family, the church, and in their living out of God's vision. For this reason Luke takes his readers from the original baptismal event on the day of Pentecost, when Peter preached the first sermon, into a description of their new life in the church. Luke tells us:

> They devoted themselves to the apostles' teaching and to the fellowship, to the breaking of bread and to prayer. Everyone was filled with awe, and many wonders and miraculous signs were done by the apostles. All the believers were together and had everything in common. Selling their possessions and goods, they gave to anyone as he had need. Every day they continued to meet together in the temple courts. They broke bread in their homes and ate together with glad and sincere hearts, praising God and enjoying the favor of all people. And the Lord added to their number daily those who were being saved.
>
> Acts 2:42–47

The immediate context in which and through which God's vision for the world is worked out is within God's family on earth. Communion with one another in the church bears an eternal meaning because it not only reflects the community of the Godhead but actually and really participates in the fellowship of Father, Son, and Spirit, which is God's goal for creation. The New Testament images of the church disclose the church's identity with Jesus, with the Spirit, and with the life of the Triune God. So the church is referred to as "the body of Christ," "the bride of Christ," "the people of God," "a chosen race," "a holy nation," a "new creation," a "new humanity," the "household of God," and even "the fullness of God." These New Testament images reveal that *God participates in human history through the church, even as the church participates in a dynamic way in the life of the Triune God.*

The church does not stand on its own in some autonomous way. It is not self-centered, does not exist for itself, does not speak for itself, does not act for itself. It is the family of God on earth called to envision community in the divine life of God and to act now in this world in the name of God revealing God's vision for the world.

Baptism in the Spirit Reveals the Mission of the Church to Witness to God's Vision for the World

When we were baptized into Jesus by the Spirit and into the life of the Triune God, sealed as God's own in this world and the next, what kind of mission did we take on? In order to understand the spiritual mission of God's family on earth, we must go back once again to the Garden of Eden, where God gave Adam and Eve, his original family, a mission in the world: "to work it and take care of it" (Gen. 2:15).

Whether the family of Adam and Eve, the family of Abraham, the nation of Israel or the church, God's family in history—God's people have always been called to the task of caring for the earth, the task of making the earth the theater of God's glory. Unfortunately the history of humanity is the opposite of God's desire for the world. Because of our rebellion against God, the cultural unfolding of humanity has made the world into a theater of all manner of sin and evil: war, violence, greed, lust, horror, and the like. Yet Jesus, the second Adam, in whom God's world is embraced and envisioned again, calls us into union with him and into a participation in God and God's purposes for the world through the Spirit, thereby re-creating man's mission for humanity and the world. We live this new life not only personally but also in the community of the church. *God's family pursues God's purposes for the world and participates in God's vision in the world by showing the world what a community of people in union with God is to look like.* In this way the church is a witness to the ultimate overthrow of the powers of evil and to the ultimate rule of God over all creation in the new heavens and the new earth.

So the baptized life has a mission in the world. It is not life-denying or life-escaping. Rather, living the baptized life is a participation in God's vision within the life of the world. It is participation that knows that there is an end to the systems of this world that deface God's world. It is to live in the hope of the new heavens and new earth.

Baptism in the Spirit Reveals the Final Victory of Christ over the Powers of Evil

Baptism in the Spirit reveals also that the power of evil has been overcome by the cross (Col. 2:15) and that those who died with Christ have died also to the "basic principles of this world" system (Col. 2:20). This system of the world, defeated by Christ on the cross, will not endure. The system itself will be destroyed (2 Peter 3:10–13). Thus a person baptized in the Spirit of Christ, whose incarnation, death, and resurrection has overcome the world, no longer embraces "the ways of this world and of the ruler of the kingdom of the air, the spirit who is now at work in those who are disobedient" (Eph. 2:2). In other words, *the spirit of the Antichrist, the evil systems that rule in the world, have been defeated in Christ and will be utterly destroyed at the end of history as we know it.* Peter tells us about the end of the powers of evil in these words: "But the day of the Lord will come like a thief. The heavens will disappear with a roar; the elements will be destroyed by fire, and the earth and everything in it will be laid bare" (2 Peter 3:10).

The view that the world itself will be redeemed typically is rejected by those who argue that all that is material is evil. For men and women holding to this Neo-Gnostic view, spirituality is a denial of living in this world, an escape from the material world to an imagined bodiless, out-of-this-world, antimaterial existence.

At first glance the above passage from Peter seems to support the view that all material will be destroyed. "God will destroy everything created" is the theological argument. But what does it mean to say "the elements will be destroyed by fire," "the heavens will disappear with a roar," and "the earth and everything in it will be laid bare"? The key to interpreting this passage is the word *elements* (*stoicha*). The elements to be destroyed are the powers of evil, not the material creation. God destroys the powers that work through people who function in the structures of existence in a way to create evil, violence, chaos, disruption of life, war, and other things that dominate our world and personal relationships. In the end it is the principalities and powers of evil that God will destroy, not creation.

Christian spirituality does not attribute intrinsic evil to creation as do the Gnostics. Nor does Christian spirituality regard creation as an extension of the divine essence, as some New Agers boldly declare. No, Christian spirituality embraces God's creation as God's good work that is now affected by the fallen state but in the end will be redeemed and restored from the present influence and corruption of all evil. Spirituality envisions the Garden of Eden restored—the union of God, humanity, and creation as God originally intended it to be.

Because creation belongs to God, it will endure. God's creation will be purged, however, of the presence and influence of the powers of evil. Christ, who overcame the powers by his cross and resurrection, will consummate history as we know it by destroying all the evil powers and systems of the world. The new heavens and the new earth will then appear, and Christ will reign as Lord of all. This is the spiritual vision by which we are called to live.

Conclusion

In this chapter I have described God's embrace that results in our spiritual identity. Our baptism marks our spiritual identity. It does not restore our spiritual communion with God; only God can do that. But baptism is the identifiable mark of our restored communion with God, and our baptism reveals a new spiritual identity—this new spiritual identity impacts our whole life. We are no longer to be identified with Adam's rebellion against God; we are no longer to be identified with the preoccupation with the self; we are no longer to be identified with a cultural unfolding that is opposite to God's desire for this world; we are no longer to be identified with the community of people who are anti-God. Our new spiritual identity, instead, is with Jesus. We Christians each wear the mark of our new baptismal identity, and that new identity is a baptism into Jesus's name. We identify with Jesus and with God's purposes for humanity that are on display in the life, death, and resurrection of Jesus.

Not only that, we are also sealed in this identity by God's Spirit. The Spirit of God, who now lives within us, seals our communion with the Triune God. Once, in the Garden, our ancestors lived in a communion, a union in the love and fellowship of the Father, the Son, and the Holy Spirit. We lost that relationship through our rebellion, but God has put his arms around us in the divine embrace and has restored our fellowship with him. His incarnate Word became one of us, and dwelling with us by the power of the Spirit, as an ancient prayer says, he opened "the windows of heaven." So now union with God's vision is restored, and the Spirit who seals that union lives within us and reveals to us how we can participate in the original purpose for which we were created. The Spirit reveals that we may live in real communion with the trinitarian activity in the life of the world as we live in God's community, the church, as we embody God's mission to the world to redeem it, as our lives become witnesses to the final victory of Christ over the powers of evil, and as we live in the hope of the resurrection anticipating the final recapitulation of all creation restored in the new heavens and the new earth.

So here we are. Receiving God's embrace is all about repentance, the continual turning away from our old identity; baptism, the mark of our continuous new identity; and the receiving of the Holy Spirit, the seal of our continuous new relationship with the Triune God, the Creator and Redeemer of all things visible and invisible. The one in whom "God was pleased to have all his fullness dwell" and through whom God "reconcile[d] to himself all things" (Col. 1:19–20) is the one in whom we now live and move and have our being. This is an incredible reality, the mark of which is baptism into Jesus Christ by the Spirit.

How do you close out a chapter that deals with such a life-changing reorientation of everything we are and do? I can think of no better summary than this ancient baptismal prayer:

Great are You, O Lord, and wondrous are Your works, and no world will suffice to hymn Your wonders. For by Your Will have You out of nothingness brought all things into being and by Your power sustain all creation, and by Your Providence direct the world. You from the four elements have formed creation and have crowned the cycle of the year with the four seasons; all the spiritual powers tremble before You; the sun praises You; the moon glorifies You; the stars in their courses meet with You; the Light hearkens unto You; the depths shudder at Your presence; the springs of water serve You; You have stretched out the Heavens as a curtain; You have founded the earth upon the waters; You have bounded the sea with sand; You have poured forth the air for breathing; the angelic Powers minister unto You; the Choirs of Archangels worship before You; the many-eyed Cherubim and the six-winged Seraphim, as they stand and fly around You, veil themselves with fear of your unapproachable Glory; for You, being boundless and beginningless and unutterable, did come down on earth, taking the form of a servant, being made in the likeness of men; for You, O Master, through the tenderness of Your Mercy, could not endure the race of men tormented by the devil, but You did come and save us. We confess Your Grace; we proclaim Your beneficence; we do not hide Your Mercy; You have set at liberty the generations of our nature; You did hallow the virginal Womb by Your Birth; all creation praises You, Who did manifest Yourself, for You were seen upon the earth and did sojourn with men. You hallowed the streams of Jordan, sending down from the Heavens Your Holy Spirit, and crushed the heads of dragons that lurked therein. Do You Yourself, O loving King, be present now also through the descent of Your Holy Spirit and hallow this water. And give to it the Grace of Redemption, the Blessing of Jordan. Make it a fountain of incorruption, a gift of sanctification, a loosing of sins, a healing of sicknesses, a destruction of demons, unapproachable by hostile powers, filled with angelic might; and let them that counsel together against Your creature flee therefrom, for I have called upon Your Name, O Lord, which is wonderful, and glorious, and terrible unto adversaries.[20]

Considering our new identity, our entrance into God's story, and the presence of God's Spirit in us, how do we go deep into God's story and participate in it day by day? This is the subject of the next chapter.

Finally, I take you back to the title of this chapter: "My Story: Coming within the Reach of His Saving Embrace." What does this suggest we are to contemplate? Certainly not *our* repentance, *our* baptism, *our* reception of the Holy Spirit. No, our contemplation is to be as that of Mary when she "treasured up all these things and pondered them in her heart" (Luke 2:19). Our contemplation is a fixed gaze on Jesus, a treasuring of that one man who voluntarily took to himself John's baptism "of repentance for the forgiveness of sins" (Mark 1:4), who was baptized for us knowing "it is proper for us to do this to fulfill all righteousness" (Matt. 3:15), and upon whom the Spirit came: "As Jesus was coming up out of the water, he saw heaven being torn open and the Spirit descending on him like a dove. And a voice came from heaven: 'You are my Son, whom I love; with you I am well pleased'" (Mark 1:10–11).

Jesus is the one man who fulfills the vision of God for humanity and for the life of the world. *He repents for all, is baptized for all, receives the Spirit for all, dies for all, is resurrected for all, and will return to establish the new heavens and the new earth. Our repentance, baptism, and reception of the Holy Spirit is our willing reception of his divine embrace. We contemplate, not ourselves, the recipients of this embrace, but he who embraced us.*

Treasure this embrace.

Ponder it in your heart.

Delight in it.

Be passionate about it.

Contemplation of God's embrace leads us to participation in God's embrace—the subject of the next chapter.

A Summary for Reflection and Conversation

Summary	Reflection
God embraces us in the incarnation, death, and resurrection.	Spirituality is to respond to God's embrace in repentance, baptism, and the reception of the Holy Spirit.
Metanoia	Repentance is not a one-time act but a continual turning away from all that is evil and death.
Baptism	The creative waters of God mark our new identity in Jesus. Baptism reveals that we have been embraced by Jesus, and united with him; we are to share his vision for the world. It is a new identity.
Holy Spirit	The Spirit, which is the seal of God's embrace, brings us into fellowship with the Triune God: a sharing in his vision for the world, a belonging to his body on earth, an anticipation of his ultimate victory over all evil.

The Challenge: Returning Spirituality to the Divine Embrace

Chapter 6   Christian spirituality is situated in God's story of the world—the story of God creating and becoming incarnate to reconcile the world to himself. The divine embrace, the story of God's incarnation, death, and resurrection, is told in the typologies of creation/re-creation, first Adam/second Adam, Exodus event/ Christ event. In the divine embrace God was united to humanity so that we might be united to God. Christ by the Spirit recapitulates the world and returns it to the Father.

Chapter 7   Baptism into union with Jesus is the sign of our new spiritual identity with the Triune God and with each other in the church. In baptism Christians embrace the new life that is the gift of God's grace through Jesus Christ by the Spirit.

Chapter 8   *The spiritual life is a living into our baptism—dying to all that is sin and death, rising through the new birth into the new life modeled by Jesus, the one who images humanity completely united to God's original purposes for creation. The spiritual life contemplates the mystery of God revealed in Jesus Christ and participates in the purposes of God for humanity.*

Chapter 9   The spiritual life is disciplined by the rule of steadfastness, fidelity, and obedience; it attends to prayer, study, and work; it meets God in daily life, in material things, and in people.

Chapter 10   The spiritual life is nourished by the church, which is the continued presence of the incarnate Jesus in and to the world. The spiritual life is nurtured by worship that sings, prays, preaches, and enacts the divine embrace in its daily prayer, weekly celebration, and yearly attention to God's saving embrace in the services of the Christian Year.

8

HIS LIFE IN MINE

Reaching Forth Our Hands in Love

Not long ago one of my former students called and asked for some advice. He had been married recently, but things were not going so well. As we conversed he slowly revealed to me that after the wedding he and his bride simply returned to their premarital lives, each continuing to live in their own apartments. At first they saw each other regularly, but as they became involved in their individual lives, they grew apart and eventually stopped seeing each other, but they kept in touch by phone. Recently, they had completely lost touch with each other. He thought the marriage was dead. He wondered what he should do about it. Should he file for divorce? Should he initiate contact again? What would I do?

My answer was very simple. You are married. You need to live together. Move out of your separate apartments lock, stock, and barrel. Stop living separate lives. Dwell together as husband and wife. Share the same vision for life. That is what marriage is all about. It will not work any other way. He took my advice. I saw him a year later and he was radiant, very much in love, and happily married.

This illustration is applicable in every detail to participation in God. The ancient fathers write that baptism is likened to a marriage. Marriage includes a renunciation, a turning away from the single life, a ritual of union, a united vision, a transformation of life as two lives are made one. Marriage implies living together. It is not an experience that, when ritualized between two people, makes no difference in their lives. When two people, united in marriage, return to their old lives, the marriage will at worst die and at best lack any kind of growing relationship according to the I-Thou dynamic.

The early church fathers saw an analogy between baptism and marriage—baptism being the rite of spiritual union with God. This rite, including its repentance, sign of union, and transformation of relationship, like marriage, establishes a residential relationship. Life in union with God now is to be lived in a partnership with God and his vision and, like marriage on the human level, requires a living relationship.

In the preceding chapter we focused on God's embrace of us, which is the divine side of our spirituality, the very source of our spiritual being. In this chapter we turn to our response to God's embrace, which is the passion of our own spiritual life. *As God has embraced us, so also we embrace God by a full, active, conscious, and passionate participation in the purposes of God for life in this world.* Like marriage, which is living in one home together, we live with God in the world, the home of his habitation, reaching our hands forth in love to God, to God's creation, and to all God's creatures.

GOD'S VISION FOR LIVING THE SPIRITUAL LIFE

I have pointed already to the separation of spirituality from God's vision for the world as the major problem with today's discussions about spirituality. Because this chapter deals with the living out of the union we have with God established by the divine embrace through Jesus Christ by the Spirit, a reminder of the separation of spirituality from God's vision is in order. When the spiritual life is divorced from God's vision for humanity and the world, it becomes subject to all kinds of fancies. Two examples will serve to warn us against creating our own version of the spiritual life.

The first comes from the pen of a Catholic writer, Peter Fink:

> I weep when the Enneagram or the Myers-Briggs analysis replaces the almost erotic intimacy with Christ described by John the Cross in his "Dark night of the soul," or the stunning challenge to discipleship and companionship presented in some of the great Ignatian meditations on the mystery of Christ. The psychological tools are fun and even helpful, but they create a fascination with oneself and in the end leave us alone with that fascination. I grow very sad when the paradoxical wisdom of our heroines and heroes is replaced by the strategies and stages of the psychological paradigm. A language that was once very large and awesomely

beautiful has been transformed into a language that is very self-centered and very small.

The same thing happens when I engage in spiritual direction myself and ask my directees what it is they are looking for. Essentially they are looking for what the gurus promise: personal growth and fulfillment, recognition and affirmation, a good feeling about one's self. They all know their Myers-Briggs letters, and most know their Enneagram numbers. But very few know the language of companionship with God both of contemplation or transformation of life born of suffering and injustice freely embraced. Very few speak of dying to themselves that others might live. I once remarked to a friend in Cambridge that I was astonished at how much time these ministry students spent watching themselves grow.[1]

My concerns were similar to Father Fink's when I read the September 5, 2005, cover essay of *Newsweek*, "Spirituality in America."[2] Pentecostal, environmentalist, Islamic, Buddhist, Catholic, and Jewish spirituality all were presented with one thing in common—the search for a transcendental experience, a focus on self, a common experience of prayer and meditation without any reference to the visions of reality or the stories that inform the experience. Spirituality, it would appear, is the common experience of the transcendent, no matter how the transcendence of a particular faith may be understood. So, according to the common view of the spiritual life, the spiritual is the search for an experience. But of what? A feeling? A mood? An atmosphere?

The Christian faith does not oppose *experience of the transcendent*, but the Christian spiritual life is not an experience *out of this world*, it is an experience of transcendent meaning here and now in this world through a passionate participation in God's vision for humanity in this world. This kind of experience was understood by the early church fathers, the Reformers, John Wesley, Jonathan Edwards, and many Christians throughout the centuries.

To demonstrate how the spiritual life is grounded in God and not an "out-of-this-world" experience, let me begin with a quote from a classic document in the Puritan tradition. In 1611 Lewis Bayly published *The Practice of Piety* with the original subtitle, *Directing a Christian How to Walk, that He May Please God*. In those days it was common to state the argument of the book up front in outline fashion. Bayly's outline speaks to the question of the relationship between theology (our convictions about God) and experience (our experience of these convictions) of the spiritual life—they are bound together as two sides of a coin:

THE PRACTICE OF PIETY consists—
    First, In knowing the essence of God, and that in respect of, (I.) The diverse manner of being therein, which are three persons—Father, Son,

and Holy Ghost. (II.) The Attributes thereof; which are either Nominal or Real,—(1.) Absolute, as, Simpleness, Infiniteness,—(2.) Relative, as, Life, Understanding, Will, Power, Majesty.

Second, In knowing thy own self, in respect of thy state of Corruption and Renovation.

Third, In glorifying God aright, (I.) By thy life, in dedicating thyself devoutly to serve him,—both privately, in thine own person; and publicly, with thy family, every day; and with the Church, on the Sabbath-day;—and extraordinarily, by fasting and by feasting. (II.) By thy death, in dying in the Lord, and for the Lord.[3]

Bayly rightly points out that to participate in God there must be some sense of what that means, otherwise we become passionate about having an experience, and that could lead us anywhere. The ancient fathers grounded spirituality as God's embrace of the world and described the spiritual life as the living out of that union. So let us turn to an examination of the mystery in which our spiritual living is situated.

GROUNDING PASSIONATE PARTICIPATION IN GOD IN GOD'S VISION FOR THE WORLD

God's vision for the world has already been presented in terms of the Triune God, creation, fall, incarnation, death and resurrection, re-creation, new heavens and new earth. These words capture the story that informs the mystery of God's vision to re-create creation and restore all things to himself through the embrace of his own two hands.

While every part of this story is a key to God's vision in that each part contributes to the whole, the key to all the keys, so to speak, is the incarnation. The incarnation is the connecting link between creation and re-creation. If God did not actually unite himself with humanity, take into himself the very creation that he made originally, the re-creation of real people and of a material world would not have taken place. His death conquers sin and death, which reigns over creature and creation. His resurrection is a new beginning for creatures and creation. God effected this recapitulation, not as a phantom who merely *stepped into* history, but as one who actually and really *became one of us*, bringing all time, space, and history into a new start. His coming again to "restore all flesh" (a phrase frequently used by the early writers) is only possible because God was made flesh. The embrace of God is an incarnated embrace. Therefore, we must ask, "What does the incarnation reveal about the spiritual life?"

The fundamental conviction of God's incarnate embrace is that God fully participated in our humanity. In Jesus, then, we see what a human being who participates in God looks like. I appreciate the way Eugene Peterson puts it. He speaks of the way "Jesus is God among us" and points out that "everything that Jesus does and says takes place within the limits and conditions of our humanity."[4] Following Peterson's lead we may say also, "Jesus is the way of man participating in God." And this way of participation, it should be pointed out, is "within the limits and conditions of our humanity." The incarnation and the life of Jesus, which flows out of it, and our spiritual life, which flows into it (the incarnational reality of God with us), is not a Gnostic or Platonic or New Age or Eastern religion life-denying, life-transcending, supraspiritual experience. *The spiritual life, like the incarnation, is participation in this world, this life, this place, in our day-to-day relationships in family, work, church, and leisure.*

Because of the incarnation, our humanity is lifted up into God, God's image within us is restored, and human nature is healed. In this sense Jesus Christ *is* "the way and the truth and the life" (John 14:6). But also, he *shows* us the way to live because he is not only the image of God among us but the image of remade humanity before God.

Before exploring the application of incarnational spirituality for our spiritual life, it is theologically necessary to make a few qualifying statements. First, Jesus is the only human being who is united to God in an incarnation. John reports, "The Word became flesh and made his dwelling among us. We have seen his glory, the glory of the One and Only, who came from the Father, full of grace and truth" (John 1:14). But second, it was a real man, a human person who bore in himself the sins of Adam—able to sin, but as Scripture tells us, "like as we are, yet without sin" (Heb. 4:15 KJV).

The ancient creeds clearly affirmed the fullness of Jesus's humanity. I am not sure we evangelicals, however, really grasp the humanity of Jesus. In our contemporary evangelical world we love to hear the words "yet without sin," but cringe at the words "like as we are." But to truly understand the spiritual life, we must come to grips with the human side of Jesus, that he truly and actually is "one who has been tempted in every way" (Heb. 4:15). The temptations of Jesus, in what Geerhardus Vos, biblical theologian of the late nineteenth century, has called the unfolding of his messianic consciousness, are every bit as real as every temptation we have ever had.

We carry around a glib portrait of Jesus, I fear. We think of him breezing through life, doing good, teaching truth, dying for us, and rising for us like a divine robot—no feeling, no struggle, hooked up to a divine energy that made his life a breeze. The creeds, fortunately, will not let us think this. The church fathers struggled with those who wanted to affirm the divinity of Jesus but deny his humanity. This is clear particularly in the monothelite controversy in which some argued that Jesus had only one will, the divine will. The affirmation of the human will in Jesus put him in our position—as one of us, struggling with his own union with God.

As one of us, real flesh and blood, Jesus reversed the wound of Adam. Beginning in the womb of Mary, and continuing throughout his entire ministry, he struggled to surrender his will to the Father. And because he succeeded in surrendering his will to the Father's will, in all things, he restored our will in his obedience. And as Jesus hung on the cross in full obedience to the Father's will, he canceled sin's debt. In his death he won a victory over death, and in his resurrection he made all things new. His work of reversing Adam's fall that corrupted humanity and all creation will be completed at the end of history when all evil will be dealt a final blow, and God's Eden, the new heavens and the new earth, will emerge with Jesus as Lord over all creation.

This brief theological description shows there to be a real, qualitative distinction between Jesus and ourselves. His struggle to remain in union with God and God's vision was the struggle to fulfill the vision of reordering the universe. Jesus alone with the Spirit has accomplished the reordering of our spiritual relation to God and of all creation in his work of recapitulation. He did not come to show us the way—as if each of us must do over again what Jesus did. No, his struggle is *for us*. He is the one single human being who has won back our original spiritual relation with God, and God does not ask us to do what his Son did either. His Son did this for all.

The spiritual relationship with God is restored by Jesus, and so to be immersed in Jesus in baptism means that our spiritual life is grounded in his accomplishments, the divine embrace, not in anything we do. Our spiritual life is defined, described, and organized by Jesus' surrender to the will of God. So the struggle to participate in God's will for our lives, the very purpose for which we were made, is, like Jesus, the struggle to surrender our will to God's will. Even as Jesus struggled to surrender his will to the Father, so also, in our own spiritual life, Jesus is the model not only for the victory but also for the struggle. Therefore we "fix our eyes on Jesus, the author and perfecter of our faith . . . ," as the writer of the book of Hebrews encourages us, "so that you will not grow weary and lose heart" (Heb. 12:2–3).

Jesus is both the subject and object of the spiritual life. As subject he has attained the spiritual life for us, that is, he alone reestablishes the unity between God and man, that unity which Adam lost. As object, we look to him to see what a human being united to God looks like. So what does the spiritual life look like? It can be said with confidence that the spiritual life is a passionate participation in God imitating the one and only human being fully united to God, Jesus.

PASSIONATE PARTICIPATION IN GOD

To be passionate about something, you need to know what you are passionate about. You cannot be passionate about a nebulous, undefined experience. But you can be passionate about the mystery of God's embrace, which establishes union with him and his vision for the world. That life is seen in Jesus and no other. As Christians we have been baptized, immersed, drenched, and soaked in Jesus in the re-creating waters of baptism and signed and rubbed in the sweet smell of the oil of the Holy Spirit. So by the two hands of God, the very hands that recovered and restored God's original creative purpose for the world, we are literally, really, and truly brought into a participation in the life of God's vision, a mystical union with God.

Since God has already accepted us in Christ, who lifted our humanity up into his, and by the Spirit has done everything necessary to make us acceptable to God, the spiritual life is a freedom to participate in God, not a duty. In Jesus we are born again to become fully human, to be what God created us to be in the first place. So the spiritual life, this marriage we have with God, is an embodied union with God and with his vision for the world revealed to us in Jesus by the Spirit. Our spiritual life, then, is not just a feeling, an idea, or a spiritual romance. No! It is an embodiment of God's vision for humanity clearly spoken in the words of Jesus and visualized in concrete ways in his actions.

The Embodied Spiritual Life

Philosophers George Lakoff and Mark Johnson, in their book entitled *Philosophy in the Flesh*, describe the embodied life. First, they make clear that an embodied life affirms an embodied soul. The soul is "located forever as part of the body, and dependent for its ongoing existence on the body." Therefore, "those religious traditions around the world based on reincarnation and the transmigration of souls, as well as those in which it is believed that the soul can leave the body in sleep or in a trance"[5] are contradicted by the Christian notion of an embodied soul.

Some Christians erroneously have succumbed to the old Greek notion of a soul independent from the body and have taught that we are inhabiting our bodies only during an earthly sojourn. Songs with lyrics such as "This world is not my home, I'm just a-passin' through" inevitably lead us to think that the holy life is only achieved by leaving earthly things behind. According to this thinking, the soul must transcend all earthly material things, all desires, all that is human so that the soul, that immaterial part of our being, may unite with God, the invisible spirit who cannot be found in the material world.

An embodied spiritual life rejects this unhealthy division between the body and the soul. This division reared its head in Gnosticism, Platonism, and the new mysticism of the late medieval era. Today this dualism is found in New Age thought, where it is believed that "humans can rise to possess immediate fellowship with the Spirit of God in the world of the spirit."[6] An embodied spirituality also rejects the pantheism of Eastern religions and paganism, in which God is identified with nature or spirituality is viewed as an absorption into the force or energy of life. Christianity, unlike New Age dualism or pantheistic monism, affirms the paradox of a Creator who is both outside creation yet within. God creates and is present to all his creation through the Spirit. God puts flesh on his word in Jesus and embodies the life of man as he created him to be.

The incarnation is the key Christian teaching of embodiment. The Christian God is not completely remote and distant from us. Even though God is transcendent and above us, he is also immanent and near. God has been embodied among us in the person of Jesus Christ: "Christ became a human being and lived here on earth among us" (John 1:14 TLB). God's embodied reality among us calls us into an embodied spirituality before him.

Lakoff and Johnson remind us, "Our body is intimately tied to what we walk on, sit on, touch, taste, smell, see, breathe, and move within. Our corporeality is part of the corporeality of the world." The mind, too, is corporeal, "but also passionate, desiring, and social." It is not culture-free. "There is much that it cannot even conceptualize, much less understand." But its "conceptual system is expandable: *it can form revelatory new understandings.*"[7]

Consider this phrase in terms of an embodied spirituality. The person—mind, heart, soul, will, all interconnected and formed in one living, breathing body—can form "revelatory new understandings." We form these "new understandings" through empathy. That is "from birth we have the capacity to imitate others, to vividly imagine being another person, doing what that person does, experiencing what that person experiences." This common experience "is a form of 'transcendence,' a form of *being in the other*."[8] In Christian spirituality, which is an in-this-world experience, we contemplate Jesus, the one perfect human being, the one in whom we have been united by virtue of God's incarnation into our skin and into our walking in this world, in this culture, in this life to show us what God created us to be. Jesus Christ is the vision of the true spiritual life. We become as baptized Christians empathetic with Jesus. We want to be like him, therefore, "the vividness, intensity, and meaningfulness of ordinary experience become the basics of a passionate spirituality."[9] Spiritual passion is not "get me out of this world" but "let me throw myself into life," swimming daily in the baptismal waters, passionately choosing to be the person God created me to be, emulating the display of perfect humanity, the embodiment of God in Jesus.

The Embodied Life of Jesus

This image of the new humanity in Jesus, a recovery of God's intent for us in the Garden, is not achieved by Jesus without a struggle. The union of Jesus with God is no mere mechanism or illustration but a true achievement on the part of Jesus for all humanity. Jesus chose by his own will to embody God's original intent for humanity. This is why the denial of the human will in the monothelite controversy was no small matter. The ancient church affirmed that Jesus, by the complete and constant surrendering of his human will reversed our fallen human will, achieved union with God for us all, and left us an example to follow.

Peter Fink describes the human struggle to surrender our will to the Father's will. It is a lengthy quote, but it states clearly a reality about the incarnation that seldom crosses our minds and speaks boldly to the passion we must bring to the incarnational dimension of our own struggle to live out God's vision for our lives:

> The affections of Christ, as all human affections, can be clustered under the two main headings of solitude and intimacy, that is, the journey inward into the mystery of God within and the journey outward into the mystery of other people. The one cluster gathers his affections toward Abba, whom he met deep within himself. The other gathers his affections toward his disciples and friends, and all others to whom Abba sent him. Since the present focus is the personal journey, we will look here only at the affections shaped in Jesus' solitude, and at the God who engaged him along the way.
>
> In a small yet powerful work entitled *Poverty of Spirit* Johannes Metz looks at the personal journey of Jesus through the lens of poverty or dependence on God. He traces Jesus' growth in this dependence, not as a given received with ease and without struggle, but as a free choice born of struggle and claimed as his own in the face of enormous inner resistance. Metz insists that Jesus' life, no different from any other human life, is a mandate from God, and that the scope of the mandate is for Jesus to become a fully human person. This "involves more than conception and birth. It is a mandate and a mission, a command and a decision."
>
> Metz's work is a reminder that the human life of Jesus had no foreordained pattern known in advance that had to be followed. Some strands of popular piety notwithstanding, Jesus did not have the security of knowing what the next step would be, nor was he in full control of the outcome. Rather, the life of Jesus, like every other human life, had to be shaped in the living. It was filled with people and events, insights and discoveries, each of which constituted a new revelation about his own human life. And each demanded

of him a choice: who shall he be, what shall he say, what will he do. Many of the choices came easily, a natural flow from the depth of the person he had already become. Some drove him back to the source of that depth, namely, the God-Abba within, where the choice had to be born of struggle, and where the struggle itself took him deeper into the mystery of his own human life and into the mystery of his God. The struggle revealed a life to which he must be faithful. In the choices which he made, faithfulness and unfaithfulness stood before him as the terms of the choice.

Metz reflects on the temptations in the desert as a paradigm of all the choices which Jesus had to make in his life. In the desert the terms of faithfulness and unfaithfulness became clear. On the one hand, there is the voice of the tempter, which carries the illusions of his own expectations and the expectations of others. "If you are the son of God . . . ," then let me tell you how the son of God should act. On the other hand, there was the voice within, the voice which was from Abba, the voice of his own human conscience and human integrity. This voice held before him the one choice which, precisely because it does not come from outside himself, but from within, is the one choice that will keep him faithful both to his own life and to his God. "I am the son of God . . . ," but God alone will tell me what that shall mean. Faithfulness is born of listening to God within. Faithfulness is obedience to the voice that is heard within.

It is difficult in our own day, when autonomy and self-actualization hold our imaginations as important values to be pursued, for us to be comfortable with the complete dependence of Jesus on Abba and the full obedience of Jesus to Abba. His life did not originate from himself; it was given to him and was guided by the design of Another. He was always free, but never autonomous. It is even more difficult for us to be comfortable with this because we have lived so long with images that have stressed the divinity of Christ and which have played down or romanticized away his total dependence on Abba. Nonetheless, however difficult it may be for us to receive the truth of Jesus' dependence on Abba, it is absolutely necessary that we do so, because such dependence on God is at its deepest, our truth also.[10]

Because Jesus struggled to perfect humanity, we are called in union with him to an incarnational spirituality. Kenneth Leech, in *Experiencing God: Theology as Spirituality*, understands the full implications of an embodied, incarnational spirituality and its many manifestations in the history of the church:

We need to relate our devotion to our humanity, to our bodies, far more than is often the case. Again, the Eastern Christians have always laid great emphasis on the physical aspects of worship, and so the "sacrament of tears" has been evident in Orthodox spirituality since Isaac of Nineveh. In the West, Augustine laid emphasis on the restlessness of the heart and on the need to discover God in the midst of human emotional turmoil.

St. Bernard's great contribution to the life of prayer lay in his insistence that "carnal love" is the first degree of the love of God. In Bernard's theology, the humanity of Christ is the gateway to union with God, and the imagination, the affections, the senses become the instruments of transformation. His devotion to the incarnation and the passion of Christ is deeply affective and rooted in the flesh. . . .

We can see the combination of affection, human warmth, and joy in the goodness of the physical world in the spirituality of St. Francis of Assisi (1181–1226). The sense of celebration of the natural creation is, of course, expressed very movingly in Francis' *Canticle of the Creatures*. Here sun and moon, earth and air, fire and water, life and death, are the vehicles of the divine.

In opening himself to the world, in taking his place among the creatures, in becoming profoundly aware of them as "brothers" and "sisters," Francis also opened himself to that obscure part of himself which is rooted in nature; unconsciously he was fraternizing with his own depths.

In Francis we see a joy in all God's works. He saw beauty itself in all things beautiful, for "he embraced all things with a rapture of unheard of devotion, speaking to them of the Lord, and admonishing them to praise him."[11]

The spiritualities of our day which pursue an otherworldly spirituality or focus on the inward experience of the self are not spiritualities rooted in God's vision for humanity and for the world. These spiritualities are questioned correctly by Hans Urs von Balthasar in these words:

The act of contemplation in which the believer hears the word of God and surrenders himself to it, is an act of the whole man. It cannot therefore assume a form in which man truncates his own being, whether for a short or longer time—for instance, by *systematically* training himself to turn from the outer world and attend wholly to the inner world, or turning from both the outer and inner senses (the imagination) to the pure, "naked" spirit. That kind of deliberate artificial restriction reduces man to a shadow of himself, and is a misunderstanding of God's demand, namely "conversion," a turning from the manifold to the essential.[12]

Likewise, Philip Sheldrake, in *Spirituality and Theology*, speaks to the oneness of the inner and outer experience of spirituality, affirming that an incarnational spirituality does not cancel the concern for the interior soul but affirms it:

Paradoxically, a widespread decline in traditional religious practice in the West runs parallel with an ever-increasing hunger for spirituality. The question at the forefront of most of the great spiritual classics used to be "What or who is God?" Nowadays the characteristic question of the contemporary spiritual seeker is more likely to be "Who am I?" Great Christian teachers

of the past such as Julian of Norwich understood quite clearly that these
two questions are inextricably linked.

And I saw very certainly that we must necessarily be in longing and in
penance until the time we are led so deeply into God that we verily and
truly know our own soul.[13]

To be led into God and to "know our own soul" are two sides of the
same coin.

This division between the inner self and the outer self that has been
so dominant in evangelical circles is changing among the younger evangelicals, those men and women who seek to retrieve an ancient faith in
our postmodern world.

Embodied Spirituality in the Emerging Church

Sociologists Richard W. Flory and Donald E. Miller have explored the
new appreciation of an embodied spirituality in an article entitled, "Expressive Communalism: The Embodied Spirituality of the Post-boomer
Generation."[14] Their research brought them to recognize "a new religious
type" that they have called "expressive communalism." There are two
groups of expressive communalism, the "cultural reappropriators," who
draw on ancient expressions of embodied spirituality and adapt them
for use in today's culture. The second group, the "cultural innovators,"
are equally concerned for an embodied spirituality, but they choose to
create new forms out of the culture of our day. A brief review of both
groups shows us the current trend to move away from the spiritualities
built on the dualisms of the secular/sacred, body/spirit dichotomies:

> *Cultural reappropriators*: "The primary characteristics of this group
> are an attraction to the visual and ritualistic elements of liturgical
> churches, a desire for a connection to a larger history of Christianity
> than what they had previously known, a desire for a small religious
> community, a commitment to a strict spiritual regimen, and a desire
> for 'religious absolutes' and a set social structure."
>
> *Cultural innovators*: This group is "expressing their desire for a more
> embodied faith by creating new traditions. . . . They are continually
> innovating in terms of their responses to the larger culture, and are
> constantly introducing new and various forms of ritual and symbol
> into their worship services and religious and community life."[15]

Common characteristics of both the reappropriators and innovators
include "emphasis on the visual representation and expression of the
sacred," "community through more intensive face to face interaction,"

"non-hierarchical authority structure," worship that is "interactive and physical, rather than the passive and (primarily) cognitive," and a "commitment to being part of the life and culture of its host city."[16]

One can see that a spirituality that embodies the vision of God incarnated in Jesus in this world is a spirituality exploding with a variety of embodied expressions.

The Variety of Expressions in an Embodied Spirituality

A disembodied spirituality has a certain appeal in contemporary culture because, like the narcissism of our day, it focuses on *self*. Disembodied spirituality *feels* spiritual to get emotional with God, to get carried away by an otherworldly experience, dream, or intuition that can be endlessly turned over in the mind.

On the other hand, the concept of an embodied spirituality appears mundane, common, too earthly, too much like daily living. In order to show that a passionate, embodied spirituality is much more than common herdlike living, let me explore the theological dimensions of living. The key to what I am about to do is to recognize that every aspect of God's relation to the world provides us with a way of an embodied spirituality. It would take another book to fully open up the embodied nature of a theologically understood life, so the best I can do is open the door to a creative application of theology to life that you can practice in your own mind and heart, and maybe you can write the book.

Consider these many paths to an embodied spirituality:

A *trinitarian spirituality* calls us to embody God's reality of a being in community to establish community with others in personal, family, work, neighborhood, and church relations through which we participate in the life of God's eternal communion.

A *creational spirituality*, like that of Celtic Christianity, calls us into a spirituality of seeing God's trinitarian expression in all of creation, to experience the beauty of God everywhere encountered in the material world in which we live.

A *revelational spirituality* embraces God's written Word as a letter from God about life. It "reads, marks, learns, and inwardly digests"[17] the Word so that life is informed by the wisdom of God made manifest in these words.

An *incarnational spirituality*, as already described, emulates the life of Christ, his self-giving, his love for others, his teachings.

A *cruciform spirituality* enters into the suffering of others to bring redemption and reconciliation.

A *resurrection spirituality* is the zestful embrace of life, the enjoyment of re-creation and newness.

An *ecclesial spirituality* (*ecclesial* comes from *ekklēsia* and means "church") loves the church, the whole church—Orthodox, Catholic, Protestant—and is characterized by an ecumenical spirit.

A *liturgical spirituality* loves the worship of the church, the memory of God's work in history, and the anticipation of God's present and future work in the world.

A *baptismal spirituality* is sensitive to union with Jesus in death and resurrection.

A *eucharistic spirituality* is open to the presence of God made known in symbol and to the kingdom that is coming made manifest, in this, the banquet of God's victory over the powers of evil.

A *social spirituality* extends God's benefits to the poor and needy, to the orphans and widows, to the homeless and friendless.

A *missiological spirituality* concerns itself with the Good News bringing salvation, reconciliation, and restoration to God to those who do not yet know Christ.

A *pneumatological spirituality* enjoys a special relationship to the third person of the Trinity.

An *eschatological spirituality* is not a spirituality that has the future figured out as in a pre- or post- or amillennial conviction, but it is one that lives eschatologically, as Peter states, "Since you are looking forward to this, make every effort to be found spotless, blameless and at peace with him" (2 Peter 3:14).

These windows into spirituality show how extensive an embodied spirituality is. It is all-inclusive of every aspect of life. An embodied spirituality, by contrast to the disembodied spiritualities of our day, calls us into a passionate embrace of God in all of life. The only one who has completely lived out this kind of embodied spirituality in union with God and God's vision for this world and for our life in it is Jesus.

We cannot explore all of these forms of spiritual embodiment here, so I will turn to explore one—baptismal spirituality, which runs through them all because it describes the pattern of the spiritual life.

BAPTISMAL SPIRITUALITY: THE PATTERN OF THE SPIRITUAL LIFE

At the age of twelve, I was sitting in the kitchen eating a snack when my father pulled up a chair, sat down beside me, and looking me in the eye said, "Robert, don't you think it is time to be baptized?" I had not given a great deal of thought to being baptized. I was a Christian, to be sure. We discussed earlier in this book that I grew up in a strict Christian home, and while my faith was the faith of the family, I had no doubt or disbelief. Still, I found my father's question to be haunting, even challenging. For the first time in my life I was asked to affirm the faith that was mine by family environment. The question raised doubt in my mind. Was this a faith I could personally embrace? I was only twelve, so the level of doubt and the quality of my questions were superficial. After a time of personal reflection I said to my father, "I *want* to be baptized."

I don't remember receiving any training before baptism. I think I saw baptism as *my affirmation of my faith*. Though baptism was taken seriously, that particular community seemed to have little understanding of how life-changing baptism could really be. So coming to baptism in the Montgomery Baptist Church in Montgomeryville, Pennsylvania, was important, but it was not nearly as significant as the Scriptures teach and as ancient Christians practiced when they taught baptism reveals the daily pattern of the spiritual life.

I do not recall everything surrounding the event. I do remember one very powerful question my father, the pastor, asked me as we stood in the water. "Robert," he said, "do you reject the devil and all his works?" I was only twelve. I did not even know all the works of the devil! Even though my dad had not reviewed this question with me, I knew what my answer was supposed to be, so I said, "I do!" not really knowing what that meant in the full sense. I certainly did not realize that I was renouncing my connection with fallen Adam and the cultures of fallenness and embracing union with Jesus and a new pattern of life revealed in his life.

Many years later as I studied the early church fathers, I came upon the rite of renunciation introduced in the previous chapter of this book. The rite, which renounces the devil, made me realize that baptism not only reveals our new identity, it also discloses our "No" to Satan and to all his forces of wickedness and death. The memory of my baptismal renunciation of evil was a marker moment in my spiritual life not only because baptism reveals a "No to evil" but also because it discloses the spiritual life, which is "Yes to the Spirit." Consequently our day-to-day, moment-by-moment experience of life in all the spiritual expressions of the embodied life mentioned above is not something we do as a matter of course. Baptism is instead a life-changing covenant, a *call* to live deeply into the pattern of death and resurrection in every area of life.

Paul puts it this way: "We know that our old self was crucified with him so that the body of sin might be done away with, that we should no longer be slaves to sin—because anyone who has died has been freed from sin. Now if we died with Christ, we believe that we will also live with him" (Rom. 6:6–8). Here then is the deep rhythm of the spiritual life: a baptism into death to sin and resurrection to a new life made possible only by the divine embrace of God, who in his incarnation became one of us to take into himself the curse of sin and death on the hard wood of the cross and to overcome it by vanquishing death at the empty tomb. The divine embrace has become for us the pattern of the spiritual life. This baptismal pattern of the embodied life in Jesus, death to sin, and resurrection to new life, is everywhere present in the New Testament teaching on the spiritual life.

A few examples of this baptismal pattern will suffice. Paul admonishes the Galatian Christians to turn their backs on sin so as to live life in the Spirit. He enumerates what the life of sin looks like: "The acts of the sinful nature are obvious: sexual immorality, impurity and debauchery; idolatry and witchcraft; hatred, discord, jealousy, fits of rage, selfish ambition, dissensions, factions and envy; drunkenness, orgies and the like" (Gal. 5:19–21). The contrast to the resurrected life of the Spirit is clear. For the "fruit of the Spirit is love, joy, peace, patience, kindness, goodness, faithfulness, gentleness and self-control" (Gal. 5:22–23). Baptism reveals that there are two ways to live: there is a former way fashioned after our identity with the first Adam, and there is a new way fashioned after our new identity with the death and resurrection of Jesus.

The same theme is presented to the Colossian church. "Put to death . . . ," Paul writes, "whatever belongs to your earthly nature." What Paul means by "earthly nature" is not our physical human self but the rebellious fallen spirit that is fashioned after our connection with the first Adam. After enumerating a similar list of sinful expressions he writes, "You used to walk in these ways, in the life you once lived." Another list follows. He concludes that you "have put on the new self, which is being renewed in knowledge in the image of its Creator." Therefore, "Clothe yourselves with compassion, kindness, humility, gentleness and patience" (Col. 3:5, 7, 10, 12; see also Eph. 2:1–10 for another striking comparison between the old way of life and the new life).

While there certainly is growth in the new, resurrected way of life, there is no ultimate perfection (except in Jesus) this side of our destiny in the new heavens and the new earth. Life here, to the very end, is characterized by the baptismal struggle of putting off the old and putting on the new. Gregory of Nyssa, a Cappadocian father from the fourth century, writes extensively of this ascent toward perfection. He wisely states that "to stop on the path of virtue is to begin on the path of evil."[18] He calls Christians, then, into the goal, the process of doing God's will in our personal life and in our social life within all the structures of existence, imitating the life and spirit of Jesus, who in his saving embrace shows us also how to live.

This vision of the spiritual life—living in the rhythm of death and resurrection—is the emphasis also of ancient Christianity. I will illustrate this by looking at the *Didache* (an early Christian document), by examining an ancient baptismal prayer, and by reviewing the teaching of the desert fathers.

The Didache: The Two Ways

In graduate school during the 1960s, I took a course on "The Apostolic Fathers" that included a study of the *Didache*, a noncanonical document that originated about AD 50. A question the professor of that course asked has stuck with me to this day. He said, "It is generally thought that Christianity shifted away from Pauline doctrine of grace to a salvation and spirituality by works by the early decades of the second century. What do you think?" This question became the lens through which I learned the course material, shaping my study of the early church writings.

My fundamentalist and evangelical background had taught me that the church fell into apostasy almost as soon as it was formed. Generally the attitude among the older evangelical professors that I had studied under was that the church remained in somewhat of an apostate condition until the Reformation. For example, once an evangelical New Testament professor, questioning my interest in the early church, said, "Webber, you act like there was never a Reformation!" I answered, "You act like there was no church history prior to the Reformation!" This exchange was in good fun, but even so, it does disclose the general Protestant attitude toward the first fifteen hundred years of Christianity and its Eastern Orthodox and Western Roman Catholic traditions.

What I found in the ancient church was this: those who were being instructed in the faith in preparation for baptism were always taught to live in the pattern of Jesus's death and resurrection. The early date of the *Didache* is important because its teaching precedes the New Testament writings. The document contains instructions for new Christians on how to prepare for baptism. These new converts to the faith were taught to turn away from their pagan lifestyle, to embrace Christ, and to enter into the pattern of dying to sin and rising to Christ. Far from being legalistic, these instructions were, in fact, expressing the spiritual life. Pagan converts to the faith had to study these two ways and learn how to live in the pattern of death and resurrection before they were baptized. Here is an excerpt from the *Didache* that describes the personal dimension of the ancient spiritual life as living in the "two ways."

There are two ways, one of life and one of death; and between the two ways there is a great difference.

Now, this is the way of life: "First, you must love God who made you, and second, your neighbor as yourself." And what ever you want people to refrain from doing to you, you must not do to them. . . .

But the way of death is this: First of all, it is wicked and thoroughly blasphemous: murders, adulteries, lusts, fornications, thefts, idolatries, magic arts, sorceries, robberies, false witness, hypocrisies, duplicity, deceit, arrogance, malice, stubbornness, greediness, filthy talk, jealousy, audacity, haughtiness, boastfulness.[19]

Next, the *Didache* is very specific about where the social struggles with evil are:

Those who persecute good people, who hate truth, who love lies, who are ignorant of the reward of uprightness, who do not "abide by goodness" or justice, and are on the alert not for goodness but for evil: gentleness and patience are remote from them. "They love vanity," "look for profit," "have no pity for the poor, do not exert themselves for the oppressed, ignore their Maker," "murder children," corrupt God's image, turn their backs on the needy, oppress the afflicted, defend the rich, unjustly condemn the poor, and are thoroughly wicked. My children, may you be saved from all this!

See "that no one leads you astray" from this way of teaching, since such a one's teaching is godless.[20]

The *Didache* presents the Christian faith not only as a confession that Jesus is Lord but a way of personal and communal life that reflects the baptismal rhythm of dying to sin and rising to new life.

An Ancient Baptismal Instruction: Warfare with the Powers of Evil

A second description of the spiritual life is found in the following baptismal instruction from the ancient church. The exact origin of these instructions is unknown, but, whatever the date, they reflect the understanding among the early Christians of the spiritual warfare. They have been handed down in the church virtually unchanged.

The Office of Holy Baptism begins with the *reception of the candidate* as a *catechumen*. The priest removes the person's clothes except for one garment. He places him with his face towards the east, breathes three times in his face, makes the sign of the cross upon him three times, lays his hand upon his head and prays for him. He says the three exorcisms, ordering the Devil to leave this person: "The Lord layeth thee under ban, O Devil: He who came into the world and made his abode among men. . . . Begone, and depart from this creature, with all thy powers and thy angels." After further prayers for delivery from evil the priest breathes upon his mouth, his brow and his breast, saying, "Expel from him every evil and impure spirit, which hideth and maketh its lair in his heart. The spirit of error, the spirit of guile, the spirit of idolatry and of every concupiscence; the spirit of deceit and of every uncleanliness. . . . And make him a reason-endowed sheep in the holy flock of thy Christ. . . ."

Then follows the renunciation of the Devil. The priest turns the person to the west and asks three times, "Dost thou renounce Satan, and all his Angels, and all his works, and all his service, and all his pride?" And each time the catechumen answers, "I do." If the person to be baptized comes from a different tradition, or is an infant, his godparent ("sponsor") answers in his place. The priest questions him three times, "Hast thou renounced Satan?" And the catechumen, or his sponsor, responds each time, "I have." He is then requested to spit upon Satan, and the priest turns him again to the east, asking him three times, "Dost thou unite thyself unto Christ?" and then, also three times, "Hast thou united thyself unto Christ?" When the catechumen has answered these questions, he recites the Nicene Creed, the Holy Symbol of the faith. This is also said three times again. When the catechumen has affirmed, for three times, "I have," the priest orders him, "Bow down also before Him!" And he answers, "I bow down before the Father, and the Son and the Holy Spirit, the Trinity, one in Essence and undivided." A short prayer of intercession concludes this part of the liturgy.[21]

Another good example of training for spiritual warfare in the ancient church is found in Augustine's instruction to those coming for baptism:

He would stress, by turns, the struggles of conversion and the gratuity of God's action. He would play on dichotomous images from the New Testament and insist that baptism meant new life, a passage from darkness to light, from slavery to freedom; yet he balanced these with developmental images, insisting that conversion was lifelong, that one only slowly acquired virtue. He also moved against inherited views and insisted that baptism marked the forgiveness of sin, not its end, that this coming to birth needed to be set within an eschatological horizon, and that on this side of eschaton the Church would remain a mix of wheat and chaff.[22]

The Desert Fathers: Guarding the Heart

One of the most distinguishing features of ancient Christianity is the rise of what became known as the *desert* tradition of spirituality. Desert spirituality has a long tradition reaching back to the prophets of the Old Testament. John the Baptist emerged from the desert to proclaim, "Prepare the way of the Lord" (Mark 1:3 RSV). Jesus himself withdrew to the desert (Mark 1:35; Luke 4:42; 5:16). So it is not surprising that when the church began to grow worldly after the conversion of Constantine, many earnest and devout Christians wishing to preserve the early Christian traditions of spirituality fled to the desert.

J. J. Von Allmen, a reformed theologian, speaks to the development of desert spirituality by saying, "God leads his people and His Son and later the anchorites and hermits [into the desert] not to cause them to flee from the world, but on the contrary to bring them into its heart so that there, in the hardest place of all, they may manifest His victory and His rights. . . . When Jesus withdrew to the desert, generally after having worked a miracle, it is not only to seek privacy but to give all the glory to God."[23]

Orthodox theologian John Meyendorff remarks that "the desert is, then, the archetypal symbol of the world that is hostile to God, subject to Satan, the dead world to which the Messiah brings new life. As his first coming was proclaimed by John the Baptist in the desert, so the Christian monks felt that their flight to the desert was an assault on the power of the evil one, heralding the second coming."[24]

Desert spirituality focuses on the heart. The desert fathers are very aware of Jesus's teaching:

> What comes out of a man is what makes him "unclean." For from within, out of men's hearts, come evil thoughts, sexual immorality, theft, murder, adultery, greed, malice, deceit, lewdness, envy, slander, arrogance and folly. All these evils come from inside and make a man "unclean."
>
> Mark 7:20–23

The fathers constantly warned against the hardness of heart that characterized wandering Israel. Jesus said of them, "These people honor me with their lips, but their hearts are far from me" (Mark 7:6). The desert fathers want instead to be the "good man" who "brings good things out of the good stored up in his heart" (Luke 6:45). Therefore, they called repeatedly for the guarding of the heart.

Now we turn to examples of guarding and training the heart from which all thoughts and actions proceed. The source for the teaching of the ancient church on these matters comes from Lorenzo Scupoli, a sixteenth-century priest who drew his inspiration from the early church fathers. His work, *Unseen Warfare*, ranks with the time-honored *Imitation of Christ* by Thomas à Kempis. The subject of the writing is the struggle with the powers of evil. Staretz Theophan aptly states, "The arena, the field of battle, the site where the fight actually takes place is our own heart and all our inner man. The time of battle is our whole life."[25]

In his introduction to the book, Scupoli presents the message of *Unseen Warfare* in these words: "The greatest and most perfect thing a man may desire to attain is to come near to God and dwell in union with him."[26]

While the author uses the words *to attain*, I do not believe he is doing so with the thought of legalistic effort. The battle with the powers of evil arises from the fact that the Spirit of God is within us, as Scupoli recognizes throughout his work. By the power of the Spirit we choose to put off evil and to put on Christ. So the choice comes from the freedom we have from the condemning power of the law and the freedom we have to live in the Spirit.

As I have shown, the union we have with Jesus is a sheer gift of God's grace. In the struggle with evil we are called, by the power of the Spirit, to grow in that union. Understanding the freedom we have not to sin and the freedom we have to choose to live in the Spirit, we turn to look more closely at the instructions on how the union with Jesus results in the pattern of dying to sin and living in the freedom of the Spirit. In brief, our union with Jesus is a call to renounce our own sinful and willful desires and live in perfect obedience to the will of God. I will comment on only a few of the issues raised by *Unseen Warfare*.

The writer tells us how to prepare our hearts for spiritual war with the powers of evil by what we *put off*. He teaches that war with spiritual enemies must be waged ceaselessly and courageously. We are, he says, "surrounded by so many enemies, whose hatred of us is so bitter, we can expect no peace or respite from them, no cessation or postponement of attacks, but must be ready for an onslaught at any moment and, when it comes, must immediately engage the enemy with courage."[27]

Scupoli points to the major enemy as a heart of self-love, which stems from the root of all sin: pride. He urges us to "wage ceaseless and coura-geous war against all passions, especially and pre-eminently against self-love, or a foolish attachment to yourself, manifested in self-indulgence and self-pity."[28] In this way he identifies the sin that from the beginning of the human race until now has turned humanity from the love and service of God.

Rebellion against God has always taken the form of self-love and self-interest. It is the devil's way of keeping us away from union with God. When we live in the pattern of self-interest, very little thought is given to living in the pattern of death and resurrection. The self-love of narcis-sism is one of the greatest problems we face today. Obviously personal care and appropriate personal attention to self is no sin. But popular culture, especially the media, constantly promotes self-interest. "It's all about me" is a slogan the Christian needs to replace with, "It's all about God." *Unseen Warfare* identifies some of the battlefronts of those who wish to live in God's pattern of death and resurrection.

First, there is the inner warfare of the *mind*. The mind must be guarded from ignorance. Ignorance "darkens the mind and prevents it from know-ing the truth which is the proper object and aim of its aspiration."[29] I find this instruction to be most helpful. There is a tendency among certain evangelicals, especially in lay Pentecostal and charismatic circles, to glorify ignorance and demean intellectual endeavors. While this is changing, it is still altogether too prevalent. In today's world the mind needs to grasp the Christian story so as to combat New Age spirituality and affirm Christian spirituality. Christians who are afraid to think and to search out are prey to the wiles of the evil one who delights in getting Christians to embrace falsehood.

Ancient Gnostic and current New Age spiritualities *sound* so spiritual. They are laden with romantic images and sentimental piety that emanate from the individual. They focus on the self, not God. They originate from self-effort and deny grace. Paul put it well when he wrote, "Do not conform any longer to the pattern of this world, but be transformed by the renewing of your mind" (Rom. 12:2). The mind is renewed by seeing the world from creation to re-creation as God sees it.

Second, the warrior should train the inner *will* "so as not to let it lean towards your own desires."[30] The goal is to bring the will into conformity to God's will to please him with a pure heart as Paul himself notes. "You will be able to test and approve what God's will is—his good, pleasing and perfect will" (Rom. 12:2).

How does one discern God's will for his or her life? When a desire to do God's work comes before you, Scupoli warns, "Do not immediately incline your will towards it and do not desire it, without previously raising your mind to God, so as to be clear whether they would be acceptable to God . . . wish it and do it, but only because God wishes it, only for the sake of pleasing Him and for his glory alone."[31]

The reason one needs to make sure it is God's will is because "the self-flattery of our nature is very subtle and few can discern it. Secretly it pursues only its own ends, though meanwhile its outward conduct is such that it seems to us we have but the single aim of pleasing God, though in actual fact this is not so."[32] This advice is particularly helpful today, and for those of us in ministry or any profession, including homemaking, there is a need to guard ourselves against building our own kingdom.

Scupoli also provides us with some good advice on knowing God's will. He speaks of waiting on God for "inner spiritual" illumination. When our will accords with God's will, we experience a "life-giving warmth, unspeakable joy, leaping of the spirit, being moved to tenderness, heartfelt tears, love for God and other blessed and God-loving feelings, produced not according to our will but coming from God, not by our own action but in our passivity." In addition, we are urged that all these feelings "must be verified by the advice and judgment of the experienced."[33]

The powers of evil desire to thwart the doing of God's will in our lives. The powers turn the focus on self, even in ministry. Resist the evil of self-gratification or self-will and wait upon God, praying and beseeching God that his will may be made known. For doing the will of God, in spite of hardships and even failures, is a most freeing way to live in the Spirit.

The warrior against evil must also guard the *senses*. Guard the *eyes*, especially against the attraction to persons of the opposite sex, for lustful looking may easily give birth in the heart to passionate lust of adultery. Be careful against paying "too much attention to rich food," or to "beautiful garments," for the psalmist writes, "Turn away mine eyes from beholding vanity" (Ps. 119:37, ancient translation).[34] Today, the eyes are under continual attack by the evil one. We are surrounded by sensual images in the media of television, movies, Internet, billboards, magazines, and the like.

Guard also the *ears*. "Do not listen to shameful and lustful speech, songs and music, which fill the soul with fancies, render it dissolute, and fan the flame of carnal lust in the heart." Do not listen to "gossip or criticism"; do not listen to "vain and empty talk"; do not listen to "flattery and the praise of flatterers." In other words, live with discernment.[35] Do not be careless in what you see or hear or smell, opening the door for the evil one to enter your life in the smallest way. For the powers of evil watch for breaks in the armor of Christians, breaks where they can enter to destroy.

Guard also the *tongue*. Take heed to the warning of James that "the tongue . . . is a restless evil, full of deadly poison" (James 3:8). "Silence," Scupoli writes, is "a great power" and a "sign of spiritual wisdom." To sustain the habit of silence, the author urges us to "reflect as often as you can on the pernicious results of indiscriminate babbling and on the salutary results of wise silence," suggesting that "when you come to taste the good fruit of silence, you will no longer need lessons about it."[36]

The fathers also deal with *imagination* and *memory*, which are seen as "one general inner sense which visualizes and remembers everything, that the five outer senses happened to experience before." The wrong kind of fantasy is "an invention of the devil, it is very welcome to him and useful in achieving our ruin." Adam fell because the devil had him imagine that he was equal with God. The power of the imagination to think more highly of the self and to recover and wallow in the remembrance of evil seen, heard, or touched is to live under their influence. "So, my brother, if you wish easily and effectively to become free of such errors and passions, if you seek to escape the varied nets and wiles of the devil, if you long to unite with God [I take this to mean in the pattern of death] . . . enter courageously into battle with your imagination and fight it with your whole strength."[37]

In summary, *putting off* and putting to death evil is a vital part of the ancient spiritual tradition. Put to death self-love, ignorance of truth, and willfulness, and guard the senses—what you see, hear, touch, smell, and feel—and put to death all wrong imaginations that arise from memory.

The calling to die to sin is a call ultimately to die to self. For here is where the powers of evil attack us. "The one exclusive means to avoid such self-deception is purity of heart, which consists in rejecting the old Adam and clothing ourselves in the new man. This is the aim and purpose of the whole unseen warfare."[38]

In addition to preparing our hearts for spiritual war by what we *put off*, the desert fathers also teach us how to *put on* the likeness to Christ. The likeness to Christ is just the opposite of the likeness to the first Adam. Paul sets up this contrast in his repeated admonitions to not only "put off" but also to "put on." The most succinct list is set before the Galatians. After admonishing the Galatian Christians to desist walking in the flesh, Paul calls them to walk in the fruit of the Spirit. They are to be about "love, peace, patience, kindness, goodness, faithfulness, gentleness and self-control" (Gal. 5:22–23).

The fathers, following Paul, set this contrast before the early church as well as for us today. They teach that if we are to live in the virtues, we must start the day with prayer. When you "wake up in the morning, pray for awhile saying, 'Lord Jesus Christ, Son of God, have mercy on me.'" To pray in the morning is important because it will "rouse against them [the evil powers] a firm resolve to conquer or die, but never to submit."[39] (This prayer of ancient origin is called the "Jesus prayer.")

If we are to acquire virtue and live in the Spirit, we must work on one virtue at a time. "Take up arms pre-eminently against the passion which troubles you most, which has often conquered you and which is ready to attack you again now . . . establish yourself in the virtue opposed to that passion. . . . As soon as you succeed in this you will, by this very fact, bring to life all the other virtues in yourself and will be clothed in them as in armor, which will then protect you from all the arrows of passion."[40]

The fathers stress the Pauline admonition to "press on toward the goal to win the prize for which God has called me" (Phil. 3:14). There must be no stopping in the pursuit of virtue. "Prepare yourself for continual labour, struggle and effort, allowing no thought of alleviation." Never for a moment imagine that "the virtue is already gained in its perfection."[41]

Also, do not assume that you can ascend to your goal quickly. "Make gradual progress your rule, moving from below upwards." Nor should you make the assumption that you can momentarily indulge in your passion and take a brief rest from your journey to attain virtue, for "during this moment of self-indulgence all passions will raise their heads and begin to wriggle like squashed worms when water is poured on them."[42]

Furthermore, you should *love* the virtues. The key to living in the resurrection arises from "a strong love for each virtue and for all virtuous life and a burning zeal for them." Reflect continually on how "pleasing to God the virtuous life is." In the morning, think on the ways you may be able to practice the particular virtue, and in the evening reflect on how well that virtue was practiced that day. Memorize Scripture that pertains to the virtue you are practicing, and "repeat them mentally as often as possible, especially when the opposite passion begins to move in you." Also, do not avoid obstacles to gaining virtue. "Meet them with a good will and the resolve to submit to their unpleasant effect on you, but at the same time prepare yourself to suffer them with unshakeable calmness of spirit."[43]

You know that you are making progress in the virtues when you are willing to follow a virtue "diligently, with a firm resolve never to leave it." When the "battle loses its intensity, the more evident becomes the progress in virtue," and "you see that your mind is not being forced, but acts freely and presses forward in good thoughts."[44] These are all signs of progress.

The desert fathers are best known for their emphasis on attention to their personal lives—of putting away sin and affirming the new life in the Spirit. One does not need to retreat from life in the normal world as the desert fathers did to live the spiritual life. The teaching of the desert fathers needs to be applied to our personal spirituality and should discipline our personal life in God in the world.

Every person whose life is characterized by the discipline of the mind, will, senses, imagination, and memory and who seeks to put on the likeness of Christ by pursuing the things of the Spirit—"love, joy, peace, patience, kindness, goodness, faithfulness, gentleness and self-control" (Gal. 5:22–23)—should be able to translate their participation in Christ into the social structures of their existence. This will be especially true for those who affirm that God's story is not only the redemption of creatures but the cosmic redemption of the entire created order.

These examples of an embodied spirituality are encouraging to all of us, but some of us may read them and be discouraged. "What about me?" someone may ask. "I constantly fail in the struggle. What happens to failures?"

Most importantly, we must remember that Jesus is not only the one who reestablishes our spiritual relation to God by uniting us with God through his incarnation, death, and resurrection, he is also the perfection of our spiritual life. We are not even capable of living a perfect spiritual life; only one man did that. It is appropriate then to end this chapter with a few comments on the ways of our imperfection.

The Ways of Our Imperfection

Simon Tugwell has addressed the problem of our failure to completely live out an embodied spirituality in his unusual work, *Ways of Imperfection*. Tugwell writes out of the understanding of an embodied spirituality represented in this book and acknowledges, as I did earlier, that by the end of the thirteenth century the criterion for spirituality was "not fidelity to the gospel, but a particular intensity of 'interiority.'"[45] In spite of this theological protest against this focus on the self, it did not make much difference. As a result spirituality today is seldom viewed as the attempt to live a serious Christian life in which our union with God is embodied in the practicalities of everyday life.

Tugwell's book explores how again and again many of the well-known names of spiritual history failed to live up to their own quests for perfection. For them and for us today, "Christianity *has* to be disappointing, precisely because it is not a mechanism for accomplishing all our human ambitions and aspirations, it is a mechanism for subjecting all things to the will of God."[46]

One example from his book will suffice: Therese of Lisieux (1873–1897). Therese "never claimed to have had a real 'vision.'" She "detested the pious trivialities" of the religious life, and she described the nuns with whom she lived as "a fine collection of old maids." On her deathbed her sister suggested "she would see troops of angels coming with Christ in all their beauty to fetch her." Therese retorted, "All these images do me no good at all. I can only find nourishment in the truth. That is why I have never desired visions. On earth it is impossible to see heaven and angels as they really are."[47]

In a letter to Leonie, Therese writes,

> I find perfection very easy to practise, because I have realised that all we have to do is take Jesus by the heart. Consider a child who has just upset his mother by losing his temper or disobeying her. If he goes and hides in a corner with a sullen look on his face and cries because he is afraid of being punished, his mother will certainly not pardon his fault. But if he comes to her and holds out his arms to her and smiles at her and says, "Give me a hug, I'll never do it again," how can his mother resist taking him fondly and pressing him to her heart, forgetting his childish wickedness? Yet she knows perfectly well that her dear child will do it again as

soon as the occasion arises, but that makes no difference; if he takes her by the heart again, he will never be punished.[48]

Tugwell informs us that "Therese had herself been tormented by scruples for more than a year" but later on came to a different conclusion about herself: Even if she committed every possible sin, she would still have exactly the same confidence in God. *She no longer needed the assurance of her own virtue.*[49]

The point here is well-taken and lies at the heart of a theologically embodied spirituality. The spiritual life is always an imperfect struggle toward the perfection accomplished only by God himself in Jesus Christ by the Spirit. In spite of all our failures, one man eternally represents us, and we who trust in him are perfected already. Therefore, we can embrace our calling to an embodied spirituality with the abandonment of heartfelt passion, participating in God's vision for our life in God's world.

CONCLUSION

This chapter has been a kind of culmination chapter to the question, "What is the spiritual life?" It answers the fundamental question of this book: "Is the spiritual life a journey into myself or is it a journey into God and God's purposes for my life?"

My concern, as I have indicated previously, is that we are surrounded by the culture of narcissism on every side of our lives. The focus on the self has attended almost every stage of our lives. We are brought up to think that everything revolves around us. We have been made to feel supreme and sovereign by advertising and consumption that appeals to our needs, our tastes, our beauty, our comfort, our success. Now this pervasive narcissism has spilled over into spirituality and focuses on a spirituality that derives from the inner self as if spirituality originates in the self.

Biblically formed ancient spirituality will have none of this! The Scriptures and early church fathers teach that spirituality is grounded in God's embrace of our human condition and the reversal of human life accomplished by God's two hands and modeled for us in Jesus. Jesus is not only the sacrifice for our sin, the victor over death for us, he is also the perfect example of the one who lives in full union with the embrace of God.[50]

Remember, the spiritual life is not a rejection of life in this world, not a denial of humanity, not a supraspirituality that is disconnected with day-to-day living. It is, rather, an intentional living into the purposes of God. I love how this vision of the spiritual life is summed up in the final morning prayer in "Daily Devotions for Individuals and Families" in the *The Book of Common Prayer,* and this prayer expresses embodied spirituality:

> Lord God, almighty and everlasting Father, you have brought us in safety to this new day: Preserve us with your mighty power, that we may not fall into sin, nor be overcome by adversity; and in all we do, direct us to the fulfilling of your purpose; through Jesus Christ our Lord. *Amen.*[51]

A SUMMARY FOR REFLECTION AND CONVERSATION

Summary	Reflection
The spiritual life	A full, active, and conscious participation in the purposes of God for life in the world.
Incarnational spirituality	The spiritual life, like the incarnation, is participation in this world, this life, this place, in our day-to-day relationships in family, work, and leisure.
Embodied spirituality	Our spiritual life flows forth from the divine embrace and embodies the vision of life modeled in Jesus. We are to imitate the life of Jesus.
Theological spirituality	Trinitarian spirituality Creational spirituality Revelational spirituality Incarnational spirituality Cruciform spirituality Resurrection spirituality Ecclesial spirituality Liturgical spirituality Baptismal spirituality Eucharistic spirituality Social spirituality Missiological spirituality Pneumatological spirituality Eschatological spirituality
The pattern of spirituality	Dying to all that is sin and death; rising to all that is new life born of the spirit.
"Put off" by guarding the . . .	Heart Mind Will Senses Eyes Ears Tongue Imagination Memory

Summary	Reflection
"Put on" Christ as you pursue the virtues.	Love
	Joy
	Peace
	Patience
	Kindness
	Goodness
	Faithfulness
	Gentleness
	Self-Control

THE CHALLENGE: RETURNING SPIRITUALITY TO THE DIVINE EMBRACE

Chapter 6   Christian spirituality is situated in God's story of the world—the story of God creating and becoming incarnate to reconcile the world to himself. The divine embrace, the story of God's incarnation, death, and resurrection, is told in the typologies of creation/re-creation, first Adam/second Adam, Exodus event/ Christ event. In the divine embrace God was united to humanity so that we might be united to God. Christ by the Spirit recapitulates the world and returns it to the Father.

Chapter 7   Baptism into union with Jesus is the sign of our new spiritual identity with the Triune God and with each other in the church. In baptism Christians embrace the new life that is the gift of God's grace through Jesus Christ by the Spirit.

Chapter 8   The spiritual life is a living into our baptism—dying to all that is sin and death, rising through the new birth into the new life modeled by Jesus, the one who images humanity completely united to God's original purposes for creation. The spiritual life contemplates the mystery of God revealed in Jesus Christ and participates in the purposes of God for humanity.

Chapter 9   *The spiritual life is disciplined by the rule of steadfastness, fidelity, and obedience; it attends to prayer, study, and work; it meets God in daily life, in material things, and in people.*

Chapter 10   The spiritual life is nourished by the church, which is the continued presence of the incarnate Jesus in and to the world. The spiritual life is nurtured by worship that sings, prays, preaches, and enacts the divine embrace in its daily prayer, weekly celebration, and yearly attention to God's saving embrace in the services of the Christian Year.

9

My Life in His

A Long Obedience in the Same Direction

I have mentioned to you already that the first seven years of my life were spent in the jungles of Africa, where my parents were missionaries, and that my growing up years were in the confines of a strict fundamentalist home, church, and school. One central conviction of my parents was that our fundamentalist way was the only faith that stood in continuity with the New Testament. All other viewpoints were distorted at best and some, especially Roman Catholicism, contained no connection with New Testament Christianity whatsoever. It should not be surprising to know that during those years and even into graduate studies in the midsixties I had no personal contact with a Catholic Christian, except for a Catholic aunt who was the black sheep of the family. But that was to change.

In graduate school one of my professors asked me to join an ecumenical prayer and fellowship community that met once a month. The group was small, but at least half of the group (six) were young Benedictine monks! Although hesitant at first because of my prejudice against Catholics (yes, even in graduate school), I joined. The first night we met I was nervous and on guard. The leader began with prayer and then asked each of us to introduce ourselves and tell something about our spiritual journey. You can imagine how shocked I was to hear these Catholic seminarians, whom I had been taught to believe were anything but true Christians, speak with warmth and passion about their faith, love, and obedience to Jesus Christ as Redeemer and Friend. I was, to use a term from Luke, "cut to the heart" with conviction about my judgmental attitude.

Over the course of the next two years, the community I experienced with these young men completely changed my view of Catholic Christians and Catholic sources of theology, worship, and spirituality. I learned, for one thing, that the hallmark of Benedictine spirituality is a deep commitment to work out a relationship to Christ through the rule of St. Benedict.[1] Although this rule was originally written for those who chose to live within the Benedictine monastery, the rule always has been applicable to the life of all Christians. This understanding is recognized today, and the rule is receiving new attention from nonmonastics. So the purpose of this chapter is to draw the principles of spiritual discipline from this extraordinary rule and apply these teachings to the discipline of our own spiritual life, the outworking of the divine embrace.

St. Benedict was born in a world very much like our own. Seventy years before his birth, Rome had fallen in AD 410 to the Huns, and for the next four hundred years Rome was to pass through what no one could have dreamed—continued invasions from the East and the complete ruin of a once great and proud society. Famine, disease, turmoil, calamity, despair, and the collapse of all stability resulted in a complete disintegration of those institutions, societies, cultures, structures, and relationships that typically ensure security, certainty, and consistency. It was within this bleak period of history that Benedict built what Esther de Waal refers to as an "ark" of safety—small and simple monasteries guided by the rule of St. Benedict. These arks of safety brought stability into an uncertain world and grew to be the most important and influential monastic community in the West.

The Benedictine rule is an extensive guide to a disciplined Christian life. While the rule is written for the monastic life, it is adaptable readily to the common Christian life in the world as we follow Jesus in the pattern of death and resurrection. We can apply this rule to the discipline of our own spiritual life by looking at three vows, three disciplines, and three means or ways to encounter Christ in all of life.

THREE VOWS: STABILITY, FIDELITY, OBEDIENCE

The word *vow* comes from the Latin word *votum*, meaning "a solemn promise in which a person is bound to an act of service or condition." Today we most commonly use the word in connection to marriage. In monasticism the word was used to voluntarily bind a person to a particular spiritual rule, "a prescribed guide for conduct of action." The principle of having a *rule of life* is still common in the churches of ancient origin, and vestiges of it are found among those Protestants who urge us to read our Bible, pray daily, go to church, and tell others about Jesus.

The word *rule* is used seldom among Protestants today. I remember, for example, meeting with a Christian from a more ancient tradition, and in the course of getting to know each other, he asked, "What is your rule of life?" I am embarrassed to say that at the time I had no idea what he was asking me. But today, with the restoration of ancient Christian practices, the idea that one would live by a rule is much more common.

While the rule of St. Benedict was originally meant for a group of men living in the community of a monastery, the rule has a long history of guiding the spiritual life of those who live outside the walls of a monastery as well. I will seek, then, to translate how the observance of the rule maintains and deepens the experience of the spiritual life of the common Christian. We begin with the vows taken by Benedictine monks, vows that are equally applicable to us. They are stability, fidelity, and obedience.[2]

Stability

We often use the word *stable* to refer to a person who is constant and consistent. We say, "You can count on her." Or, in Christian terms, we may think of the writer of Hebrews, who admonishes new Christians to endure to the end (Heb. 4:11).

The monastic concept of stability translated into our spiritual life means "stay in your baptism" and "continue to live out of the death and resurrection of Jesus by continually dying to sin and rising to the new life of the Spirit staying in God's divine embrace." Obviously such a vow should not be taken lightly.

For Benedict, the ability to maintain stability in the monastic way was essential. Therefore, he made the monastic way difficult to enter. A person who wanted to live under the Benedictine rule had to pass through a ritual process that tested his will to enter. For example, the aspirant to the monastic life was first required to knock on the door of the monastery for several days before he was allowed to enter. Upon entrance the rule of the monastic life was read to the one seeking entrance. After two months of being warned of the difficulties and austerities of the monastic life, the rule was read to him again, followed again by another reading four months later. Then if the novitiate chose to remain, the rule was read once again. After this repeated presentation of the rule, the novitiate was then accepted into the monastic life in the full knowledge of the new life now embraced.

For those in the modern world, Christianity has been made too easy in comparison to those living in the Benedictine rule. The emphasis has been too much on "believe these truths" or "accept Jesus as your Savior," almost as if the Christian life primarily is an idea or knowledge disassociated from life itself. In the premodern world and now again in the postmodern world within which we live, Christian faith is being presented once again, however, not as mere ideas to be defended by reason or science but as a story to be embodied, that is, to be lived. Like the ancient monk who took a vow to live in the stability of his baptism into Christ through the embodied life of the monastic community, so we who have been baptized into the death and resurrection of Jesus should vow to remain stable in our living into the pattern of death and resurrection.

One's vow to the rule's stability, steadfastness, endurance to the end is grounded in the faithfulness of God. It is affirmed that God remained faithful to the covenant he made with the Hebrews and now with us. So faithfulness to God's covenantal embrace is a necessity today. God's steadfast nature has been translated into one of the most popular hymns of our day, "Great Is Thy Faithfulness." Over the years I have been in numerous communities where this hymn has been sung—and it seems to me that it is sung always with great conviction and fervor, expressing the unity of worship and spirituality.

Stability refers to our vow to remain stable in a life lived in the pattern of death and resurrection. I love the saying, "a long obedience in the same direction," popularized by Eugene Peterson's book by the same title, and I find that phrase popping up in my conscience and being formed on my lips again and again as temptations arise to be slothful, to wallow in discouragement, or to yield to temptation. We all wrestle with the same problem.

For example, the International Consultation on Discipleship bemoans the fact that "Christians are not different from the culture around them," they "are not living lives of biblical purity, integrity and holiness."[3] By taking a vow to be stable, to live always out of the embrace of God, and to embody that in every facet of life, we can begin to address the problem noted concerning the Protestant evangelical church that faith is an inch deep and a mile wide.

The good news is that we do not have to enter a monastery to live in God's embrace. We recall from this book's earlier discussions that the spiritual life is not an escape from life but an affirmation of God's way of life in the struggles we meet in our personal thoughts, in the relationships we have in the family, among our neighbors, at work, and in our leisure. This Christian life is an embodied life. It affirms that all of life belongs to God, and God is everywhere in life. We can choose to be stable following Jesus in all places, at all times, among all situations, and among all people. The vow of stability always is to live out of our baptism into God's embrace in the incarnation, death, and resurrection of Jesus.

Fidelity

At first glance the idea of stability and fidelity appear to be the same. They are not, although they are related. Stability is the vow. Fidelity is to remain in the vow. The word derives from the Latin *fides* that means "faith." Its derivative means "trust." The word is used today to refer to the *fidelity* of an electronic device such as a radio or a television. Thus, a person who takes a vow of fidelity is someone you can count on. Therefore, in what sense do you become a person whom others count on? What is it about your character, your personality, your way of living that can be counted on?

The rule of St. Benedict is practical and does not state a rule for Christian discipline without giving some specifics. Like Paul's instructions to young Christians, Benedict provides instructions for a Christ-centered life written down in a list of seventy-two rules to guide fidelity. He calls these the "tools of our spiritual craft." I have included all of them for your meditation. Remember, meditation differs from contemplation. Contemplation is a delight in God as revealed in the wonder and awe of God's story. Meditation, on the other hand, is a *searching out*. Take time to search out the following guidelines and to examine yourself in their light. Ask, "Am I faithful to the new life in Christ? Can someone count on me to be like this?"

1. To love the Lord God with all our heart, soul, and strength.
2. To love one's neighbor as oneself.
3. Not to kill.
4. Not to commit adultery.
5. Not to steal.
6. Not to covet.
7. Not to bear false witness.
8. To respect all men.
9. Not to do to another what one would not have done to oneself.
10. To deny oneself in order to follow Christ.
11. To chastise the body.
12. Not to love pleasure.
13. To love fasting.
14. To comfort the poor.
15. To clothe the naked.
16. To visit the sick.
17. To bury the dead.
18. To aide those in trouble.
19. To comfort the sad.
20. To reject worldliness.

21. To love Christ above all else.
22. Not to become angry.
23. Not to show temper.
24. Not to keep deceit in one's heart.
25. Not to make a false peace.
26. Not to forsake charity.
27. Not to swear, for fear of committing perjury.
28. To speak the truth with heart and lips.
29. Not to return an evil for an evil.
30. Not to injure anyone, but to accept patiently any injury oneself.
31. To love one's enemies.
32. Not to insult those who insult one, but to praise them.
33. To suffer persecution for the sake of justice.
34. Not to be proud.
35. Not to drink to excess.
36. Not to be a glutton.
37. Not to love sleep.
38. Not to be slothful.
39. Not to murmur.
40. Not to slander.
41. To put one's trust in God.
42. To attribute to God the good one sees in oneself.
43. To recognize that the evil in oneself is attributable only to oneself.
44. To fear judgment day.
45. To fear hell.
46. To desire eternal life with all one's spirit.
47. To see death before one daily.
48. To monitor one's activity ceaselessly.
49. To know for certain that God sees all everywhere.
50. To dash one's evil thoughts against Christ immediately, and to reveal them to one's spiritual advisor.
51. Not to speak evil or wicked speech.
52. Not to speak much.
53. Not to speak idly nor so as to cause mirth.
54. Not to love boisterous laughter.
55. To enjoy holy reading.
56. To often partake of prayer.
57. To confess past sins to God daily in humble prayer and to avoid these sins in future.
58. Not to succumb to the desire of the flesh.
59. To despise one's own will.

60. To obey the abbot's commands in all things, even if he strays from his own path, mindful of the Lord's command: "What they say, do, but what they do, do not perform" (Matt. 23:3).
61. Not to desire to be called holy before the fact, but to be holy first, then called so with truth.
62. To fulfill God's commandments in one's activities.
63. To love chastity.
64. To hate no one.
65. Not to be jealous or envious.
66. To hate strife.
67. To evidence no arrogance.
68. To honor the elderly.
69. To love the young.
70. To pray for one's enemies for the love of Christ.
71. To make peace with an adversary before sundown.
72. Never to despair of God's mercy.[4]

These rules reveal the nature of the spiritual life. The spiritual life is not a sentimental way of speaking about God; it is not an escape from the reality of living in the community of the world; it is not a strange way of being. The spiritual life is, as Esther de Waal states, a life "earthed in Christ."[5] Christ is the embodied story of God, the one in whom God became human and showed us what humanity was intended to be. The faithful life is the life that seeks to live the Jesus way. The vow of fidelity means you can count on me to be Jesus to you. And when I fail, which we all do, you can count on me to repent and return to my intent to be faithful to living in the pattern of death and resurrection.

Obedience

Stability in Jesus and fidelity to Jesus are not grounded in the self but are grounded in obedience to the voice of God. Obedience begins, says St. Benedict, with *listening*. The *Prologue* to the rule of St. Benedict begins, "Listen, my son, and with your heart hear the principles of your master."[6] This instruction reminds us, as Esther de Waal points out, that "we go to God by the road to obedience."[7] But we must ask, "How do we travel this road to obedience? What are the steps of our journey?"

The first step toward obedience is cheerful servanthood, a glad and willing heart to be under the rule of God. "Orders," writes Benedict concerning rule 5, "should be carried out cheerfully for 'God loves a cheerful giver' (2 Cor. 9:7). God will not be pleased by the monk who obeys grudgingly, not only murmuring in words but even in his heart."[8]

The second step to a listening obedience is humility. To be humble, choose to live under the commandments of God, "never ignoring them, and fearing God in his heart." Thus "humility is reached when a man, not loving his own will, does not bother to please himself, but follows the injunctions of God."[9]

Other steps to humility include obedient submission to a superior, putting up with things that inflict life, confession to a superior, the practice of silence, restraint from frivolity, the learning of gentleness, and an embrace of "humility in his heart and in his appearance." This kind of obedience results in an inner freedom, for it is as rule 71 states "a blessing" because it forms "habits" that are "derived of virtue."[10]

These are the vows that will shape the life that embodies the life of Jesus. What these vows say is that the spiritual life is not simply automatic. It is true that God has made us spiritual, not by anything we do, but by becoming one of us and through the incarnation lifting our humanity up into union with himself and doing for us in his suffering, death, and resurrection what we cannot do for ourselves. It is true that by these actions God has initiated our union with him so that we can enjoy a real, true, participation in his life by fulfilling his purpose for our life through an obedience to his will.

We are to make those choices that live out this union. In order to stay in this life of God and to experience the freedom to become what God has called us to become as "new creatures," we must choose from the inner self, from the very chamber of the heart, from the resolve of the will to embrace the vows of stability, fidelity, and obedience. But these vows need to be made to a community of accountability. Find two or three friends where intimacy can be shared freely, where honesty and openness permit a sharing of life and a mutual accountability to each other, a group in which a mini-monastic rule of life is lived out in mutual respect and concern.

THREE DISCIPLINES: PRAYER, STUDY, WORK

We are all familiar with the relationship between a vow and a discipline. How do you keep a vow, a solemn promise? By discipline, of course.

The subject of spiritual disciplines has become popular among Christians since Vatican II. It was the publication of *The Celebration of Discipline* by Richard Foster that alerted evangelicals to their value.[11] Disciplines, once relegated to the monastic life, are now practiced by lay Christians throughout the world. Yet how do we understand a spiritual discipline?

There is one common misunderstanding that I found among many who practice the spiritual disciplines. They view the disciplines as the *source* of spirituality. "If only I could be more consistent with my Bible study and my prayer, I would be more spiritual." Or, on the other hand, some people who practice the spiritual disciplines seem to have an air of superior spirituality about them. Maybe they use "the Lord this and the Lord that" language. Or maybe they speak or act judgmentally about others.

The corrective to all this "Lordy, Lordy stuff" is to return to the divine embrace. It is here, in God's incarnate action to restore the world by his own two hands, that true spirituality is situated. We are spiritual not because we practice the disciplines or use pious words but because we are united to Jesus who has restored our union with God. So our goal is never to *become spiritual* but to *live out* the spirituality we have in Jesus through the choices that spring forth from continually living in God's embrace affirmed in baptism. Look at these disciplines of the rule of St. Benedict, then, not as sources of spirituality but as disciplines that help us fulfill the spiritual life to which we have been called in Christ.

The rule of St. Benedict is a Christ-centered rule. Benedict himself was not setting forth the rule as a means of achieving spirituality but as a way of practicing the presence of Christ and participating in the life of God in the life of the world. The rule of Benedict presents the disciplines of prayer, study, and work, not as something that runs alongside of life but as something integrated with life in the world. The monks themselves were not isolated individuals living in caves or up in trees. They lived in community, in relationships in the rhythm of a day-to-day, week-to-week schedule. For this reason the disciplines can be easily translated to our own lives within the routine of our day-to-day lives of family, work, and leisure. So how do the disciplines of prayer, study, and work serve the spiritual life that we live day to day?

Prayer

The common understanding of prayer is that we do it in a time set apart from life. We steal away to talk to God, and when finished, we return to life, charged by the moments we have had with God.

It is not wrong to pray this way. But the assumption that prayer only occurs when we stop life and withdraw to pray is not the biblical nor the Benedictine way. The rule of Benedict affirms the goodness of God's creation and thus the presence of God everywhere. Consequently, the fundamental disposition of prayer is that all of life is lived in God's presence. Prayer is an openness to hear God and dialogue with God in every moment, every thought, every action, every relationship, every transaction of every day.

Benedict also knows that specific times set aside for prayer keep the monks aware that life is lived always before God in Jesus by the Spirit.

Consequently, the monks of the Benedictine monasteries practice the seven daily offices of prayer.[12] The rhythm of the monastic day was punctuated by a communal prayer that continually kept the monk in the vision of God with eyes fixed firmly on Christ. Chapter 16 of the rule of St. Benedict says, "The prophet says: 'Seven times daily I have sung Your praises' (Ps. 119:164). We will cleave to this sacred number if we perform our monastic duties at Lauds, Prime, Tierce, Sext, None, Vespers and Compline. The same prophet says of the Night Office: 'I arose at midnight to confess to You' (Ps. 119:62). In the Day Office, therefore, we ought praise our Creator for His just judgments, and at night we will rise to confess to Him."[13]

How do we apply the rule of Benedict on prayer into our daily lives? First, we must simply be open to the presence of God in all of life. To know that God's purposes are being worked out in history, that creation is not evil but good because it is created by God and sustained by the Holy Spirit, who is the Lord, the giver of life, is itself the fundamental disposition of prayer. Prayer is the conviction of the permeating presence of God and the awareness that evil is a rebellion against God's presence. Prayer is a weapon God has given his people in the struggle against those evil impulses that drive a person to focus on self and self-interest. Prayer is the choice to do God's will on earth as it is in heaven. Prayer is the thankful response for daily bread, the forgiveness of those who trespass against us, the resistance of evil, and the doing of God's purposes in life. This kind of prayer is a continual conversation and dialogue with God, an unceasing language of relationship that anticipates the goal of history—the eternal worship of God.

But how does the ordinary person pray seven times a day? Certainly it is not possible to stop wherever we are and gather in community seven times a day as the monks do. Let me make a suggestion. Read and become acquainted with the Daily Office of the church.[14] Learn the moments of the office and the spirit of each office. Then, memorize one prayer from each office, and during the day, wherever you are, repeat the prayers in your mind, or better yet, voice the prayer so that you not only say it but hear it.

By attending to the daily prayers, you affirm God's story of the world— creation, incarnation, death, resurrection, and the new heavens and the new earth. These moments of prayer recount the story of God and form it in the heart and mind. They frame the day and intensify the experience of the presence of God in all of life.

Study

The common understanding of study is that it is an activity of the mind, an intellectual exercise that analyzes, dissects, systemizes, and categorizes information. While there is an aspect of study that is ana-lytical, the approach of St. Benedict is that the study of God's ways, the second of the three disciplines, arises out of praying the Scriptures. "More or less four hours a day are assigned to *Lectio Divina*, prayerful private reading and *Meditatio*, the memorization, repetition, and reflec-tion of Biblical texts."[15]

Today, the church is shifting from a mere intellectual study of Scrip-ture. This is why the ancient *Lectio Divina*, a method of a prayerful reflec-tion on Scripture, has been recovered and is gaining a new prominence, especially among young men and women. Consequently, a word about this ancient practice and some comments on how to engage in Scripture praying is in order.

The goal of *Lectio Divina* is union with God through a *meditative* and *contemplative* praying of Scripture. Through this form of Scripture prayer, the world of God can take up residence within and form you into the image of Christ. Thelma Hall, in *Too Deep for Words*,[16] distinguishes between meditative and contemplative prayer.

The word *meditation* refers to a discursive reading process in which words, events, etc. are prayerfully pondered and reflected upon with the object of drawing from them some personal meaning or moral. It is basically an activity of the intellect and reason, aided by grace.

Contemplation is variously described as a "resting" in God, a "loving gaze" upon him, "knowing beyond knowing," or a "rapt attention" to God. All such attempts at verbalizing the experience necessarily fail to express the reality for the simple reason that contemplation transcends the thinking and reasoning of meditation as well as the emotions and feelings of the affective faculties. It is basically a prayer and experience of pure faith.

Lectio Divina is primarily a subjective, prayerful listening for the voice of God in Scripture. The monastic method of reading Scripture spiritually was captured by the medieval mystic, St. John of the Cross, who paraphrased Luke 11:9 into the four steps of *Lectio*:

Seek in *reading*,
And you will find in *meditation*.
Knock in *prayer*,
And it will be opened to you in *contemplation*.

To gain a better understanding of the method follow this procedure:
Read and listen to a text (*Lectio*). Choose a text of Scripture to read slowly. *Listen* to the text with your heart and mind. *Hear* the Lord speak-ing to you in the text. Allow yourself to simply *be* with the text in an open and vulnerable way.

Reflect on the text (*Meditatio*). By faith assume this text is *addressed to you*. Because God has translated himself into our humanity in Jesus, Jesus truly speaks to us by the Spirit in a language we can understand. At the *Meditatio* level it is important to ask, "What is it that you want me to hear?"

Let the word touch your heart (prayer, *Oratio*). In *Oratio*, the Word of God goes deeper into the self and becomes the prayer of the heart. In this prayer, open your heart so that his light may enter. The goal is like that of St. Augustine, who cried, "O God, our hearts are made for thee, and they shall be restless until they rest in thee." There emerges within the heart a holy desire, a longing for the text, the Word of God, to be concretized in reality.

Enter into contemplation (*Contemplatio*). *Contemplatio* shifts praying the Scripture into a new language (silence). This silence does not ask us to do anything, it is a call to *being*. Thomas Merton says, "The best way to pray is: Stop. Let prayer pray within you, whether you know it or not."[17]

This four-fold process is described by a French Benedictine monk in the following way:

We read (*Lectio*)
Under the eye of God (*Meditatio*)
Until the heart is touched (*Oratio*)
And leaps to flame (*Contemplatio*).

As you read these Scriptures that lead you into a walk with the Spirit, open your heart and mind to the voice of God met in the words and images of Scripture. Take time to reflect, to ruminate, to chew on what you hear. Have a good walk and allow yourself to be formed more deeply by your companion, the Holy Spirit,[18] remembering,

In the same way, the Spirit helps us in our weakness. We do not know what we ought to pray for, but the Spirit himself intercedes for us with groans that words cannot express. And he who searches our hearts knows the mind of the Spirit, because the Spirit intercedes for the saints in accordance with God's will.

Romans 8:26–27

Work

Unfortunately, rather than one of the ways to embody God's purposes for life, many people view work as drudgery. The technological and compartmentalized world in which we live has reduced work for many people to meaningless, rote tasks that fail to participate in the larger picture of God's story. However, many do engage in work that is fulfilling and meaningful. But in the Benedictine rule, as in Scripture, work is one of the disciplines that participates in the vision of God. So work is one of the disciplines that stands alongside of prayer and study.

The opposite of work is idleness. St. Benedict clearly warns, as does 2 Thessalonians 3:6, against idle minds, hearts, and hands. "Idleness," Benedict writes, "is an enemy of the soul."[19] Still, the work of our hands is not to occupy the whole of life. The frenzy of the workaholic is to be feared as much as idleness. But work is set alongside of prayer and study to establish a stable approach to life.

Because of creation and the mandate given in the Garden of Eden to work and care for God's good earth, work, in the best sense, is an engagement with God in the outworking of God's will, even as prayer is a dialogue with God and study is a meditation of God.

How do we translate the vision of work into our own work today? To begin, it is important to recognize that work is not the result of the fall, as some suppose. Work, instead, is a source of encounter with God because work tends to and participates in the care and the unfolding of God's good creation. Work, of course, can join with the forces of evil and oppose the priestly ministry of work given by God. Work that oppresses the poor, marginalizes the weak, takes advantage of people (especially women and children), dehumanizes the dignity of the worker, and results in injustice accomplishes the purposes of the evil one.

God has called the Christian to do work, not only in order to maintain body and soul and care for the family, but to do work that results in the common good of civilization and in the promotion of the dignity of every human being. Working, in God's story, unfolds civilizations and cultures in a way that contributes to making the world the theater of God's glory. Work is union with God in action, springing forth from our union with God's purposes for creation.

These three—prayer, study, and work—are disciplines in the rule of St. Benedict that order the spiritual life. The result of these disciplines is an encounter with Christ in our daily lives, in the material reality of life itself, and in relationships with people.

Three Means to Encounter Christ: In Daily Life, in Material Things, in People

Back in the 1970s, religious posters became popular. Almost everyone had a poster in their office or out in the hallway for people to see when they passed. In religious bookstores you could buy posters presenting Scripture sentences or pithy statements by theologians or church leaders.

My favorite poster was a saying by Catholic theologian Tielhard Chardin. The poster was huge, with a solid, dark blue background and white letters that proclaimed, "Because of Creation and even more because of Incarnation, there is nothing profane for those who know how to see." This poster captures the ancient and historic Christian emphasis on the goodness of creation, not only because God created it but because God was actually united with his creation to restore creation to himself. This theme underlies the conviction of Benedictine spirituality in its approach to daily life, material things, and people. God is present *everywhere*, not as in pantheism (a philosophy that affirms God and the material realm are one), but as in the Holy Spirit, who, as the Nicene Creed confesses, is "The Lord, the giver of life."

Christ Encountered in Daily Life

Many of us are acquainted with the writing of Brother Lawrence, who wrote of meeting the presence of God in the chores of the kitchen and in the cleaning of the bathroom. Brother Lawrence spelled out in detail what is foundationally implied in the Benedictine rule. "The Rule presents no abstract or remote theological treatise on God and his mysteries. Instead it is pervaded with the idea of sacramental encounter with Christ in the circumstances of daily life."[20] Consequently the rule speaks to weekly kitchen service stating, "The brothers should wait on one another."[21]

What underlies this rule is the assumption that God is experienced most clearly in a well-ordered day. God is the God of order, not chaos. A chaotic day in which there is no purpose and intention leads to a troubled and dislocated life, a life irritated by the events of the day because they control and run one's life. The structure of the day gives purpose, intent, and meaning as God is encountered in the events of daily life. When the day is ordered, serendipitous events may change the course of the day, but God's presence in these events more readily is seen because the day has been ordered, and the eyes and heart have been watching.

A well-ordered day is a way, of course, to see life, to perceive reality that arises from faith. God is seen in the ordering of the day, the rising and setting of the sun; the ordering of purpose, not chaos. By ordering the day through prayer, we remember God's act of creation in the morning, the crucifixion at midday, the rest of God from his labors at night. In an ordered day we see God in everyone because all are created in the image of God; God is encountered in every event, for the day discloses God even in those events of evil that are revelatory of the continued struggle with the powers. God is experienced in the weekly rhythm of Sunday, a day of rest and re-creation; God is met throughout the year as time reveals the meaning of all history in the services of the Christian Year. As the saving events of God are proclaimed and enacted, in the very rhythm of life itself God is continually manifest for those who know how to see.

Christ Encountered through the Care of Material Things

Because the God who created became incarnate in the material world, uniting himself with humanity and all creation in Jesus, the material things of this world are capable of revealing God. This axiom does not affirm materialism, which is the love of consumption and the commitment of one's life to accumulation. It is the realization, instead, that this material world is owned by God and should be treated with dignity and shared because God by his life-giving Spirit is disclosed everywhere in the visible creation.

The Benedictine rule on property and utensils states that the abbot "will choose brothers whose lives and virtue are reliable to care for clothes, tools, and other monastic property." The same rule states, "No one shall treat monastic property carelessly or in a slipshod manner."[22] On the surface one sees a simple, practical admonition to care for the material property of the monastery, but underneath the rule one sees the conviction that "the gardening tools are as worthy of attention as the altar vessels."[23]

The rule speaks also against all private ownership. "No one," without the abbot's permission, "shall dare give, receive or keep *anything*—not book, tablet or pen—nothing at all. . . . All things are to be common to everyone."[24]

How does this emphasis on material things and the communal life apply to those of us who live outside the walls of an ancient monastery in a world governed by a capitalist economy? What are the principles that govern a spirituality that cares for material things?

The first principle is that the material world is good and not to be despised. Paul states, "Since the creation of the world God's invisible qualities—his eternal power and divine nature—have been clearly seen being understood from what has been made" (Rom. 1:20). We are to receive what we have—food, clothing, and shelter—as gifts from God, and we are to love the God who gives us these benefits. In receiving these benefits, then, we are to care for them, not as *things* to be treated carelessly but as *gifts* to be treasured and cared for because they come to us by God's very own hand.

Does the rule, however, require us to become socialists or communists, owning nothing? By no means. We must remember that the monks came to the monastery to give their lives to God in this particular community and in this particular way. People not in monasteries may equally give their life to God and live within any economic system, whether socialist, communist, or capitalist. The issue for those living in a capitalist society is to treat material wealth in a Christian way. For one, the accumulation of wealth is not the primary goal of life; the primary goal of life is the service of God. When wealth comes our way, we are to receive it as a gift and use that wealth appropriately, giving a portion to the poor and needy, supporting the ministries and outreach of the church, caring for the needs of the world that many times are in our own neighborhood. This is a principle for all of us to follow, especially those who have been blessed with wealth. For wealth itself is not a sin. It is the love of wealth and the accumulation of wealth for the sake of consumption and power that leads to the misuse of wealth. Those who receive material blessings as gifts from God, the source of the material world itself, and use this wealth for the sake of God's kingdom experience God in the care of material things and in the sharing of material wealth with others.

Christ Encountered in People

The rule of St. Benedict bears no idealism about people. Benedict clearly recognizes the fallen nature of humanity, the deviousness in which people engage, those who are slothful and lazy, those who would control and bully others, those who would cheat others for self-gain. All these kinds of people can also be found within the monastery, under the same rule. The rule states, "If a brother is found to be stubborn, disobedient, proud or a murmurer, or at odds with the Holy Rule, or scornful of his elder's directions, he should be admonished by his superiors."[25] What lies beneath this injunction is the conviction that we have all been made in the image of God and are called to grow into God's icon, Christ, who reveals to us what humanity was meant to be.

But persons who are called to grow into Christ, and thus reveal Christ, are also fallen. We all struggle with some form of sinfulness—whether pride, stubbornness, grasping for wealth, seeking power—and in these and other ways reveal evil and wickedness. Therefore, the rule disciplines persons so that they may grow in Christlikeness and reveal Christ by their words and actions. The emphasis on growing into Christlikeness is made clear in the rule, where the qualities of the abbot are set forth. "Most important," writes Benedict, "the Abbot must not under value or overlook the salvation of his charges. Thus he must always remember his task is the guidance of souls."[26]

So what does this rule say to us? First, we are to affirm people because all are made in the image of God and, therefore, God may be disclosed in people. Certainly the fall means that people by their actions also reveal the presence of evil, and that is not to be disregarded. So all people, even though they are made in the image of God, reveal both the good that comes from God and the evil that comes from the powers of wickedness. Second, we ought always and in every way to encourage the good and discipline the bad within ourselves, within our families in the nurturing of our children, and within our churches through preaching and the appropriate use of Christian discipline.

Conclusion

I wanted to conclude this chapter with an example of how a layperson puts the rule of St. Benedict into practice in everyday life. So, I asked my former Wheaton student Mark Clatterbuck, who became an oblate (a layperson living under the vows) of the Benedictine order, to reflect on his experience living the rule. Mark, the chaplain at Moravian Academy in Bethlehem, Pennsylvania, and a doctoral candidate at Catholic University in Washington, DC, shared the following:

> I carry a palm-sized *Rule of Saint Benedict* with me every day to work. My spiritual journey has led me to regard this modest sixth-century text as a miniature treasure trove where the choicest gems of Christian spirituality are found gathered together in a single rule for daily life. Moderation is at the heart of the Benedictine tradition. In this regard, Benedict joins wisdom teachers from Lao-tzu to Aristotle in believing that virtue lies between extremes in any direction, and that a love for moderation should mark our way in literally all things: in speech, in work, and even in prayer itself. The *Rule* is also tireless in reminding us that no one journeys alone. Whether we have trouble getting ourselves out of bed for morning prayers, or have difficulty getting to the dinner table on time, Benedict gently reminds us that we all require encouragement and accountability from others along the way, and that each of us possesses his fair share of quirks and deficiencies. It is therefore little wonder that among Benedict's closing admonitions is the gentle charge to "support with the greatest patience one another's weaknesses of body or behavior." The Benedictine tradition is equally marked by a pursuit of authenticity in all things. "Never give a false peace" says Benedict, for one's tongue should speak only when moved by a conviction of the heart. For this reason, we are instructed to keep our prayers "short and pure" since it is purity of heart, and not our many words, which attracts the attention of God.
>
> The genius of Benedict's ability to integrate moderation, community, and authenticity into a single spiritual vision is surely validated by the *Rule's* enduring attraction a full 1,500 years after his own time. Yet the most transformative aspect of the Benedictine tradition for me continues to be its unflinching commitment to an earthy, gritty spirituality which has done more than anything else to heal a long-standing fracture in my own soul. For all the benefits I still carry today from the rich tradition of my evangelical upbringing, I also inherited from that tradition a lot of baggage from an ugly divorce I witnessed daily between spirit and body,

heaven and earth, sacred duty and worldly responsibilities. I was taught a great deal about saving souls, but precious little about saving the homeless. I learned much about waging "spiritual warfare" against virtual forces of darkness, but failed to see how those efforts related to the more immediate battle against actual forces of hunger and racism.

The day my curiosity led me through the doors of St. Procopius Abbey in Lisle, Illinois, thirteen years ago, I was unwittingly taking the first step on a long journey toward reconciling these two long-estranged spheres of my life. I began attending evening Vespers, and soon became an oblate of the community. The Benedictine tradition is marked by a spirituality rooted deeply, intentionally in the issues and activities which confront us every day. These include the seemingly endless quotidian chores which fill the greater part of most of our days. Working. Eating. Caring for the sick and providing for the poor. Talking. Reading. Dealing with difficult people, just like ourselves. The *Rule* emphatically validates the sanctity of these efforts, drawing them up into the same sphere of holy activity as prayer, and meditation on sacred Scripture. Kitchen utensils and garden tools of the monastery are to be treated no differently than the sacred vessels of the altar. Guests are to be welcomed as one would welcome Christ himself. Rather than drawing lines between sacred and profane, or attempting heroic theological gymnastics to keep the high work of spirituality unspotted from the lowly tasks of this world, the *Rule* unabashedly weds life in Christ to life in the sanctified dust and sweat of our daily-grind existence.

While recently attending a *shabbat* service at a local synagogue, I had a curious encounter with an elderly member of the congregation I only met that evening. When he learned that I was a Christian, he said to me without hesitation: "You know what the problem is with Christianity? It spends so much time preparing people for the next world that it forgets how to live in this one." I would have set him straight if he hadn't just described the single greatest failing of my own Christian upbringing. In Benedict, I have found something of an antidote to this other-worldly obsession. Benedict erases any artificial distinction between the holy and the mundane. At one point in the *Rule*, body and soul are described as two sides of a single ladder. We read that together they lead us every day either toward, or away from, heaven. It's as if Benedict anticipated the words of Emily Dickinson taped to my desk at work: "Who has not found the heaven below / Will fail of it above."

Several years ago I attended a retreat for oblates at St. Benedict's Abbey in Atchison, Kansas. During one of the sessions, an attendee was visibly perplexed to discover that a Protestant had infiltrated the ranks of the monastery. "Why are *you* a Benedictine oblate?" he asked, half accusingly. Caught off guard at the time, I had little to say. Today, I would tell him that Benedict has finally helped me make some sense of Jesus's elusive phrase, "The kingdom of God is among you."

Drawing from the rule of St. Benedict, I have demonstrated, not in depth but at least in principle, the way our spiritual life that springs forth from our union with God may be disciplined toward a fulfillment of God's purposes for our life in this world.

The practical application of the three vows (stability, fidelity, obedience), the three disciplines (prayer, study, work), and the three ways to encounter God (in daily life, in material things, in people) are all grounded in God's story of the world and the meaning of human existence. When we enter into God's embrace through conversion and baptism, we are made spiritual through Christ and the Spirit who unites us to God. But this is not the end; it is the beginning of the spiritual life. The spiritual life, the living out of the life of Christlikeness by the power of the Spirit is not automatic. It is a learned life that comes from a transformed heart. This new spiritual life, however—which is a joyous affirmation of life, not an escape into a private, withdrawn life—is ordered by the disciplines. So the disciplines are not the source of the spiritual life, Christ is, and the disciplines order and organize our life into more and more of the fullness of God's embrace of our humanity and the vision for life exhibited for us in Jesus himself.

A Summary for Reflection and Conversation

Summary	Reflection
Three Vows:	
Stability	The faithfulness of God calls us to faithfulness in God's embrace.
Fidelity	Seventy-two ways to remain in the vow
Obedience	Servanthood; humility; live under the commandments of God
Three Disciplines:	
Prayer	All of life is lived in the presence of God; specific times of daily prayer inform all of life.
Study	*Lectio Divina*
Work	Work arises from God's mandate in the Garden.
Three Means to Encounter Christ:	
In daily life	Sacramental encounter with Christ in every moment of the day
In material things	Because God is Creator, the material things of nature and the products of our hands reveal God and are to be well cared for.
In people	All people are made in the image of God. How we treat other persons is our treatment of God.

THE CHALLENGE: RETURNING SPIRITUALITY TO THE DIVINE EMBRACE

Chapter 6 Christian spirituality is situated in God's story of the world—the story of God creating and becoming incarnate to reconcile the world to himself. The divine embrace, the story of God's incarnation, death, and resurrection, is told in the typologies of creation/re-creation, first Adam/second Adam, Exodus event/ Christ event. In the divine embrace God was united to humanity so that we might be united to God. Christ by the Spirit recapitulates the world and returns it to the Father.

Chapter 7 Baptism into union with Jesus is the sign of our new spiritual identity with the Triune God and with each other in the church. In baptism Christians embrace the new life that is the gift of God's grace through Jesus Christ by the Spirit.

Chapter 8 The spiritual life is a living into our baptism—dying to all that is sin and death, rising through the new birth into the new life modeled by Jesus, the one who images humanity completely united to God's original purposes for creation. The spiritual life contemplates the mystery of God revealed in Jesus Christ and participates in the purposes of God for humanity.

Chapter 9 The spiritual life is disciplined by the rule of steadfastness, fidelity, and obedience; it attends to prayer, study, and work; it meets God in daily life, in material things, and in people.

Chapter 10 *The spiritual life is nourished by the church, which is the continued presence of the incarnate Jesus in and to the world. The spiritual life is nurtured by worship that sings, prays, preaches, and enacts the divine embrace in its daily prayer, weekly celebration, and yearly attention to God's saving embrace in the services of the Christian Year.*

10

LIFE TOGETHER

Rediscovering Our Mystical Union with God

I conversed recently with a pastor who was agonizing over the conflict between his head and heart. Even though this person is a well-trained seminary graduate with an appetite to know and teach the Scripture and has a comprehensive view of the Bible, his heart feels empty and dry. "I've even attended to the disciplines of spirituality," he said, "but they don't do anything for me. I can't seem to feel what my head knows."

Eventually this pastor put his finger on the real problem. "I've done everything I can to make myself spiritual," he said, "but nothing seems to work."

I knew how he felt. Like him, I at one time thought my spirituality depended on what I did or did not do. Like him, as I discussed in chapter 4, I grew up with the admonition that to become spiritual I must read my Bible regularly, keep all the rules, pray fervently, be in the church every time the door is open, and witness to everyone I meet. If only I would do all these things, I was told, I would feel spiritual. I have discovered that this viewpoint assumes that spirituality arises from the self, that is, as an autonomous human being I should be able to stretch toward God and reach God with spiritual tools that please God and cause him to turn toward me affirming his satisfaction with my attempts to be spiritual.

I frequently hear this myth proclaimed in the pulpit, read it argued for in current Christian books, and experience it presented in retreats on spirituality. It is a view that seems to permeate the evangelical culture.

I counseled this minister whose heart felt empty and dry to cease striving to be spiritual and see spirituality as a gift to contemplate. "Delight," I told him, "in the mystery of God revealed in Christ, who, by the Spirit, is united to our humanity and opens the way to our union with God. Delight in the incarnation of God in Jesus, in his sacrifice for our sins, his victory over the powers of evil, and the good news that everything that needs to be done to unite us with God and establish our spiritual relationship with God is done through grace by faith in our Lord and Savior, Jesus Christ. Affirm that Jesus, in union with God, dwells in you and you in him, and see the world through God's divine embrace. Then live in your freedom to participate in God in the life of the world!"

I think this pastor and others like him have a hard time connecting head and heart and, as a result, experience the contradiction between what they *know* and what they *feel* for two reasons. First, they situate spirituality in something other than God's embrace. Second, they look for spiritual nourishment outside of the church and its worship. Let me explain what I mean.

First, if we situate spirituality in ourselves and not God's divine embrace, we feel responsible to nourish our own spirituality. We apply the word *nourish* to ourselves in the way the word is commonly used, "the care of the self." For example, we nourish our bodies by eating right, exercising regularly, and sleeping eight hours a night. We nourish our minds by reading books, engaging in intelligent conversation, and opening ourselves to new ideas. So it is natural for us to think that we approach the nourishing of our spirituality in the same way. We ask, "What should *I* do to nourish my spiritual life?" And we are told, "Do this and that and you will be spiritual."

The point is, of course, that we are made to feel responsible for our own spiritual growth. What *we* do is most important. The message is that the time and energy we give to these disciplines and others will determine our spiritual condition.

I am asking you to see Christian nourishment in a different way. When we situate spirituality in God's embrace, the church and its worship are seen as sources that nourish the spiritual life, not by what the church and its worship demand of us but by what they *reveal to us*. The church and its worship are sources of nourishment precisely because they embody God's story and witness to God's divine embrace and constantly keep God's vision of a restored people and renewed earth before us.

As I urged the pastor with whom I had been speaking, I urge us all to stop looking at ourselves for the nourishment of our own spirituality and turn to the church and its worship to disclose God's embrace and thus nourish our spirituality. The church, by its very existence, is the life of God's embrace, and worship, when properly understood, is the continual experience of God's embrace, reaching out from the hard wood of the cross. When the church and its worship are situated in the story of God's embrace, our hearts will be nourished, our emotions will respond with delight, and our lives will intentionally participate in the life of God.

The problem for this pastor and for many others of us is that we turn things around and instead of seeing church and worship as the means of nourishing our mystical union with God, we see our life in the church and in worship as *our work*. We subvert God's way of nourishing our union with him by looking to self as if we sustain the union, only to grow weary in our own self-righteousness.

THE CHURCH, SITUATED IN GOD'S EMBRACE, NOURISHES THE SPIRITUAL LIFE

The Crisis of Today's Church

The current crisis of the church is that many define it out of the world's narrative. In recent years the church has become a business, with Jesus as the commodity to be marketed and advertised. I remember standing on the campus of Wheaton College conversing with the person who later became the architect of the market model of the church. He spoke of his graduate training in marketing and said, "We need to apply principles of successful business to the church. I have seen these principles work in business; I know they can work in the church as well."

The architects of the business model of the church meant well. I do not fault them. The problem goes much deeper. It reaches into the loss of God's story; an antihistorical mentality that disregards the past; a distaste for the tradition of the church, seeing it as valueless; and the enterprising spirit of the American entrepreneur who asks, "What's next?" These leaders of the CEO model of the church are visionaries with a heart for God and a longing to see people come to Christ. They did not foresee how the business model of church would be shaped by consumerism. They envisioned *big, successful, relevant, effective*. This has always been the evangelical way, and while it has resulted in numbers, it struggles to form depth.

Many leaders of these successful churches are *on top of the world* and feel that all churches should go this route. And to be fair, many lives have been changed through the ministry of the business model church. These churches do reach out to numerous people with shipwrecked lives. So why not jump on the bandwagon and go the CEO way?

I engaged in a private conversation with a pastor in one of these churches recently. He said, "I'm burned out. It just doesn't feel real to me anymore. I'm not seeing a real transformation in people's lives, not even my own. Our whole staff is discussing this question. It's like the church has become a big horde of people enthusiastically looking for entertainment. What's next? We've done it all."

It does appear that the cycle that began in the eighties has run the course and that the excitement for the business model of the church is waning. For example, Tom Cheatham, a Presbyterian campus minister at Mississippi State University, wrote to me, "It doesn't seem to matter if one speaks of a congregation (of whatever size) or a presbytery, the concern is always numbers, power, and control." He compares being in the church to "being in any other club or secular organization" and tells of a colleague, a second-career minister, who "touts his 'management experience' as qualifying him to make judgments about campus ministry." He concludes that "vulnerable, authentic leaders who model the struggle" will be eaten alive by the "predators in the church" who "consider them weak."[1]

Alan Wolfe, an avowed unbeliever and a student of religious trends, notes in *The Transformation of American Religion*,

> American religion survives and even flourishes not so much because it instructs people in the ways to honor God but because people have taken so many aspects of religion into their own hands. . . . Evangelical popularity is due . . . [to] its determination to find out exactly what believers want and to offer it to them. The biggest challenge posed to American society by the popularity of megachurches and other forms of growth-oriented Protestantism is not bigotry but bathos [sudden appearance of the commonplace]. Television, publishing, political campaigning, education, self-help advice—all increasingly tell Americans what they already want to hear. Religion, it would seem, should now be added to that list.[2]

From Wolfe's perspective we see the problem: too many local churches reflect the narrative of culture. The church has become a big business, an enterprise to sell Jesus to a consumer market.

Consequently Wayne Stacey, pastor of Southside Baptist Church, notes, "(1) The nature and mission of the church is 'up for grabs,' and (2) The best models and images . . . we can come up with for what the church is and should be are all derived from what we see in the secular world."[3] The point we must consider is this: churches formed by culture will nourish culturally formed Christians. As the old hymn goes, "The church's one foundation is Jesus Christ her Lord," and as such, what we want is a church so nourished by Christ that it nourishes its people into a Christ-formed spiritual life. *A people shaped by the embrace of God, then, is the alternative to a people shaped by culture.*

The Church Shaped by the Divine Embrace of God

What lies at the heart of biblical Christianity is God restoring creation, the place of his habitation, and calling into being a family of his own. God's desire is a place of dwelling and a people in whom he dwells and they in him. The book of Genesis tells us that God appointed Israel to be a particular place and a particular people of God's dwelling (Genesis 12). In the New Testament, Paul recounts that the work of Christ for Jew and Gentile alike expands the Israel type to the church and the whole world (Rom. 3:1–21). The story of Israel and the church are types pointing to the eschatological future when evil will be put away forever and God's new heavens and new earth will be the place of his dwelling and the people of heaven will be God's family, living in the glory of the Triune God, praising him eternally.

In the meantime, here on earth the church is to be the witness to this ultimate vision of the world. Here in the church is the primary dwelling of God. The church is the family of God, called to live the baptized life in a world that is rebellious against God and continues to do battle against God's purposes for the world and its people. "We were all baptized," Paul writes to the Corinthian church, "by one Spirit into one body. . . . You are the body of Christ" (1 Cor. 12:13, 27). The implication of 1 Corinthians 12 is not only that we participate in the body with the gifts God has given us to exercise, but that we are nourished in the body for in it the present and active disclosure of the life of Jesus is being continually manifest. Since this is true, we need to ask, "How does the body of Christ nourish the way we think, feel, and act?"

First, there is a need to rediscover the very nature of the church as the continuation of the presence of God in the world. Reclaiming the incarnate nature of the church will shift us away from the business model of the church and help us focus on the church as the continuation of God's vision for the world. This will result in congregations asking, "How can we witness to God's vision for the world?"[4] For example, theologian George Lindbeck suggests the return of our society to the Christian faith will not come from the accommodation *to* culture but *from* "the development of an Israel-like understanding of the church."[5] This "Israel-like" understanding of the church is clearly the perspective of the New Testament writers and of the ancient church as well. Peter reminds the Christians in exile,

> You are a chosen people, a royal priesthood, a holy nation, a people belonging to God, that you may declare the praises of him who called you out of darkness into his wonderful light. Once you were not a people, but now you are the people of God; once you had not received mercy, but now you have received mercy.
>
> 1 Peter 2:9–10

Peter's words capture the essence of Israel, even as they capture the essence of the church. The point is that God has established a community of people in the world who have as their responsibility a communal calling to show the world what the new humanity looks like. This is the "Israel-like" mission of the church referred to by George Lindbeck. The church is to be a countercultural community (like Israel) who have as their personal and corporate mission the calling to be the people of God on earth. Peter says, "I urge you, as aliens and strangers in the world, to abstain from sinful desires, which war against your soul. Live such good lives among the pagans that, though they accuse you of doing wrong, they may see your good deeds and glorify God on the day he visits us" (1 Peter 2:11–12). His words carry the message of the spiritual life: God has raised up a people in a fallen culture to be a *showcase* of his desire for humanity—a people living in union with his purposes and in praise of his glory.

Peter describes what a countercultural spiritual life looks like. It is to show respect to everyone, to love the brotherhood, to fear God, and to honor those in authority. In other words, the countercultural life is to follow Jesus, the one true human being in whom we find our spiritual identity and from whom our individual and collective life spring forth. It is to die with him to the powers of evil and to rise with him to a new way of life (read 1 Peter 2:13–5:11).

In summary, the vision of the church as the context in which spiritual nourishment occurs is this: the church is to live out the new humanity as a corporate people, calling others into its life, nourishing an identity in Jesus, and teaching the pattern of living into his death and resurrection. In addition to Peter's admonition we can identify three prominent ancient images of the church that speak to the experience of the church as a place of nurture. They are the church as womb, mother, and community.

First, *the church is a womb*. The church is likened to the waters of the Jordan in which Jesus was baptized. The Jordan River was like a womb, from which Jesus came forth as the Messiah. So the church, like the Jordan, is the womb from which the new babe in Christ comes forth. The fathers of the church do not reduce the baptism of Jesus to slogans like, "The baptism of Jesus teaches us that like him, we too should be baptized." No, the fathers see the Jordan as a "womb" that discloses the beginning of the "larger mystery in which the Trinity was revealed, the creation renewed in power, the church united to Christ, the rebellious powers condemned and sin and evil destroyed." Kilian McDonnell remarks that "Jesus' baptism not only opens up our baptism, our rebirth as children of God, but opens up the whole economy of salvation."[6] As for the womb's birthing waters, St. Gregory writes, pointing to the image of water, that just as God made "the first earth emerge from the waters" of creation, and by the freshness of water all plants, reptiles, and wild animals were fattened, so "by treading the waters with his own footsteps" at the Jordan "he made green the womb of regeneration so that the second earth 'might be renewed through the spirit by the waters.'"[7]

In the beginning the Spirit moved over the waters, thus setting out "the order of creation." At the baptism of Jesus, the Spirit, who "dwells in the water," sets out the order of the new creation for those who are born children of God. "The invisible Spirit opened again the womb by the visible water," bringing children to rebirth, to "the glory of adoption."[8] The church is the womb that nourishes new life. The waters of the womb protect and care for the new creation that is being formed. As Jesus was disclosed in the waters of the Jordan as the second Adam, so too the waters of the church reveal our new birth in him. The church is the womb in which our spiritual life is gestated.

The second ancient image that speaks to the nurturing nature of the church is *the church as mother*. In Scripture, the image of mother is prominent (Matt. 12:46–50; Mark 3:33–34; John 19:25–27). Even the attitude of Jesus toward Jerusalem is likened to the mothering of the hen who "gathers her chicks under her wings" (Matt. 23:37), so it is no wonder that the fathers of the church likened the church to a mother who nourishes and cares for her young. Cyprian writes, "He cannot have God for his father who does not have the church for his mother." He speaks of the church "that keeps us for God" and "that steals for the Kingdom the Sons whom she bore."[9] St. Augustine writes of the marriage of Christ and the church and warns those who say they love Christ but blaspheme the church. He admonishes them to "love our Lord God" and to "love His church," to love "Him as a Father, her as a Mother; Him as a Master; her as His Handmaid; for we are the children of the Handmaid herself."[10]

The church as community is the third ancient image to express the nurturing nature of the church. The importance of this nurturing image of the church as community is expressed by the interesting and compelling point made by Luke. Immediately after calling new converts to "save yourselves from this corrupt generation" (Acts 2:40), Luke shows us what an embodied community of God's people looks like. The message of spirituality is to be in union with the purposes of God for humanity and to do it in community! The community that Luke describes in Acts 2:42–47 is characterized by worship, the apostolic teaching, the Eucharist, prayer, fellowship, signs and wonders, sharing of common life, and eating together.

The church in Jerusalem described by Luke was a story-formed group of people who seem to have lived together communally. At the very least they shared much of their lives together in each other's homes, at the table eating, and in the mutual sharing of possessions.

While the Jerusalem model is not the only model of community in the early church, certainly it is the most striking and radical of the models. Today many young people—singles and young marrieds—are choosing the Jerusalem model.[11] But what about those who are older, more established with families, homes in the suburbs, jobs within society? Are we to expect them to give up their place in life to assume a radical poverty-defined life in the city? While the Jerusalem model is a significant and powerful model of a story-formed witness in a corrupt society, it is not the only model presented in the New Testament. It is possible for a church, a community of people, to have a story-formed witness without each person selling all their possessions and moving into a "shared purse" community.

For this model of a countercultural church as community witness, we turn to the Epistles. When we read the instructions on Christian living at the end of each of Paul's Epistles, we note they describe the pattern of spirituality for the many of us who do not live in the Jerusalem model of community. For example, to live in submission to each other—husbands and wives, parents and children, employers and employees (Eph. 5:22–6:9)—is a form of spiritual living in union with God. Obeying the mandate of Paul in Ephesians 5:1–2, "Be imitators of God . . . live a life of love, just as Christ loved us and gave himself up for us," is a communal life. Spiritual living is not a difficult thing to grasp. In this case it means to serve one another, not to be a dominating husband or parent or boss but to live by the model of Jesus, who came not to be served but to serve and to give his life for us.

The husband who yells at his wife and kids and demands unswerving obedience because "I am the head of the house" is living as the world lives, is following the dominant model of a male culture, and is being shaped by a pattern of relationship that is ungodly and unspiritual. Again and again Paul turns the dominant culture on its head and calls us into a practical living that dies to self-interest and rises to the new life in the Spirit exemplified by Jesus. Take a moment to read the following passages of Scripture and see firsthand what a story-formed spirituality that springs forth from union with God's purposes for life looks like. It is not strange and bizarre behavior but a choice to live as God called us to live in union with his purposes.

Romans 12:1–15; 14:1–23
Galatians 5:16–6:10
Ephesians 4:1–6
Philippians 3:1–4, 9
Colossians 2:6–4:6

1 Thessalonians 4:1–12
2 Thessalonians 2:13–3:14
1 Timothy 5:1–6, 21
2 Timothy 3:1–17
Titus 1:5–3:11
Philemon 1–22
Hebrews 6:1–12; 10:19–39; 12:1–17; 13:1–10
James 1:2–5:20
1 Peter 2:11–5:11
2 Peter 1:3–11; 3:14–18
1 John 1:5–2:17; 3:4–20, 24
2 John 5
3 John 3–4, 11
Jude 17–25

These passages all describe baptismal identity and spirituality. The spiritual life is walking in the ways of union with God, following the path of restored fellowship, and participating in the purposes of the Triune God together with others.

The church is a family of people who have a history rooted all the way back into Israel and spread around the world and who are called to live in the world, in the structures of the world—political, economic, family, institutional, educational, artistic—all of life is open to the Christian. The spiritual life walks within the story of God; shaped by the narrative of God, redeeming and rescuing the world through Jesus Christ; with the church, his body, being an embodied presence of God in the world.

Considering these examples from the early church—the church as mother, womb, and story-formed community, we must ask ourselves the question: what type of church should we become in order to nourish spiritual identity in Jesus Christ as well as the spiritual pattern of dying to sin and rising to new life in Christ by the Spirit?

We must become a church that nurtures disciples—birthing and mothering to create story-formed communities. In order for a church to be story-formed, the focus needs to be on people, not on buildings.

David Hill uses an interesting illustration to demonstrate how many churches today emphasize the building, not the people: "If you ask a five–year-old to draw a church, you will get a house-like structure with a steeple on top, maybe topped by a cross. Many churches identify themselves with pictures of their edifice. This is because most American churches spend a significant portion of their money on their building. If you ask a five-year-old to draw a family, then you get a picture of people. . . . Churches seem to be about buildings and families seem to be about people."[12]

To be a story-formed community, the focus of the church needs to be on a process of Christian formation of people, not on programs. Perhaps the question most frequently asked of churches today is "What kind of programs do you have to meet the needs of people?" Consumers want programs—programs for children, youth, singles, divorced, widowed, alcoholics, drug abusers. Name a need. Create a program. I realize most of the programs are ministries, and I do not suggest churches should not reach out. But nowhere in the Epistles do you find the apostolic writers urging the church to develop programs. Instead all the teaching is about a *way of life*, and that way of life is taught and caught in the church as it sees itself as the continuation of God's story in the world. For example, in the spirit of Paul calling us to be imitators of Christ daily, one might ask, "Who am I discipling? Who is discipling me? Am I a disciple of Jesus Christ?"

Younger evangelical Craig Gilbert writes, "If we are to make disciples, then we are called to long-term care, feeding and education of the soul that we evangelize. To not integrate them into the body of Christ, the church, is to not fulfill the great commission. To fail to faithfully live the example in fellowship and study, prayer and worship, and thereby give the convert a tangible model to emulate, is to fail in our calling."[13]

Gilbert's concern seems to be the new consensus. The problem of conversions without discipleship was addressed by an International Consultation on Discipleship that met in September of 1999 in Eastbourne, England. On that occasion 450 evangelical leaders from fifty-four countries and nearly ninety Christian fellowships and denominations met to discuss the failure of evangelical communities to nourish disciples. They define discipleship as "a process that takes place within accountable relationships over a period of time for the purpose of bringing believers to spiritual maturity in Christ."[14] Note that when you break down the primary tenants of this definition, all arise from the image of *womb* and *mothering*:

- process
- within accountable relationships
- over a period of time
- for the purpose of . . . spiritual maturity
- in Christ

But where do we go to find a model for nurturing that is designed particularly to form new Christians over a period of time into spiritual maturity?

A model that nurtures new converts was developed in the early church. I propose that we adapt that model for use in our twenty-first-century churches. Note that my proposal is to *adapt* the model, not to just copy the model without a concern to translate it into our language and cultural situation.

I have written on this model before,[15] so I will briefly summarize the model here: The model is a process that evangelizes, disciples, spiritually forms, and assimilates new converts into the church. Each stage of formation is marked by a passage rite. The culminating rite is baptism. A sponsor or mentor walks through side by side with the converting person. This sponsorship fulfills all the aspects of the definition of discipleship set forth by the International Consultation on Discipleship. It is a "process . . . over a period of time" within "accountable relationships . . . for the purpose of . . . spiritual maturity in Christ."

Below is the most simple way to see this process from beginning to end. It remains true to the ancient model, and it translates that process of use for any church.

Step 1. Evangelize the seeker.
        Rite of conversion
Step 2. Disciple the new believer.
        Rite of covenant
Step 3. Spiritually form the maturing Christian.
        Rite of baptism
Step 4. Assimilate the maturing Christian into the full life of the church.

This ancient process of discipleship reflects the nature and mission of the church, which is to raise up a people of God who embody the story of God and witness to the validity of God's work to rescue creatures and creation by living in union with God's purposes for humanity. The church is to disciple this way of life and through that discipleship nourish the spiritual life of its people, young and old.

The church needs to be realigned to the intent of Christ, but it does not need to be reinvented. Reinventing the church is what we do when we allow the culture to shape the church. We reinvent the church to fit modern science and rationalism, reinvent it to fit the culture of consumerism and entertainment, reinvent it to fit postmodern relativism. Obviously the church must speak to the culture. It only speaks authentically and with integrity, however, when speaking out of the story of God. The moment the church capitulates to the culture and speaks out of one or more of the culture's stories and not out of the story of God, the church loses its nature and mission and ceases to be salt and light to the world.

The problem of a burnout between head and heart that results in a "what's it all about anyway" attitude, where the nature and mission of the church is "up for grabs,"[16] can be solved as we turn away from a culture-formed understanding of the church to once again see the church as it truly is—the people of God who live in the world out of God's story. To make that shift and become a womb, mother, and community that nurtures the baptized life, we, the people of the church, must turn to the contemplation of God's divine embrace of the church and to participation in the church.

To contemplate the church, we must do more than think about the church as a fact of life; we must delight in the church through the lens of God's story. The early church delighted in the church as the soul of the world. In spite of all the warts of the church, some of which have been mentioned here, it is the unique people of God who circle the globe, people who are present in nearly every culture, every language, every geographical area. The church, called forth to be God's unique people, is to be the salt of the world and the light of the world. They are my brothers and sisters in our family of God. They are Catholics, Orthodox, Protestants, charismatics, fundamentalists. They all belong to me and I to them. My Christian brothers and sisters are the body of Christ, and as a result, the presence of Jesus to the world. I am to take delight in this belonging and stand in awe of the body of interconnected people throughout history, around the globe, and in the heavens. For through the presence of the church in the world, Jesus Christ, the Savior of the world, is being revealed.

The spiritual life not only springs forth from God's union with us in the church, the spiritual life also delights in its union with God in the church. The spiritual life participates also in the life of God made real by the church in the life of the world. This world is God's world, and the church is by no means an escape from the world. Instead it is (1) the womb that prepares us to live in the world as Christ's followers and (2) the breasts that nourish our living. God's purpose for the world—to be the theater of his glory—is to happen now in this community of people, who live as God's family on earth, pursuing the purposes of God.

WORSHIP SITUATED IN THE STORY OF GOD'S EMBRACE NOURISHES THE SPIRITUAL LIFE

The Crisis of Worship in Today's Church

In recent years worship has been wrenched from the story of God and has been formed by some of the narratives of contemporary culture. Culturally formed worship is illustrated by the experience of a deeply committed evangelical professor who sought out an evangelical church:

Everywhere we went, we found the same basic atmosphere, patterns, and attitudes. . . . Each church we visited caused us to ask the same set of questions. . . . What were the practical benefits of attending and participating in an evangelical church? . . . *What we were asking had to do with our spiritual walk, with sanctification, and with spiritual maturity.* Were we being helped, encouraged, uplifted by the music? Hardly, since church music seemed designed to exalt the performers more than God. Could the bizarre scenes of stage performers undulating sensually to taped background music designed to allow them to do that for which they had no talent, be honoring to our God? Did the casual, "user-friendly" services facilitate worship or were they merely self-centered pep-rallies? I shall never forget my consternation at hearing that most irreverent expression of pseudo-piety the "Jesus Cheer." Were we supported by the fellowship with other believers?

What fellowship? Social interaction based on convenience and conformity can hardly pass for the communion of God's people. Or should we have focused our desire for spiritual nourishment on the ordinances, in particular the Lord's Supper? But here too, we were disappointed. The infrequently celebrated sacraments had long since been reduced to mere symbols, i.e., gutted of all divine power and mystery. But there was always the truth as presented in the teaching of the Word. But, poorly prepared, badly delivered homilies filled with jokes, platitudes and the individual interpretations did little to enhance growth and maturity. With what authority did our self-authenticating "pastors," "bishops," and "popes" teach?

And on it went. It soon became apparent that most of our questions were being answered in the negative, i.e., the answers consistently pointed to a desultory form of religious activism practically devoid of spiritual benefit. So it was that our quest for an authentic expression for Christian Church began.[17]

This description cannot be dismissed as the evaluation of a disgruntled Christian. Here is a deeply committed Christian professor in an evangelical seminary looking for spiritual nourishment in the worship of a local evangelical church. But he finds only a cultural manifestation of Christianity that bears no mark of spiritual nourishment or sustenance.

Me-oriented worship is the result of a culturally driven worship. When worship is situated in the culture and not in the story of God, worship becomes focused on the self. It becomes narcissistic. Christopher Lasch points to narcissism as a "metaphor of the human condition."[18] Certainly from a biblical perspective, sin is fundamentally a rebellion against God, a rebellion that places self at the center. Therefore, we must ask whether it is really a fact that much of our worship has shifted from a focus on God and God's story to a focus on me and my story.

This question is answered by the research of Lester Ruth, professor of worship at Asbury Seminary. Dr. Ruth examined the seventy-two top contemporary songs over a fifteen-year period of time with his primary question being, "Are these songs rooted in the Triune nature and activity of God?" His conclusions are alarming: "None of the songs in the corpus of seventy-two explicitly refer to the Trinity or the Triune nature of God. . . . Only three songs refer to or name all three persons of the Trinity." While Jesus is named in thirty-two of the songs, the Holy Spirit is named in only two songs. "With so few of the songs naming or worshiping all three persons of the Trinity, it is therefore not surprising to find little remembrance of Triune activity in the corpus." This results in a "de-emphasis on commemorating God's saving activity."[19]

By not situating worship in a recollection of the trinitarian activity to redeem and restore the world, the shift in worship, revealed in this study, is to turn God into an object of worship. Consequently the "overwhelming character of the songs" is that of the worshiper "expressing love, adoration, and praise to the direct object of their worship."[20]

The real underlying crisis in worship goes back to the fundamental issue of the relationship between God and the world. If God is the object of worship, then worship must proceed from me, the subject, to God, who is the object. God is the being out there who needs to be loved, worshiped, and adored by me. Therefore, the true worship of God is located in me, the subject. I worship God to magnify his name, to enthrone God, to exalt him in the heavens. God is then pleased with me because I have done my duty.

If God is understood, however, as the personal God who acts as subject in the world and in worship rather than the remote God who sits in the heavens, then worship is understood not as the acts of adoration God demands of me but as the disclosure of Jesus, who has done for me what I cannot do for myself. In this way worship is the doing of God's story within me so that I live in the pattern of Jesus's death and resurrection. My worship, then, is the free choosing to do what Paul admonishes us to do: "Offer your bodies as living sacrifices, holy and pleasing to God—this is your spiritual act of worship. Do not conform any longer to the pattern of this world, but be transformed by the renewing of your mind" (Rom. 12:1–2).

Here is the shift: the biblical God, Father, Son, and Holy Spirit is not the God who sits in the heavens but the one who *acts* in this world. The Triune God creates, becomes involved with creation, becomes present in Israel, becomes incarnate in Jesus, dies for sin, is victorious over death, ascends to heaven, and calls the church into being by the Spirit to witness to his work of redeeming the world. This same God will restore creatures and creation and rule over all in the new heavens and the new earth. Biblical worship tells and enacts this story. Narcissistic worship, instead, names God as an object to whom *we* offer honor, praise, and homage.

Narcissistic worship is situated in the worshiper, not in the action of God that the worshiper remembers through Word and table.

The current focus on worship originating in the self is probably a reaction against truth without passion and is what happened to me as a result of the Enlightenment and what happened to me when my learning of Scripture through the scientific method left me dry. The traditional worship of the fifties is more confessional, concerning itself with making truth statements about God. Unfortunately, these truth statements often are based on an Enlightenment method that privileges reason, science, and fact. Consequently, worship based on these truths is often dispassionate, intellectual, and dry. Contemporary worship is more characterized by passion. It has to do with the heart, with relationship, with an intimacy; it elicits feelings, emotion, tears, and intensity; it lacks substance. Worship needs both truth and passion. Truth without passion is dry. Passion without truth is empty. Where do we go to find both truth and passion? I suggest recovering worship as the proclamation and enactment of God's story.[21]

Worship Proclaims and Enacts God's Story

There seems to be a great deal of confusion about the purpose of worship. I talk to many men and women who think worship arises from inside themselves. Worship, like spirituality, springs forth from the story of God. Worship does God's story. It proclaims God's story in the reading and preaching of the Word; in prayer, the church prays for the world God has reclaimed; in the Eucharist, the church ascends into the heavens and experiences the consummation of God's story in the new heavens and the new earth. There is a personal dimension to worship. Worship is the contemplation, the delight in our own heart that comes from hearing and enacting the story of how God renews the face of the earth through his Son and Spirit. The other response to worship is the choice we make to participate in purposes of God for the world that worship celebrates. This is how song, Scripture, prayer, and Eucharist nourish our spiritual life.

Scripture Nourishes the Spiritual Life

The reading and preaching of Scripture in worship nourishes our spiritual life as it interprets the whole world through the story of God's embrace.[22] This means that we cannot read the Bible through any other story. We cannot embrace the story of rationalism and science, on the one hand, and bring it to the story of the Bible as if the story of the Bible *needs* the story of reason and science to shore it up and make it acceptable. The whole method of making the Bible sensible through other disciplines—be they reason, science, sociology, psychology, or whatever—must be turned on its head and seen for what it is. Scripture calls us to delight in the story as true, stand inside the story, and let the story interpret science, philosophy, sociology, and all other disciplines. Scripture sees everything in life through the story.

God does not say, "Come and read the Bible through existentialism or postmodern philosophy or sociology and see if you can make it fit." No. Scripture presents the story as true and says, "Look at the world and all its structures and relationships and dysfunctions through the eyes of God." Scripture says the story of God is itself a philosophy, an anthropology, a sociology, a reason, a science. Scripture frees the Christian to see the world through the eyes of God's story as a true commentary on the origin of life, the problem of evil, the restoration of true humanity, the meaning of life, the destiny of history.

Reading the biblical story is not enough. To be fully nourished by Scripture, one must enter into it and participate in God's story. We must become the word, by living the Word. The Scripture as God's Word *tells* us how we are to live in the pattern of death and resurrection, but Jesus, who is the living Word of God, has embodied true humanity and *shows* us how we are to live, following the Word and doing as Jesus did for others.

The benediction at the end of the book of Hebrews, a book that urges its readers to embody the living Word, declares,

> May the God of peace, who through the blood of the eternal covenant brought back from the dead our Lord Jesus, that great Shepherd of the sheep, equip you with everything good for doing his will, and may he work in us what is pleasing to him, through Jesus Christ, to whom be glory for ever and ever. Amen.
>
> Hebrews 13:20–21

It does not get much clearer than this. The spiritual life is not nourished by faith in an abstract idea. Rather, the spiritual life is made real as we embody the written and living Word of God by dying to all that is evil and by being birthed to all that is in the service of God.

Worship as the Prayer of the Church Nourishes the Spiritual Life

In the early church the public worship of the church was a prayer of praise and thanksgiving directed not to the people but to God.[23] Seeing worship as prayer is a paradigm shift from the current presentational notion of worship. Today worship is frequently seen as a presentation made to the people to get them to believe in the first place, to enrich and edify their faith, and to bring healing into their lives. But the ancient church did not design (a contemporary word) worship to reach people, to educate people, or to heal people. Yet in their worship, which was a prayer of praise and thanksgiving offered to God, people were indeed nourished by offering God's mighty acts of salvation as a prayer to God for the life of the world. The point is, of course, that worship as prayer shapes who we are. But how so?

First, worship as prayer focuses on historical events. God is known to us in this world, in the revelation of himself in creation, in the salvation history of Israel, and ultimately in God made visible in Jesus. Worship prayer focuses on God's self-giving love through which he recapitulates the human condition, restores our union with God, and promises a restored creation in the new heavens and the new earth. This history that we pray is not dead but alive and active, for it is God's activity, God's presence, God's reality working within history to redeem and restore the world.

Second, the prayer of worship is done not with the language we mortals create but with the language of God. Worship prayer does God's history in this world using the language that is particular and peculiar to the Christian story. The language of prayer is the language of *creation, fall, covenant, Passover, tabernacle, prophetic utterance, incarnation, death, resurrection, church, baptism, Eucharist, eschaton*. These words are necessary because they speak God's voice and presence. They are not common to the other religions of the world, and they are not generic. They are the specific words of God, and consequently, they constitute the language of worship, prayer, contemplation, and participation. There are no comparable words, no substitutes, no adaptations. The relationship between God and humanity must be articulated with these words, for they constitute the only true relationship between God and creation and, therefore, are the language of Christian prayer.

Third, the prayer that we do is situated in God's story and discloses this story. Prayer does *not* proceed out of an inner language that we create in the depth of our own person, as if we have the capacity to form and establish our own personal prayer detached from the story of God. No. The church prays, instead, God's story in the language of God's voice; our prayer is always anchored in the public voice of the church. Our personal prayer is dependent on the faithfulness of the church to articulate for us what we can only say in a fumbling way. The personal praying of the public prayers of the church is a necessary component of our prayer. The public prayer is the bridge to the personal prayer. There is a process through which this public prayer takes place.

Augustine refers to that process as *memoria—intellectus—voluntas*.[24] First, the prayer of the church makes an impression upon our mind. We recall through *memory* the particular story of God and the world. The story itself grasps our intellect, envelops it, overwhelms it with wonder and astonishment (contemplation), and then produces within us the determination of the will to find our place within the prayer, to let that prayer define the meaning of the self, of human existence, of the world, of human history, of the cosmos. The prayer urges us to enter into the historical flow of God's story, to find our personal meaning within God's story of the world—especially in the climax of world history in the divine embrace of Jesus Christ—and to live in the world in the embrace of the one who shows us the fullness of human meaning. Then prayer engages the will as we act (participation) as the continuation of Jesus in the world, the affections become engaged, and we love as Jesus loved.

Yet one more thing: in the prayer of the church that does the saving acts of God in history, it is not the acts of God that constitute our personal prayer but the wonder and astonishment of the God who reveals his nature through this historical action culminating in the God who becomes incarnate, suffers for us, and is risen for us to reclaim us and the world to himself. We marvel in the kind of glorious God whose overwhelming love leads to these actions that reveal his very nature. And our nature, lifted up into the nature of Jesus in prayer, is through him united to God and changed, transformed, and transfigured into the original nature created in the image of God, for in him we are to live, to move, and to have our being. What wondrous splendor is the prayer of the church, which we pray and through which we contemplate and participate in God.

The Eucharist Nourishes the Spiritual Life

In order to be nourished by Christ at bread and wine, most Christians I know will have to go through a paradigm shift.[25] My circle of Christian and non-Christian friends are formed so deeply by Enlightenment rationalism that they only see bread and wine. It is as though they are looking at a snapshot photo of what Christ told us to eat and drink. They live with such a truncated and desupernaturalized faith that wants a *reason* to believe that Jesus is disclosed at bread and wine. In this demand they do what I have been decrying from the start of the book. They bring their Enlightenment worldview that privileges reason and science to God's story and demand that God's story be accountable to a scientific worldview rather than the other way around. To them I say, you must denounce the priority you give to a false worldview and step into the story of God and see Eucharistic bread and wine from *within* the story. The story says, "You do not live in a natural world explained by reason and science." God's story says, "You live in a supernatural world of wonder and mystery. Stand in this world and receive the mystery of bread and wine, disclosing to you the goodness of creation and the union of the human and divine embodied for the restoration of the whole world in Jesus, now made tangible to you and disclosed in this piece of bread and drink of wine. Be free from the constraints of reason and science and meet the true meaning of life in the mystery of these elements."

Now, how do bread and wine draw us into a participation in the life of God in the world? Bread and wine disclose the union we have with Jesus, which, as I have said earlier, is not a mere standing but a true and real participation that is lived out in this life as we become the story of God in this world individually in all our ways and corporately as the people of God. First, we are to ingest eucharistic bread and wine. In contemplation we look on with steadfast delight in all that bread and wine disclose, pulling back the curtain to the divine embrace. In participation we first reach out and take the whole world into our hands. We lift the Alpha and Omega to our mouth. We take God's whole story into our stomach, let it run through our bloodstream, let it then energize our entire living—our relationships, our work, our pleasure—all of life is to be lived now as Jesus lived his life for us, and for our sake, dying for us, rising for us, showing us how to live in the pattern of his dying and rising. As he took into himself the suffering of all humanity, so we are to take into ourselves the suffering of the world and do something about it. As he rose above all that is evil in the world through his resurrection, so we, too, are to rise to the new life by the Spirit of God. All our death to sin and rising to life finds its true and ultimate meaning in him who lives in us, living in our sufferings, living in our struggles with evil, living in our resurrections to new life.

So bread and wine is no abstract object out there, no *thing* to be observed as an object of interest, no mere ritual to be taken in a perfunctory or mechanical way. No. We move from a delightful contemplation of all that bread and wine disclose to participate in God's story by letting the Jesus who comes to us by bread and wine be given anew and poured out again to the world through our individual lives and through the community of the people of God, the church.

CONCLUSION

Let us go back to my pastor friend. Why did he experience such a disparity between his mind and his heart? My inclination is to say that his head was wrapped around a culturally formed view of Christianity—perhaps an Enlightenment, proof-oriented view of the faith, a business model of the church, and a presentational approach to worship. These culturally formed models of faith and practice have no soul, no heart. In time they become mechanistic, dry, and dead. Lacking roots in the life-giving source of God's divine embrace, these culturally formed models have no power to nourish the heart, the mind, and the soul for either pastors or people.

The only hope to nourish ministry is to return to God's story in which the church and its worship are situated and recover the true nature and mission of the church as a community called to be the continuation of God's story living out of the purposes of God for humanity within community—proclaiming and living out the Good News. The images of people of God, new creation, fellowship in the faith, and the body of Christ all refer to the church as an Israel-like, story-formed community. The ancient images of *womb*, *mother*, and *community* speak to the church's work as a birthing and nurturing ministry. The church here on earth is an alternative, countercultural community, whether living as a communal household or scattered into the various vocations of life. God's people live out of a particular antithesis to the values of the fallen world, and they do so as the "soul" of the world, transforming life to envision God's redemption accomplished in the divine embrace when God the Son, by the power of the Spirit, stretched out his arms of love on the hard wood of the cross and won back the world to the Father.

When worship does God's story, our contemplation is simply a delight in the story that worship does. The delight of worship is not expressed in words like "That was a great program," or "I loved the music today," or "What an entertaining sermon," or "I really felt like I was worshiping today," or "That sure was fun dancing around, shouting 'Amen!' and giving my neighbor a high five." These are descriptions of delight in self as if "I did it; I broke through; I really worshiped." Worship that generates that kind of response is not worship that glorifies God and his story. Rather, that kind of worship glorifies the self as if the self has generated worship.

True worship generates the sense of "What a great story," or "I can't believe that God would do that for the world and for me," or "What a God to become human and to restore all things through Christ." For some people the truth declared in worship will be received with exuberance, and for others the truth of God's story will be received with reserve, with a quiet sense of joy, or even with relief. But for us all, a worship that sings, proclaims, and enacts God's story should result in a delight that produces an ongoing participation in the purposes of God in life.

Because God is the subject who acts upon me in worship, my participation is not reduced to verbal response or to singing. Rather, my participation is living in the pattern of the one who is revealed in worship. God as the subject of worship acts through the truth of Christ proclaimed and enacted in worship to form me by the Spirit of God to live out the union I have with Jesus by calling me to die to sin and to live in the resurrection. Worship forms me and transforms my life to do God's purposes in this life in this world, to the glory of God who created me in the first place, and re-created me and the whole community of faith to be the people of his own glory in this world now, and in the life of the world to come, forever.

So then the church and its worship, and indeed all its ministries, will nourish the life of all God's people when situated in the story of God as the continuation of that story and a witness to God's reconciliation of the world to himself.

A Summary for Reflection and Conversation

Summary	Reflection
A personal conflict	We have been taught that the source of spiritual nourishment lies in the self.
The church nourishes the spiritual life.	When the church is shaped by God's story of divine embrace, God nourishes the spiritual life.
Worship nurtures the spiritual life.	God is not the object of our worship but the subject who forms us as we sing, tell, pray, and enact God's story in worship.

Postscript

No Story but God's; No God but the Father, Son, and Spirit;
No Life but the Baptized Life

One Lord, one faith, one baptism;
one God and Father of all,
who is over all and through all and in all.

Ephesians 4:5

few days before I wrote this postscript, I received a phone call from Rev. Richard Crabtree, pastor of First Christian Church in Oden, Indiana. "Bob," he said, "I've called to tell you a story."

That summer I had spoken at the Christian Church Convention in Lexington, Kentucky, and Rev. Crabtree had been in attendance. I was in the middle of writing this book. Since its content was steadily present in my heart and on my mind, my talk emphasized the story of God's embrace. Pastor Crabtree wanted to tell me how affected he was by recovering the story and especially how the story was particularly applicable in the recent funeral of a teenager who had been killed in an auto accident.

Pastor Crabtree said,

I told them that I needed to tell them two stories. The first story is about my poor sense of direction. Every time I drive from Oden to Indianapolis, everything inside of me tells me I am going north. The fact is I am driving east, but it looks like and feels like I am driving north. It feels so north to

241

me that I've even checked the map, and sure enough the map tells me I am going east.

Right now, everyone of us here wonders where God is in the death of Rebecca. On the one hand we feel that God is not here, not close to us, not caring for us. Yet God really is. We feel one thing, but God's map, the Scriptures, tells us that God is near to the brokenhearted, to those whose spirits have been crushed. To know this I must tell you another story, the story of God.

God, who dwells in the eternal community of love, is so overflowing with love that he chose to share his love with others. He created a world, a place to inhabit, a place to show forth his glory. And he created a people, Adam and Eve, to live in union with him doing his purposes in the world.

But Adam and Eve chose to rebel against God. The result was a catastrophe. The relation between man and God was broken; the relationship of people to people became dysfunctional; even nature rose up against humanity. The world became a hostile place full of death, war, greed, lust, and sin of every kind. Humanity was now in a terrible fix, and there was nothing they could do about it.

But God in his mercy chose to do something about the human situation. He chose not to simply step into the world but to become a human and reverse the human situation from the inside. He became one of us in the womb of the Virgin Mary. He lived in every stage of our lives. As an infant he suckled at Mary's heart; as a boy he was taught to fear God; as an adult he inaugurated his ministry at his baptism. But his own people to whom he came turned against him. They sentenced him to die on the cross. He gave up his life willingly, and there in his death, he destroyed death, rising triumphantly from the grave.

Today it is hard to believe that God is close to us as we mourn the loss of Rebecca. We are in deep sorrow, but we must look at the map, at God's story. When Martha was grieving the death of Lazarus, Jesus said to her, "I am the resurrection and the life." The one who came into the world to fix it and make it new gives us this message today.[1]

"I noticed," Pastor Crabtree told me, "that as I told the story of God's identification with us, of the pain God himself experienced in the death of his son, that the weeping stopped, that people, including Rebecca's mother and father and fourteen-year-old brother leaned forward in their seats and listened intently. God's story was touching them where they hurt most and giving them hope.

"Many people in this small town were deeply touched by the story of God. A high school history teacher, for example, said to me, 'What I took home from that funeral message was this: this world is turned upside down, and Jesus is the only one who can fix it.'

"'You got it,' I said, and he answered, 'Yes I did!'"

What can I say? There is no story in this world that is more profound than the story of God's embrace. My dinner companions heard the gospel in a new way. And each of them, in their own way, is growing in the life-changing embrace of God, as I am and I trust you are too. For there is no story but God's; no God but the Father, Son and Spirit; and no life but the baptized life.

NOTES

Chapter 1: Introduction

1. The primary proof for the Christian faith throughout history has been what Yale theologian George Lindbeck identifies as "intratextual." After the Reformation of the church in the sixteenth century a plurality of authorities appeared, all claiming to be true on the basis of the Bible. Efforts were made to find proof for the Christian faith outside of the Bible. Following the lead of René Descartes, the new foundation for truth was located in reason. The followers of this method are known as "foundationalists." They defended Christianity with reason, but in time reason and science became opponents of the Scripture. And now, in the postmodern world, the collapse of reason and science as foundations for truth no longer make theological foundationalism valid. Thus the rejection of "extratextual" arguments for the Christian faith and a return to God's story as a true interpretation of life, but not provable through the enlightenment method of reason and science. See George A. Lindbeck, *The Nature of Doctrine: Religion and Theology in a Postliberal Age* (Philadelphia: Westminster, 1984).

2. In recent years there has been a great deal of discussion about Universalism. New attention to the incarnation focuses on God becoming one of us that we might be reunited to him through Jesus by the Spirit. Furthermore, the recent embrace of the unity of spirit and matter emphasizes that God in the incarnation not only took on humanity, God also became this creation subject to sin and death. Having united himself to fallen humanity and a creation affected by sin and death, God in Christ reconciled all things to himself through his death and resurrection. Does this imply universal salvation?

Calvinists who espouse the origin of salvation in the decrees of God argue that God became incarnate for those who are elect; Arminians who emphasize the importance of free will say that God became incarnate for all, was crucified and resurrected for all, and makes a universal offer of salvation, which may be appropriated by all who believe. Radical Universalists would argue that God's work is effective for all and that in the end of history all people and all creation will be united to God by the work of Jesus and the Spirit. There are also those who follow Karl Rahner in affirming the following biblical paradoxes: "We must maintain side by side and unwaveringly the truth of the omnipotence of the universal salvific will of God, the redemption of all by Christ, the duty of all men to hope for salvation and also the true possibility of eternal loss." Karl Rahner, "Holle" [Hell], *Sacramentum*

Mundi, vol. 3 (New York: Herder and Herder, 1969), 8, quoted by Hans Urs von Balthasar, *Dare We Hope: "That All Men Be Saved"* (San Francisco: Ignatius, 1988), 212.

Current books on the question of Universalism include Dennis L. Okholm and Timothy R. Phillips, *Four Views on Salvation in a Pluralistic World* (Grand Rapids: Zondervan, 1996); Robin A. Perry and Christopher H. Partridge, *Universal Salvation? The Current Debate* (Grand Rapids: Eerdmans, 2003); Terrance L. Tiessen, *Irenaeus on the Salvation of the Unevangelized* (Metuchen, NJ: Scarecrow Press, 1997); and Terrance L. Tiessen, *Who Can Be Saved? Reassessing Salvation in Christ and World Religions* (Downers Grove, IL: InterVarsity, 2004).

3. "Spirituality in America" (cover title), *Newsweek*, September 5, 2005, 9.

4. For a good overview of the story of God, I suggest Gabriel Fackre, *The Christian Story: A Narrative Interpretation of Basic Christian Doctrine*, rev. ed. (Grand Rapids: Eerdmans, 1984).

5. The image of the "two hands of God" originates in a quote by Irenaeus, the most outstanding Christian theologian of the second century. In his work, *Against Heresies*, Irenaeus writes, "Having been molded at the beginning by the hands of God, that is, of the Son and of the Spirit, [man] is made after the image and likeness of God." Here, in the very creation of humanity, matter and spirit are united. See Alexander Roberts and James Donaldson, eds., *Ante-Nicene Fathers*, vol. 1 (Grand Rapids: Eerdmans, 1973), 557. Thanks to Jim Salladin, Regent College, for locating this quote for me.

6. For the history of spirituality as union with God, see the book by Fuller Seminary professor Veli-Matti Kärkkäinen, *One with God: Salvation as Deification and Justification* (Collegeville, MN: Liturgical Press, 2004).

7. Dallas Willard, *The Divine Conspiracy: Rediscovering Our Hidden Life in God* (San Francisco: HarperSanFrancisco, 1998), 11.

8. Philip Sheldrake, *Spirituality and Theology: Christian Living and the Doctrine of God* (Maryknoll, NY: Orbis Books, 1998), 35.

9. Bernard McGinn, *The Foundations of Mysticism: Origins to the Fifth Century* (New York: Crossroad, 1991), 65. For an excellent summary of mysticism in the New Testament, especially the Synoptics, Paul, and John, see pages 66–83.

10. Ibid., 65.

11. For a philosophy of embodiment, see George Lakoff and Mark Johnson, *Philosophy in the Flesh: The Embodied Mind and Its Challenge to Western Thought* (New York: Basic Books, 1999). "Truth is mediated by embodied understanding and imagination" (6).

The material dimension of the Christian faith is set forth in "the rule of faith," an early Christian guideline, for the interpretation of God's story. This "rule," which is found in many areas of the Roman world in various forms, is the precursor to the Apostles' Creed. Below is the common rule of faith summarized by Irenaeus in his debate with the Gnostics, who rejected the union of spirit and matter and espoused a "spiritual" Christianity in which matter is evil and in conflict with spirit, which is good. Note how Irenaeus emphasizes the union of flesh and matter:

> Now the Church, although scattered over the whole civilized world to the end of the earth, received from the apostles and their disciples its faith in one God, the Father Almighty, who made the heaven, and the earth, and the seas, and all that is in them, and in one Christ Jesus; the Son of God, who was made flesh for our salvation, and in the Holy Spirit, who through the prophets proclaimed the dispensations of God—the comings, the birth of a virgin, the suffering, the resurrection from the dead, and the bodily reception into the heavens of the beloved, Christ Jesus our Lord, and his coming from the heavens in the glory of the Father to restore all things, and to raise up all flesh, that is, the whole human race, so that every knee may bow, of things in heavens and on earth and under the earth, to Christ Jesus our Lord and God and Saviour and King, according to the pleasure of the invisible Father, and

every tongue may confess him, and that he may execute righteous judgment on all. The spiritual powers of wickedness, and the angels who transgressed and fell into apostasy, and the godless and wicked and lawless and blasphemers among men he will send into the eternal fire. But to the righteous and holy, and those who kept his commandments and have remained in his love, some from the beginning [of life] and some since their repentance, he will by his grace give life incorrupt, and will clothe them with eternal glory. Irenaeus, *Against Heresies*, book 1, chap. 10, par. 1, quoted in *Early Christian Fathers*, ed. Cyril C. Richardson, vol. 1, The Library of Christian Classics (Philadelphia: Westminster, 1953), 360.

12. St. Augustine, *On Sacred Virginity*, quoted in Ramero Cantalamessa, *The Eucharist: Our Sanctification* (Collegeville, MN: Liturgical Press, 1993, 1995), 54.

13. Hugh of St. Victor, quoted in ibid., 62.

14. St. Bonaventure, quoted in ibid.

15. Ibid.

16. *The Book of Common Prayer* (New York: Seabury Press, 1979), 101 (italics mine).

17. I am indebted to Alan Kreider for these summary words. See his book *The Change of Conversion and the Origin of Christendom* (Harrisburg, PA: Trinity, 1999), 92.

Chapter 2: A Historical Perspective 1 (AD 30–1500)

1. The history of spirituality has been presented in brief form in Cheslyn Jones, Geoffrey Wainwright, and Edward Yarnold, SJ, eds., *The Study of Spirituality* (New York: Oxford University Press, 1986). A more extensive history of spirituality is found in the twenty-five volumes of *World Spirituality: An Encyclopedic History of the Religious Quest* (New York: Crossroad, 1986–). Three of these volumes cover the history of Christian spirituality: Bernard McGinn and John Meyendorff, eds., *Christian Spirituality I: Origins to the Twelfth Century* (New York: Crossroad, 1986); Jill Raitt, ed., *Christian Spirituality II: High Middle Ages and Reformation* (New York: Crossroad, 1987); Louis Dupré and Don E. Saliers, eds., *Christian Spirituality III: Post-Reformation and Modern* (New York: Crossroad, 1989).

2. Sheldrake, *Spirituality and Theology*, vii. Sheldrake is one of a few contemporary authors who understand spirituality as an ancient applied theology. I fully recommend this book and Philip Sheldrake, *Spirituality and History: Questions of Interpretation and Method*, rev. ed. (1991; repr., Maryknoll, NY: Orbis Books, 1998).

3. Sheldrake, *Spirituality and Theology*, 3.

4. Bengt Hägglund, *History of Theology*, trans. Gene J. Lund (St. Louis: Concordia, 1968), 33. I highly recommend this one-volume work on historical theology. Hägglund writes from the perspective of the ancient "rule of faith" and has a helpful grasp on those movements that modify classical applied theology.

5. *The Book of Common Prayer*, 120.

6. The origin of the Apostles' Creed lies in "the rule of faith"—early second-century creeds written to express what Christians believe over against Gnostic faith. The rule of faith evolved into "the interrogatory creed." This creed constituted the three questions asked of those who were being baptized. Baptism was and still is a baptism into the life of the Triune God. Baptism, in the early church, does not emphasize "my story" but God's story, in which we have been united by the incarnate Word and the Spirit. Below is the earliest full record of baptism into the faith of the church.

When the one being baptized goes down into the waters the one who baptizes, placing a hand on him, should say thus: "Do you believe in God the Father Almighty?"

And he who is baptized should reply: "I believe."

Let him baptize him once immediately, having his hand placed upon his head. And after this he should say: "Do you believe in Christ Jesus, the son of God, who was born of the Holy Spirit and Mary the virgin and was crucified under Pontius

Pilate and was dead [and buried] and rose on the third day alive from the dead and ascended in the heavens and sits at the right hand of the Father and will come to judge the living and the dead?"

And when he has said, "I believe," he is baptized again.

And again he should say: "Do you believe in the Holy Spirit and the holy church and the resurrection of the flesh?"

And he who is being baptized should say: "I believe." And so he should be baptized a third time.

And afterwards, when he has come up from the water, he is anointed by the presbyter with that sanctified oil, saying: "I anoint you with holy oil in the name of Jesus Christ."

And afterwards, each drying himself, they shall dress themselves, and afterwards let them go into the church. (Dix:22) And the bishop, laying his hand on them invokes, saying:

"Lord God, you have made them worthy to deserve the remission of sins through the laver of regeneration: make them worthy to be filled with the Holy Spirit, send your grace upon them that they may serve you in accordance with your will; for to you is glory, to the Father and the Son with the Holy Spirit in the holy church both now and to the ages of ages. Amen."

After this, pouring the sanctified oil from his hand and putting it on his head he shall say: "I anoint you with holy oil in God the Father Almighty and Christ Jesus and the Holy Spirit." And signing him on the forehead he shall give him the kiss and say: "The Lord be with you." And he who has been signed shall say: "And with your spirit." And thus he shall do to each. And thenceforth they shall pray with all the people; they shall not pray with the people until they have performed all these things. And after they have prayed they should give the kiss of peace. Hippolytus, *On the Apostolic Tradition*, an English version with introduction and commentary by Alistair Steward-Sykes (Crestwood, NY: St. Vladimir's Seminary Press, 2001), 110–12.

7. The debate with Arius has been revived in the new interest in the Trinity. Although the Nicene Creed is known as the creed that established the Trinity—which it did—the debate, then and now, is essentially a soteriological debate. Who saved us? If Jesus is God incarnate, then God saved us. This conclusion led the church into greater clarity, affirming the triune nature of the God revealed in the biblical story. To read more on the soteriological dimension of the Nicene debate, see Catherine Mowry La Cugna, *God For Us: The Trinity and Christian Life* (San Francisco: HarperSanFrancisco, 1991). For an original source, read St. Athanasius, *On the Incarnation* (Crestwood, NY: St. Vladimir's Seminary Press, 1998). See also Anselm of Canterbury, *Why God Became Man*, trans. Joseph M. Colleran (Albany, NY: Magi Books, 1969).

8. Hägglund, *History of Theology*, 80.

9. *The Book of Common Prayer*, 358–59.

10. See Henry Bettenson, ed., *Documents of the Christian Church* (New York: Oxford University Press, 1956), 75. This work of primary sources contains a section on the debate between Pelagius and Augustine with extended quotes from both, 74–87.

11. Ibid., 77.

12. Ibid., 86. The subject of human ability in the early church fathers is more broadly summarized in J. Patout Burns, SJ, *Theological Anthropology* (Philadelphia: Fortress, 1981).

13. *The Book of Common Prayer*, 864 (italics mine).

14. A broad and helpful work on Christology is David F. Wells, *The Person of Christ: A Biblical and Historical Analysis of the Incarnation* (Wheaton: Crossway Books, 1984).

15. *Service Book of the Holy Orthodox-Catholic Apostolic Church* (Englewood Cliffs, NJ: Antiochian Orthodox Christian Archdiocese, 1983), 583.

16. For the monothelite controversy as well as the other debates and resulting creeds of the ancient church, see Leo Donald Davis, *The First Seven Ecumenical Councils (325–787): Their History and Theology* (Collegeville, MN: Liturgical Press, 1990).

17. Gregory of Nyssa, "Commentary on the Canticle," / PG 44.873 D—87617, quoted in Jean Danielou and Herbert Musurillo, eds., *From Glory to Glory: Texts from Gregory of Nyssa's Mystical Writings* (New York: Charles Scribner's Sons, 1961), 55.

18. Kallistos Ware, *The Orthodox Way* (Crestwood, NY: St. Vladimir's Seminary Press, 1980), 98. There are numerous books on Orthodox spirituality. I especially recommend the book written by A Monk of the Eastern Church, *Orthodox Spirituality: An Outline of the Orthodox Ascetical and Mystical Tradition* (Crestwood, NY: St. Vladimir's Seminary Press, 1996).

19. Sheldrake, *Spirituality and Theology*, 16–17.

20. There are, of course, nuances of difference between the fathers of the church. But they work with the common biblical structure affirmed by the major creeds of the church. See John D. Zizioulas, "The Early Christian Community," and Charles Kannengiesser, "The Spiritual Message of the Fathers," in McGinn and Meyendorff, *Christian Spirituality I*, 23–44, 61–86.

21. Irenaeus, *Against Heresies*, book 4, chap. 20, par. 7, in *Early Christian Fathers*, ed. Richardson. This quote appears in many Orthodox writings in slightly different translations. I am not certain where the original quote is found. An example of its translation is found in George A. Maloney, *The Breath of the Mystic* (Denville, NJ: Dimension Books, 1974), 15. His translation reads: "The glory of God—a man living to the fullest."

22. Athanasius, *Against the Arians*, preface (p. 25, col. 692A), quoted in McGinn and Meyendorff, *Christian Spirituality I*, 65.

23. Vladimir Lossky, *The Mystical Theology of the Eastern Church* (Crestwood, NY: St. Vladimir's Seminary Press, 1976), 8.

24. Plato quoted in Dom Cuthbert Butler, *Western Mysticism: Augustine, Gregory and Bernard on Contemplation and the Contemplative Life* (Mineola, NY: Dover, 2003), 201–2 (italics mine).

25. Plato, *Phaedrus*, quoted in ibid., 247.

26. John Meyendorff, *St. Gregory Palamas and Orthodox Spirituality* (Crestwood, NY: St. Vladimir's Seminary Press, 1974), 16–17.

27. Ibid., 26.

28. See the article "Benedictine Spirituality," in *New Catholic Encyclopedia*, 2nd ed., vol. 2 (Detroit: Thompson-Gale, 2003), 265.

29. Herbert McCabe, OP, *God Matters* (London: Geoffrey Chapman, 1987), 20, quoted in Mark McIntosh, *Mystical Theology: The Integrity of Spirituality and Theology* (Malden, MA: Blackwell, 1998), 16.

30. Rowan Williams, *The Wound of Knowledge: Christian Spirituality from the New Testament to St. John of the Cross*, 2nd ed. (Cambridge, MA: Cowley Publications, 1991), 1, quoted in McIntosh, *Mystical Theology*, 17.

31. McIntosh, *Mystical Theology*, 43.

32. Ibid., 63.

33. Ibid.

34. T. Corbishley and J. E. Bieshler, "Mysticism," *New Catholic Encyclopedia*, 2nd ed., vol. 10 (Detroit: Thompson-Gale, 2003), 111.

35. Philip Sheldrake, *Spirituality and History*, rev. ed. (1992; repr., Maryknoll, NY: Orbis Books, 1998), 46. Citations are to the 1998 edition.

36. There are numerous books available on the history of mysticism. Of all these books, I recommend the five-volume work by Bernard McGinn, *The Presence of God: A History of Western Christian Mysticism* (New York: Crossroad, 1991–1998). Three of these volumes are available at the time of this writing. In volume 3, *The Flowering of Mysticism: Men and Women in the New Mysticism 1200–1350* (New York: Crossroad, 1998), McGinn deals particularly with the new mystics, their renunciation of this life, and their visions, which "were often (though not always) mystical, involving personal, deeply emotional and even erotic encounters with Jesus, the Divine Lover" (28). He cautions us to "remember that Medieval mystics placed far less value on the significance of 'experience' than many modern theories of mysticism do" (29).

37. See the descriptions of this change in McIntosh, *Mystical Theology*, 68.

38. See the three steps, ibid., 72–73.

39. Ibid., 73.

40. McGinn, *Flowering of Mysticism*, 12.

41. Ibid., xii.

42. Dorothy Sayers, *The Mind of the Maker* (San Francisco: Harper, 1941), xiii.

43. Catherine La Cugna, "Trinitarian Spirituality," in *The New Dictionary of Catholic Spirituality*, ed. Michael Downey (Collegeville, MN: Liturgical Press, 1993), 968, quoted in Sheldrake, *Spirituality and History*, 18.

44. Henry Scougal quoted in James B. Torrance, *Worship, Community and the Triune God of Grace* (Downers Grove, IL: InterVarsity, 1996), 32.

45. McGinn, *Flowering of Mysticism*, 157.

Chapter 3: A Historical Perspective 2 (1500–1900)

1. Louis Bouyer, *The Spirit and Forms of Protestantism*, trans. A. V. Littledale (London: Harvill Press, 1956), 10.

2. From "A Treatise on Christian Liberty," *Works of Martin Luther*, vol. 2, cited in Hugh T. Kerr, ed., *A Compend of Luther's Theology* (Philadelphia: Westminster, 1953), 100.

3. St. John Chrysostom, quoted in William A. Jurgens, *The Faith of the Early Fathers*, vol. 2, no. 1185 (Collegeville, MN: Liturgical Press, 1979).

4. Carl E. Braaten and Robert W. Jenson, eds., *Union with Christ: The New Finnish Interpretation of Luther* (Grand Rapids: Eerdmans, 1998), 2 (italics mine).

5. Ibid., 11.

6. Ibid.

7. From the "Small Catechism," Lenken edition, vol. 24, cited in Kerr, *Compend of Luther's Theology*, 164.

8. John Calvin, *Institutes of the Christian Religion* (Grand Rapids: Eerdmans, 1997), book 4, chap. 15, 515.

9. Cornelius J. Dyck, William E. Keeny, and Alvin J. Beachy, *The Writings of Dirk Philips, 1504–1568*, Classics of the Radical Reformation 6 (Scottdale, PA, and Waterloo, Ontario: Herald Press, 1992), 145–46, quoted in Kärkkäinen, *One With God*, 69–70.

10. Ibid.

11. Bouyer, *The Spirit and Forms of Protestantism*, 23–24.

12. For a good overview of hymnody, see Paul Westermeyer, *Te Deum: The Church and Music* (Minneapolis: Fortress, 1998).

13. This information was supplied by David Gorming, email message to author, Fall 2005. Gorming's source is the works of John Wesley, *A Collection of Hymns for Use of the People Called Methodists*, Franz Hildebrandt and Oliver A. Beckerlegge, eds. vol. 7 (Nashville: Abingdon, 1983), hymn 138.

14. Ibid., hymn 153.

15. William Chillingworth, *The Religion of Protestants, A Safe Way of Salvation* with excerpts from *Charity Maintained* by Edward Knoff [Matthew Wilson] (London: Bohn Library, 1854), quoted in Clyde L. Manschreck, ed., *A History of Christianity: Readings in the History of the Church*, vol. 2, *The Church from the Reformation to the Present* (Englewood Cliffs, NJ: Prentice-Hall, 1964; repr., Grand Rapids: Baker, 1981), 225. Citations are from the Baker edition.

16. John Toland, *Christianity Not Mysterious: Or, A Treatise Shewing, That There Is Nothing in the Gospel Contrary to Reason, Nor Above It: And That No Christian Doctrine Can Be Properly Call'd A Mystery*, quoted in Manschreck, *A History of Christianity*, vol. 2, 228–31.

17. James C. Livingston, *Modern Christian Thought: From the Enlightenment to Vatican II* (New York: Macmillan, 1971), 256.

18. Walter Rauschenbusch, *Christianizing the Social Order* (New York: Macmillan, 1912), quoted in ibid., 263.

19. See W. E. Wiest, "Schleiermacher, Friedrich," in *New Catholic Encyclopedia*, 2nd ed., vol. 12 (Detroit: Gale-Thompson, 2003), 740.

20. See "The Rise of Evangelical Pietism," in Manschreck, *A History of Christianity*, vol. 2, 263–314.

21. Ibid., 268.

22. Philip Jacob Spener quoted in Hägglund, *History of Theology*, 327.

23. David W. Lotz, "Continental Pietism," in Jones, Wainwright, and Yarnold, *The Study of Spirituality*, 450.

24. John Wesley, quoted in John H. Tyson, "John Wesley's Conversion at Aldersgate," in Kenneth J. Collins and John H. Tyson, *Conversion in the Wesleyan Tradition* (Nashville: Abingdon, 2001), 37.

25. John Wesley quoted in ibid., 37.

26. Clarence H. Faust and Thomas H. Johnson, eds., *Jonathan Edwards: Representative Selections* (1935; repr., New York: Hill and Wang, 1962), quoted in Robert Handy, "Some Patterns in American Protestantism," in Jones, Wainright, and Yarnold, *The Study of Spirituality*, 474–75.

27. Ibid., 475.

28. William Law, *A Serious Call to a Devout and Holy Life* (Boston: Larkin, Greenough, Stebins, 1808), quoted in Manschreck, *A History of Christianity*, vol. 2, 281.

29. This admonition is still quoted in the Methodist Discipline: *Doctrines and Disciplines of the Methodist Church* (New York: Methodist Publishing House, 1940–1960), quoted in Manschreck, *A History of Christianity*, vol. 2, 288–89.

30. Sheldrake, *Spirituality and Theology*, 37.

Chapter 4: A Modern Dislocation (1900–2000)

1. See Robert Webber, *The Younger Evangelicals* (Grand Rapids: Baker, 2002). The movement I refer to is popularly known as the "emerging church." Its chief architect is Brian McClaren. Two widely read books by McClaren are *A New Kind of Christian* (San Francisco: Jossey-Bass, 2001), and *Generous Orthodoxy* (Grand Rapids: Zondervan, 2004).

2. Alan Wolfe, *The Transformation of American Religion: How We Actually Live Our Faith* (New York: Free Press, 2003), 36.

3. The best critique of legalism I have ever read was written nearly fifty years ago. I read and reread this book as I struggled with the legalism of my fundamentalist background. If you are wrestling with legalism in your own life, I highly recommend Daniel B. Stevick *Beyond Fundamentalism* (Richmond: John Knox, 1964). Stevick grew up in fundamentalism and graduated from Wheaton College in the 1950s. This book has been out of print for years but will be well worth the search to find a copy.

4. Pat Allison, email message to author, Spring 2003.

5. Carol McDaniel, email message to author, Spring 2003.

6. Merril Smoak, email message to author, Spring 2003.

7. Marie Wonders, class paper, Northern Seminary, Lombard, Illinois, May 5, 2004.

8. Dale Buss, email message to author, Spring 2003.

9. One of the burdens of the radical orthodoxy movement is to return the Christian faith to a vision of the world that does not depend on reason and science for its self-verification. See James K. A. Smith, *Introducing Radical Orthodoxy: Mapping a Post-Secular Theology* (Grand Rapids: Baker Academic, 2004); and John Milbank, *Theology and Social Theory: Beyond Secular Reason* (Malden, MA: Blackwell Publishing, 1990).

10. Christopher Lasch, *The Culture of Narcissism: American Life in an Age of Diminishing Expectations* (New York: Norton, 1991).

11. Mike Lueken, email message to author, Spring 2003.

12. Richard J. Foster, *Streams of Living Water: Celebrating the Great Traditions of Christian Faith* (San Francisco: HarperSanFrancisco, 1998), xvi.

13. Dallas Willard, *Divine Conspiracy*, 11.

14. Eugene H. Peterson, *Christ Plays in Ten Thousand Places: A Conversation in Spiritual Theology* (Grand Rapids: Eerdmans, 2005), 5–6.

15. Dallas Willard, *The Spirit of the Disciplines: Understanding How God Changes Lives* (San Francisco: HarperSanFrancisco, 1988), xi–xii.

Chapter 5: A Postmodern Provocation (2000–)

1. Francis Schaeffer, *How Should We Then Live? The Rise and Decline of Western Thought and Culture* (Wheaton: Crossway Books, 1976).

2. J. Jacobi quoted in Paul C. Vitz, *Psychology as Religion: The Cult of Self-Worship* (Grand Rapids: Eerdmans, 1977), 3.

3. Chuck Fromm, *New Song: The Sound of Spiritual Awakening: A Study of Music in Revival*, unpublished papers presented to Oxford Reading and Research Conference, July 1983, Oxford, England, 16.

4. William Strauss and Neil Howe, *The Fourth Turning: What the Cycles of History Tell Us About America's Next Rendezvous with Destiny* (New York: Broadway Books, 1997), 136.

5. Peter L. Berger, ed., *The Desecularization of the World: Resurgent Religions and World Politics* (Grand Rapids: Eerdmans, 1999), 2.

6. Wade Clark Roof, *Spiritual Marketplace: Baby Boomers and the Remaking of American Religion* (Princeton: Princeton University Press, 1999), 3.

7. This and the quotations in the following four paragraphs are taken from Lama Surya Das, *Awakening to the Sacred: Creating a Spiritual Life from Scratch* (New York: Broadway Books, 1999), 12–13.

8. An excellent one-volume work on the religions of the world is Huston Smith, *The World's Religions* (San Francisco: HarperSanFrancisco, 1991).

9. James A. Herrick, *The Making of the New Spirituality: The Eclipse of the Western Religious Tradition* (Downers Grove, IL: InterVarsity, 2003), 26.

10. George Koch, email message to author, September 2005.

Chapter 6: God's Story

1. Ken Wilbur, *A Brief History of Everything* (Boston: Shambhala, 1996). The spiritual dualism of Wilbur's book rejects the material world in order to find spirituality in what it deems to be the antithesis to the material world—the spirit. Historic Christian spirituality affirms the unity of matter and spirit. A very helpful work in understanding this union is Lakoff and Johnson, *Philosophy in the Flesh*. They write, "The concept of spirituality in

our culture has been defined mostly in terms of disembodiment and transcendence of this world. What is needed is an alternative conception of embodied spirituality that at least begins to do justice to what people experience" (564). *The Divine Embrace* does not focus on an otherworldly spirituality, as if one should seek to escape this world and this life as a way of coping with human existence. Instead, this world, the very place where we live and the people with whom we live, is the arena of our spiritual existence. God's story is the story of this world and our life in it. Here in this life is where spirituality is actualized. This perspective has been developed in what is called a Christian worldview. An excellent work is David N. Naugle, *Worldview: The History of a Concept* (Grand Rapids: Eerdmans, 2002). Naugle writes, "Narrative, not free floating, independent selves, is the most basic category. Stories are necessary to make sense of one's life and the lives of others" (301). God's story, I argue, is not a set of intellectual propositions to be proven by history and science, but as Rollo May writes, "a way of making sense in a senseless world . . . narrative patterns that give significance to our existence . . . [a] way of finding this meaning and significance." Rollo May, *The Cry for Myth* (New York: Norton, 1991, New York: Bantam Doubleday Dell, Delta, 1992), 15, quoted in Naugle, *Worldview*, 298. The primary structure of this story, as I have indicated, is creation, incarnation, re-creation. The ancient church fathers read the world through this framework. See St. Irenaeus of Lyons, *On the Apostolic Preaching*, trans. and intro. John Behr (Crestwood, NY: St. Vladimir's Seminary Press, 1997). In Behr's introduction he points out that "Irenaeus does not present Christianity in the way we have come to think of it, as a system of theological beliefs. . . . Irenaeus follows the example of the great speeches in Acts, recounting all the various deeds of God culminating in the exaltation of his crucified son, our Lord Jesus Christ, and the bestowal of His Holy Spirit, and the gift of a new heart of flesh" (7).

2. Wilbur, *A Brief History of Everything*. To read more on the story of God, I especially recommend David Bentley Hart, *The Beauty of the Infinite: The Aesthetics of Christian Truth* (Grand Rapids: Eerdmans, 2003). His understanding of the story is not only consistent with the ancient church, it is also a thoughtful interaction with the issues raised by postmodern thought.

3. The material of these pages summarizes an enormous amount of theological thinking. It sets forth a personal God who lives in community, who made creatures to be in community with himself, who, when they rebelled against him, became involved in history to restore union with himself. In this action we find the meaning of our existence: to be in union with God, fulfilling his purposes in creation. The most helpful book that expands this notion and interacts with postmodern thought is Stanley S. Grenz, *The Social God and the Relational Self: A Trinitarian Theology of the Imago Dei* (Louisville: Westminster John Knox, 2001).

4. The typological reading of Scripture is consistent with the recovery of an embodied experience of spirituality. It permeated the hermeneutic of the ancient church, but in modern times it has been replaced by the grammatical, historical, and theological method of interpreting the Bible. The current distancing from a more scientific approach to hermeneutics has resulted in the recovery of typological interpretation. See especially Christopher R. Seitz, *Figured Out: Typology and Providence in Christian Scripture* (Louisville: Westminster John Knox, 2001); and John David Dawson, *Christian Figural Reading and the Fashioning of Identity* (Berkeley: University of California Press, 2002). The return to a typological interpretation of Scripture is a return to the ancient way of reading the Bible. Consider, for example, the following instruction on typology given by the fourth-century father, St. Basil:

> Divine things are very often prefigured by means of shadowy types. Typology points out what is to be expected, indicating through imitation what is to happen before it happens. Adam was a type of Him who was to come; "the Rock was Christ"

typologically, and the water from the rock was a type of the living power of the Word, for He says, "If anyone thirst, let him come to Me and drink." The manna was a type of the living bread which came down from heaven, and the serpent suspended on the pole was a type of the saving passion accomplished on the cross, since the life of every one who looked at the serpent was preserved. Similarly, the history of Israel's exodus was recorded to typify those who would be saved through baptism. The firstborn of the Israelites were saved in the same way as the bodies of the baptized: through grace given to those who were marked with blood. The blood of the lamb is a type of the blood of Christ, and the firstborn is a type of the first-formed man. Since the first-formed man necessarily exists in each of us and will continue to be transmitted among us until the end, it is said that in Adam we all die, and the death reigned until the fulfillment of the law and the coming of Christ. The firstborn were preserved by God from the destroyer's touch to show that we who are made alive in Christ no longer die in Adam. At the time of the exodus, the sea and the cloud led the people from amazement to faith, but they also typified the grace which was yet to come. "Whoever is wise, let him understand these things": how the baptism in the sea which brought about Pharaoh's demise typifies the washing which makes the devil's tyranny depart. The sea killed the enemy in its waves, and baptism kills the enmity between us and God. The people emerged from the sea unharmed, and we come up from the water as alive from the dead, saved by the grace of Him Who has called us. The cloud is a shadow of the Spirit's gifts, for He cools the flames of our passions through the mortification of our bodies. Saint Basil the Great, *On the Holy Spirit* (Crestwood, NY: St. Vladimir's Seminary Press, 1980), 53.

5. Mitchell Stephens, *The Rise of the Image, the Fall of the Word* (New York: Oxford University Press, 1998), 22.

6. Ibid., xi.

7. For many Western Christians the teaching of the new creation is a new paradigm. I suggest you first read Bernhard W. Anderson, *From Creation to New Creation: Old Testament Perspectives* (Minneapolis: Fortress, 1994), to gain a perspective from Hebrew literature. For a compelling theological interpretation of the same theme, read Georges Florovsky, *Creation and Redemption*, vol. 3 of *Collected Works of George Florovsky* (Belmont, MA: Nordland, 1976).

8. John Calvin, *Calvin's Commentaries: The Epistle of Paul the Apostle to the Romans and to the Thessalonians*, trans. Ross Mackenzie (Grand Rapids: Eerdmans 1948), 172, 174.

9. The dualism between spirit and matter will always see the spirit in conflict with the material. But the Christian perspective is that the sin is a rebellion against God, not the substance of the material world. I have particularly appreciated the clarification of this in Gregory Boyd, *God at War: The Bible and Spiritual Conflict* (Downers Grove, IL: InterVarsity, 1997).

10. The teaching that Jesus Christ is the second Adam reversing the sin of the first Adam through his death and resurrection was the dominant interpretation of the atonement for the first thousand years of Christianity. This view did not reject the understanding that Jesus's death was a sacrifice for sins but, rather, affirmed that by his sacrifice he won a victory over the powers of evil and restored the fallen nature of humanity and recovered God's claim over the created order. I suggest two books: Vladimir Lossky, *In the Image and Likeness of God* (Crestwood, NY: St. Vladimir's Seminary Press, 1974), to understand the restoration of human nature, and Gustav Aulen, *Christus Victor* (Eugene, OR: Wipf and Stock, 2003), to grasp the cosmic implications of Christ's victory over the power of evil. I also suggest the work of Larry W. Hurtado, *Lord Jesus Christ: Devotion to Jesus in Earliest Christianity* (Grand Rapids: Eerdmans, 2003).

11. A study of the comparison of the Exodus event to the Christ event is an enormous study that covers nearly the entire content of both the Old Testament and New Testament materials. The ancient fathers frequently draw on the Exodus event/Christ event typology. I particularly recommend the following ancient writings: St. Basil the Great, *On the Holy Spirit*; St. Ephrem the Syrian, *Hymns on Paradise*, intro. and trans. Sebastian Brock (Crestwood, NY: St. Vladimir's Seminary Press, 1990); St. Irenaeus of Lyons, *On the Apostolic Preaching*; and St. Maximus the Confessor, *On the Cosmic Mystery of Jesus Christ*, trans. Paul M. Blowers and Robert Louis Wicken (Crestwood, NY: St. Vladimir's Seminary Press, 2003).

12. Irenaeus, *Against Heresies*, book 1, preface, par. 2, in Richardson, *Early Christian Fathers*, 359.

13. Ibid., book 5, chap. 19, 389–90.

14. Ibid., chap. 20, 390.

15. Ibid., chap. 21, 390–91.

16. Ibid., 390–91.

17. Ibid., chaps. 1–2, 386.

18. To read on the elements of story, I suggest William J. Bausch, *Storytelling: Imagination and Faith* (Mystic, IN: Twenty-Third Publications, 1984).

Chapter 7: My Story

1. Repentance is not a one-time act to be done with and then get on with life. Throughout the history of the church it has been recognized that repentance is a continuous turning away from our rebellion against God and the specific sins that express this development. Numerous books have been written on continuous repentance. For a broad overview, I especially suggest James Dallen, *The Reconciling Community: The Rite of Penance* (New York: Pueblo, 1986). For a specific study of the theological content of repentance, I suggest Kenan B. Osborne, OFM, *Reconciliation and Justification: The Sacrament and Its Theology* (New York: Paulist, 1990).

2. Cyril of Jerusalem, quoted in Edward Yarnold, SJ, *The Awe-Inspiring Rites of Initiation: Baptismal Homilies of the Fourth Century* (Slough, England: St. Paul Publications, 1971), 69–70.

3. Martin Luther, "A Mighty Fortress Is Our God," in *Hymns for the Living Church* (Carol Stream, IL: Hope Publishing, 1974).

4. Turning from one identity to another is developed from a New Testament perspective in *Made Not Born: New Perspectives on Christian Initiation and the Catechumenate, from the Murphy Center for Liturgical Research* (Notre Dame, IN: University of Notre Dame Press, 1976). Referring to the Pentecost event, the authors write, "Their baptism was, so to speak, their total immersion into the Christ event" (10).

5. There is an enormous amount of material on baptism in the New Testament and the early church. I especially recommend the research of Maxwell E. Johnson, *The Rites of Christian Initiation: Their Evolution and Interpretation* (Collegeville, MN: Liturgical Press, 1999), and Maxwell E. Johnson, *Images of Baptism: Forum Essays* (Chicago: Liturgy Training Publications in cooperation with the North American Forum on the Catechumenate, 2001). Patristic practices of baptism are especially found in Yarnold, *Awe-Inspiring Rites of Initiation*. The ancient process of initiation into God's story through baptism is interestingly presented in William Harmless, SJ, *Augustine and the Catechumenate* (Collegeville, MN: Liturgical Press, 1995). A very helpful book on baptism in the New Testament period alone is G. R. Beasley-Murray, *Baptism in the New Testament* (Grand Rapids: Eerdmans, 1962). Those who wish to read more from the pens of the early church fathers will also be interested in Edward Yarnold, SJ, *Cyril of Jerusalem* (New York: Routledge, 2000). Yarnold is "mostly concerned with the instruction of candidates for baptism, and focusing on the creed and

the liturgical rites" (introductory page). Also, if you are interested in more information on sermons to the prebaptized, read Thomas Macy Finn, trans. and commentator, *Quodvultdeus of Carthage: The Creedal Homilies* (New York: Newman Press, 2004). Quodvultdeus was a young colleague and deacon to Augustine. His sermons are brilliant presentations of the practical nature of the Apostles' Creed in the pagan setting of the Roman world.

6. St. John Chrysostom quoted in Yarnold, *Cyril of Jerusalem*, 168.

7. The word *Didache* means "teaching." It is a noncanonical document dated by some scholars as early as AD 50.

8. Ron Morrell, email message to author, Summer 2004.

9. *The Book of Common Prayer*, 306–7.

10. Irenaeus, *Against Heresies*, book 1, chap. 21, par. 4, in Richardson, *Early Church Fathers*, 366.

11. Ibid., par. 3.

12. Tertullian, *On Baptism*, quoted in Colman J. Berry, *Readings in Church History*, vol. 1, *From Pentecost to the Protestant Revolt* (Westminster, MA: Newman Press, 1960), 53–58.

13. Ibid.

14. Ibid.

15. Ibid.

16. Cited in Meyendorff, *St. Gregory Palamas and Orthodox Spirituality*, 31.

17. Jack Boyd, email message to author, Summer 2004.

18. For an excellent study on the forgiveness of sin, see L. Gregory Jones, *Embodying Forgiveness: A Theological Analysis* (Grand Rapids: Eerdmans, 1995).

19. The role of the Spirit in birthing the new Christian, the work of the Spirit in baptism, and the ongoing activity of the Spirit in the Christian life and in the collective life of the church permeates the New Testament writings and the patristic literature. Because there are numerous books on the work of the Spirit, it is difficult to reduce my recommendation to a few select works. For the Spirit in the New Testament, I suggest Gordon D. Fee, *God's Empowering Presence: The Holy Spirit in the Letters of Paul* (Peabody, MA: Hendrickson, 1994). For early church studies, particularly in relation to baptism, read Maxwell E. Johnson, ed., *Living Water, Sealing Spirit: Readings on Christian Initiation* (Collegeville, MN: Liturgical Press, 1995). Read also the classic patristic work, St. Basil the Great, *On the Holy Spirit*. Then, too, read *Baptism, Eucharist and Ministry: Faith and Order Paper No. 111* (Geneva: World Council of Churches, 1982). This document, also known as the *Lima Text*, is based on fifty years of ecumenical research, especially in the early church. Regarding the Holy Spirit, the text states: "The Holy Spirit is at work in the lives of people before, in and after their baptism. It is the same Spirit who revealed Jesus as the Son (Mark 1:10–11) and who empowered and united the disciples at Pentecost (Acts 2). God bestows upon all baptized persons the anointing and the promise of the Holy Spirit, marks them with a seal and implants in their hearts the first installment of their inheritance as sons and daughters of God. The Holy Spirit nurtures the life of faith in their hearts until the final deliverance when they will enter into its full possession, to the praise of the glory of God (2 Cor. 1:21–22; Eph. 1:13–14)." *Baptism, Eucharist and Ministry*, 2.

20. This ancient prayer is found in Max Thurian and Geoffrey Wainwright, *Baptism and Eucharist: Ecumenical Convergence in Celebration* (Grand Rapids: Eerdmans, 1983), 12.

Chapter 8: His Life in Mine

1. Peter E. Fink, SJ, *Worship: Praying the Sacraments* (Washington, DC: Pastoral Press, 1991), 152. I have been reluctant to use the analogy of marriage to the union we have with God. My resistance to this analogy has been the overt romantic and even sexual innuendo of medieval mystical writings and the sentimental romanticism of many of today's songs and choruses. However, romantic feelings aside, the image of marriage is the best analogy

for the mystical union we have with God. This analogy is set forth in the Song of Songs. Jewish exegetes see the Song as expressing the love of God for Israel. Christians read it as an allegory of the love of God for the church and for its individual members. Early Christians viewed the Song, along with the Psalms and the Gospels, as the writings that most clearly set forth God's relationship to the believer. A book that collects both ancient and medieval commentary on the Song of Songs is Richard A. Norris Jr., ed., *The Song of Songs: Interpreted by Early Christian and Medieval Commentators* (Grand Rapids: Eerdmans, 2003). A reading of this work shows that the ancient fathers did not interpret the Song in a subjective romantic way but interpreted the Song in a typological manner, referring to the word of God and the sacraments, whereas the medieval mystics interpreted the Song in an exuberant personal and romantic way. The opening phrase, "Let him kiss me with the kisses of his mouth" (Song of Songs 1:2), is interpreted by Origen, an ancient father, in the following way: "Pour into my mouth the words of his mouth, that I may hear him speaking . . . for the kisses of Christ are those that he bestowed on the Church when in his advent he himself, present in the flesh, spoke to it words of faith and of love and of peace, just as, when sent ahead of time to the bride, Isaiah promised by saying that 'the Lord himself shall save them' (Isa. 33:22), and not a representative or an angel" (ibid., 21). Compare this typological interpretation to the romantic personalism of the eleventh-century mystic, Rupert of Deutz, to the same passage: "What means this cry, so loud, so startling? An overflowing joy, O blessed Virgin, a powerful love, a rush of delight wholly seized you, wholly captured you. It intoxicated you deep within" (ibid., 24–25). Origen's interpretation focuses on God. Rupert focuses on me and my experience with God. The shift is profound. Other early church fathers like St. Basil interpret the marriage passages in the Song as types of baptism and the intimacy passages as types of the Eucharist. In this sense baptism is union with God, whereas the Eucharist is the divine kiss. The marriage analogy can be used effectively without pursuit of a sexually explicit relationship with God.

2. "Spirituality in America" (cover), *Newsweek*, September 5, 2005.

3. Lewis Bayly, *The Practice of Piety* (1611; repr., Morgan, PA: Soli Deo Gloria Publications, 1995), 1.

4. Peterson, *Christ Plays in Ten Thousand Places*, 34.

5. Lakoff and Johnson, *Philosophy in the Flesh*, 563.

6. George Knight, *Christ the Center* (Grand Rapids: Eerdmans, 1999), 3.

7. Lakoff and Johnson, *Philosophy in the Flesh*, 565–66 (italics mine).

8. Ibid.

9. Ibid., 567.

10. Fink, *Worship*, 191–92. This includes a quotation from Johannes Metz, *Poverty of Spirit*, trans. John Drury (Glen Rock, NJ: Newman Press, 1968).

11. Kenneth Leech, *Experiencing God: Theology as Spirituality* (San Francisco: Harper & Row, 1985), 262.

12. Hans Urs von Balthasar, *Prayer* (San Francisco: Ignatius, 1986), 191, quoted in Leech, *Experiencing God*, 264.

13. Sheldrake, *Spirituality and Theology*, 5.

14. Richard W. Flory and Donald E. Miller, "Expressive Communalism: The Embodied Spirituality of the Post-boomer Generation," *Congregations*, Fall 2004, 31–35.

15. Ibid., 32–33.

16. Ibid., 33.

17. *The Book of Common Prayer*, 261.

18. This quote originates in Gregory of Nyssa, *The Life of Moses*, and is found in *From Glory to Glory: Texts from Gregory of Nyssa's Mystical Writings*, selected and with an intro. by Jean Daniélou; trans. and ed. Herbert Musurillo (New York: Scribner, 1961), 82. This collection provides a very helpful introduction to the theology of Gregory of Nyssa and

illustrates how the spiritual life is situated in theological reflection in the writings of the ancient fathers. The spiritual life described by many of the mystics of the medieval period shifts toward the contemplation of the journey into self more than the journey into God.

19. *Didache*, 1; cited in Richardson, *Early Christian Fathers*, 171, 173.

20. Ibid., 173–74.

21. Thurian and Wainwright, *Baptism and Eucharist*, 9.

22. Harmless, *Augustine and the Catechumenate*, 295.

23. J. J. Von Allmen, *Vocabulary of the Bible* (London: Lutterworth, 1958), 283, quoted in Meyendorff, *St. Gregory Palamas and Orthodox Spirituality*, 14.

24. Meyendorff, *St. Gregory Palamas and Orthodox Spirituality*, 14.

25. Lorenzo Scupoli, *Unseen Warfare: The Spiritual Combat and Path to Paradise of Lorenzo Scupoli*, ed. Nicodemus of the Holy Mountain and revised by Theophan the Recluse, trans. E. Kadloubovsky and G. E. H. Palmer (Crestwood, NY: St. Vladimir's Seminary Press, 1995), quoted from the back cover, 77.

26. Ibid., 70.

27. Ibid., 112.

28. Ibid., 110.

29. Ibid., 90.

30. Ibid., 94.

31. Ibid., 95.

32. Ibid., 96.

33. Ibid., 96–97.

34. Ibid., 140.

35. Ibid.

36. Ibid., 146–47.

37. Ibid., 147, 149–50.

38. Ibid., 96.

39. Ibid., 113.

40. Ibid., 176.

41. Ibid., 177.

42. Ibid.

43. Ibid., 181–82, 184.

44. Ibid., 190.

45. Simon Tugwell, O. P., *Ways of Imperfection: An Exploration of Christian Spirituality* (Springfield, IL: Templegate Publishers, 1985), vii.

46. Ibid., 1.

47. Ibid.

48. Ibid., 219.

49. Ibid., 220 (italics mine).

50. Several popular works that see the spiritual life as being what we are called to be include Philip D. Kenneson, *Life on the Vine: Cultivating the Fruit of the Spirit in Christian Community* (Downers Grove, IL: InterVarsity, 1999); Eugene H. Peterson, *A Long Obedience in the Same Direction: Discipleship in an Instant Society* (Downers Grove, IL: InterVarsity, 1980); and Samuel M. Powell and Michael E. Lodahl, eds., *Embodied Holiness: Toward a Corporate Theology of Spiritual Growth* (Downers Grove, IL: InterVarsity, 1999).

51. *The Book of Common Prayer*, 137.

Chapter 9: My Life in His

1. There are numerous studies on the Benedictine order and its rule. The classical study of the order is Edward Cuthbert Butler, *Benedictine Monasticism*, 2nd ed. (1923, repr., Cambridge: Cambridge University Press, 1961). For a detailed study of the rule itself, see

Dom David Parry, OSB, *Households of God* (London: Darton, Longman & Todd, 1980). One of the best short introductions to the spirituality of the rule is Adalbert de Vogue, *The Rule of Saint Benedict: A Doctrinal and Spiritual Commentary* (Kalamazoo, MI: Cistercian Publications, 1983). To see how the Benedictine rule may be applied to all Christians, see Maria Boulding, *A Touch of God: Eight Monastic Journeys* (London: SPCK, 1982). See also Esther de Waal, *Seeking God: The Way of St. Benedict* (Collegeville, MN: Liturgical Press, 1984). There are many editions of the rule itself without commentary, except for the introduction. I have drawn from Anthony C. Meisel and M. L. del Mastro, trans. and intro., *The Rule of St. Benedict* (New York: Doubleday, 1975).

2. My summary of the three vows, three disciplines, and three ways to encounter God draws from the work of de Waal, *Seeking God*.

3. The text of the International Consultation on Discipleship is found in Robert Webber, *Ancient-Future Evangelism: Making Your Church a Faith-Forming Community* (Grand Rapids: Baker, 2003), appendix 4, 181–84.

4. Meisel and del Mastro, *The Rule of St. Benedict*, 52–54.

5. De Waal, *Seeking God*, 34.

6. Meisel and del Mastro, *The Rule of St. Benedict*, 45.

7. De Waal, *Seeking God*, 45.

8. Meisel and del Mastro, *The Rule of St. Benedict*, 55.

9. Ibid., 55, 57–58.

10. Ibid., 58–61.

11. Richard Foster, *The Celebration of Discipline* (San Francisco: HarperSanFrancisco, 1978).

12. Maxwell E. Johnson has compiled and edited a new edition of the daily office and other prayers in the Benedictine tradition. This over 2,000-page volume of prayers is "intended for those with some form of association with or attraction to Benedictine monasticism." Maxwell Johnson, *Benedictine Daily Prayer: A Short Breviary* (Collegeville, MN: Liturgical Press, 2005), vi.

13. Meisel and del Mastro, *The Rule of St. Benedict*, 66.

14. The Daily Office I refer to is found in *The Book of Common Prayer*. The morning prayer is found on p. 137, the noon prayer, p. 138, the early evening prayer, p. 139, and prayer at the close of the day, p. 140. Memorize these prayers, which are short, and you will be able to speak them in your heart during the day at the appropriate times wherever you are.

15. De Waal, *Seeking God*, 146–47.

16. Thelma Hall, *Too Deep for Words: Rediscovering Lectio Divina* (New York: Paulist, 1988).

17. Thomas Merton, *Seeds*, ed. Robert Inchausti (Boston: Shambhala, 2002).

18. The preceding, which summarizes the material of Hall, *Too Deep for Words*, is taken from Robert Webber, *Walk in the Spirit* (Wheaton: IWS Resources, 2001), introduction.

19. Meisel and del Mastro, *The Rule of St. Benedict*, 86.

20. Brother Lawrence quoted in de Waal, *Seeking God*, 115.

21. Meisel and del Mastro, *The Rule of St. Benedict*, 77.

22. Ibid., 75.

23. De Waal, *Seeking God*, 118.

24. Meisel and del Mastro, *The Rule of St. Benedict*, 26.

25. Ibid., 70.

26. Ibid., 50.

Chapter 10: Life Together

1. Tom Cheatham, email message to author, Spring 2004.

2. Wolfe, *Transformation of American Religion*, 36.

3. Wayne Stacey, "A Pastor's Vision Statement for Southside Baptist Church," unpublished paper.

4. One of the most important new books on the church as situated in the story of God is the recent release of Dietrich Bonhoeffer's doctoral thesis, written when Bonhoeffer was twenty-one years old. *Sanctorum Communio* (Minneapolis: Fortress, 1998) is volume 1 of the Dietrich Bonhoeffer works. In this extraordinary theological dissertation Bonhoeffer writes: "The cord between God and human beings that was cut by the first Adam is tied anew by God, by revealing God's own love in Christ, by no longer approaching us in demand and summons, purely as You, but instead by *giving God's own self as an I, opening God's own heart. The church is founded on the revelation of God's heart*," 145. The other book on the church by Bonhoeffer that I recommend is Dietrich Bonhoeffer, *Life Together* (San Francisco: HarperSanFrancisco, 1954). Other valuable discussion on the church that situates God's story in the church includes Stanley Hauerwas and William H. Willimon, *Resident Aliens: A Provocative Christian Assessment of Culture and Ministry for People Who Know That Something Is Wrong* (Nashville: Abingdon, 1989).

5. George A. Lindbeck, *The Church in a Postliberal Age*, ed. James J. Buckley (Grand Rapids: Eerdmans, 2003), 7.

6. Kilian McDonnell, OSB, *The Baptism of Jesus in the Jordan: The Trinitarian and Cosmic Order of Salvation* (Collegeville, MN: Liturgical Press, 1996), 103.

7. St. Gregory the Great quoted in ibid., 102.

8. Ibid., 103.

9. St. Cyprian, *The Unity of the Catholic Church*, quoted in Jurgens, *Faith of the Early Fathers*, vol. 1, 221.

10. St. Augustine, *Psalms*, quoted in Jurgens, *Faith of the Early Fathers*, vol. 3, 19.

11. See The Rutba House ed. *School(s) for Conversion: 12 Marks of a New Monasticism* (Eugene, OR: Cascade Books, 2005).

12. David Hill, email message to author, Spring 2004.

13. Craig Gilbert, email message to author, Spring 2004.

14. See the "Eastbourne Consultation on Discipleship" in Webber, *Ancient-Future Evangelism*, appendix I, 181–84.

15. See Robert Webber, *Journey to Jesus: The Worship, Evangelism, and Nurture Mission of the Church* (Nashville: Abingdon, 2001), and Webber, *Ancient-Future Evangelism*.

16. Stacey, "A Pastor's Vision Statement."

17. Ed Rommen, "Reflections on Becoming Orthodox," *Occasional Bulletin of the Evangelical Missiological Society* (Spring 1999), http://missiolog.org/EMS/bulletins/rommen.htm (accessed Spring 2004). The author of this article has since become a priest in the Orthodox Church in America.

18. Lasch, *Culture of Narcissism*, 31.

19. Lester Ruth, "Lex Amandi; Lex Orandi: The Trinity in the Most Used Contemporary Christian Worship Songs," paper presented at the conference on "The Place of Christ in Liturgical Prayer: Christology, Trinity and Liturgical Theology at Yale Institute of Sacred Music," February 27, 2005, 3, 7, 9. To be published in the collection of papers from the conference.

20. Ibid., 11.

21. See Robert Webber, *Worship Old and New*, 2nd ed. (Grand Rapids: Zondervan, 1994); Robert Webber, *Worship Is a Verb*, 2nd ed. (Peabody: Hendrickson, 1992); Robert Webber, *Planning Blended Worship* (Nashville: Abingdon, 1998). See also Gordon W. Lathrop, *Holy People: A Liturgical Ecclesiology* (Minneapolis: Augsburg, 1999), and Aidan Kavanagh, *On Liturgical Theology* (New York: Pueblo, 1981).

22. See Ellen F. Davis and Richard B. Hays, eds., *The Art of Reading Scripture* (Grand Rapids: Eerdmans, 2003), and Stephen E. Fowl and L. Gregory Jones, *Reading in Community* (Eugene, OR: Wipf and Stock, 1998).

23. See Alexander Schmemann, *For the Life of the World* (Crestwood, NY: St. Vladimir's Seminary Press, 1997).

24. Augustine, quoted in Balthasar, *Prayer*, 133.

25. See Alexander Schmemann, *Eucharist* (Crestwood, NY: St. Vladimir's Seminary Press, 1987).

Postscript

1. Richard Crabtree, personal message recorded on CD and sent to the author, December 15, 2005.

SELECTED BIBLIOGRAPHY

Allen, Joseph J. *Inner Way: Toward a Rebirth of Eastern Christian Spiritual Direction*. Grand Rapids: Eerdmans, 1994.

Ambrose, Isaac. *The Christian Warrior: Wrestling with Sin, Satan, the World and the Flesh*. Morgan, PA: Soli Deo Gloria Publications, 1997.

Appleton, George, ed. *The Oxford Book of Prayer*. New York: Oxford University Press, 1985.

Arseniev, Nicholas. *Russian Piety*. Translated by Asheleigh Moorhouse. Clayton, WI: American Orthodox Press, 1964.

Bakke, Jeannette. *Holy Invitations: Exploring Spiritual Direction*. Grand Rapids: Baker, 2000.

Balentine, Samuel E. *Prayer in the Hebrew Bible: The Drama of Divine-Human Dialogue*. Minneapolis: Fortress, 1993.

Ballester, Mariano. *Introduction to Profound Prayer*. Collegeville, MN: Liturgical Press, 1997.

Balthasar, Hans Urs von. *Prayer*. San Francisco: Ignatius Press, 1986.

———, ed. *The Scandal of the Incarnation: Irenaeus against the Heresies*. San Francisco: Ignatius Press, 1990.

———. *Truth Is Symphonic: Aspects of Christian Pluralism*. San Francisco: Ignatius Press, 1987.

Barron, Robert. *The Strangest Way: Walking the Christian Path*. Maryknoll, NY: Orbis Books, 2002.

Barry, William A., and William J. Connolly. *The Practice of Spiritual Direction*. San Francisco: HarperSanFrancisco, 1986.

Basil the Great, Saint. *On the Holy Spirit*. Crestwood, NY: St. Vladimir's Seminary Press, 1980.

———. *On the Human Condition*. Crestwood, NY: St. Vladimir's Seminary Press, 2005.

Bayly, Lewis. *The Practice of Piety: A Puritan Devotional Manual*. Morgan, PA: Soli Deo Gloria Publications, 1995.

Beasley-Topliffe, Keith. *Surrendering to God: Living the Covenant Prayer*. Brewster, MA: Paraclete Press, 2001.

Bernstein, Eleanor, ed. *Liturgy and Spirituality in Context: Perspectives on Prayer and Culture*. Collegeville, MN: Liturgical Press, 1990.

Bonaventura, Saint. *The Mind's Road to God*. Translated with an introduction by George Boas. Indianapolis: Bobbs-Merrill, 1977.

Bouyer, Louis. *Liturgy Piety*. Notre Dame, IN: University of Notre Dame Press, 1954.

Bowe, Barbara E. *Biblical Foundations of Spirituality: Touching a Finger to the Flame*. Lanham, MD: Rowman and Littlefield, 2003.

Braaten, Carl E., and Robert W. Jenson, eds. *Union with Christ: The New Finnish Interpretation of Luther*. Grand Rapids: Eerdmans, 1998.

Bradshaw, Paul F. *Daily Prayer in the Early Church*. New York: Oxford University Press, 1982.

———. *Early Christian Worship: A Basic Introduction to Ideas and Practices*. Collegeville, MN: Liturgical Press, 1996.

Braso, Gabriel M., OSB, ed. *Liturgy and Spirituality*. Collegeville, MN: Liturgical Press, 1971.

Brianchaninov, Bishop Ignatius. *On the Prayer of Jesus*. Liberty, TN: Saint John of Kronstadt Press, 1995.

Bunge, Gabriel, OSB. *Earthen Vessels: The Practice of Personal Prayer According to the Patristic Tradition*. San Francisco: Ignatius Press, 2002.

Burion-Christie, Burton. *The Word in the Desert: Scripture and the Quest for Holiness in Early Christian Monasticism*. New York: Oxford University Press, 1993.

Butler, Dom Cuthbert. *Western Mysticism: Augustine, Gregory and Bernard on Contemplation and the Contemplative Life*. Mineola, NY: Dover, 2003.

Byrne, Lavinia. *Tradition of Spiritual Guidance*. Collegeville, MN: Liturgical Press, 1990.

Callen, Barry L. *Authentic Spirituality*. Grand Rapids: Baker, 2001.

Capps, Walter Holden, and Wendy M. Wright, eds. *Silent Fire: An Invitation to Western Mysticism*. New York: Harper & Row, 1978.

Carmichael, Alexander. *Carmina Gadelica: Hymns and Incantations: Collected in the Highlands and Islands of Scotland in the Last Century*. Edinburgh, Scotland: Floris Books, 1992.

Chambers, Oswald. *Christian Disciplines*. Grand Rapids: Discovery House Publishers, 1995.

Chariton, Igumen of Valamo, compiler. *The Art of Prayer: An Orthodox Anthology*. Translated by E. Kadloubovsky and E. M. Palmer. Edited with an introduction by Timothy Ware. London: Faber & Faber, 1997.

Chrysostom, St. John. *Baptismal Instructions*. Translated and annotated by Paul W. Harkins. New York: Paulist, 1963.

Church, F. Forrester, and Terrence J. Mulry. *The Macmillan Book of Earliest Christian Prayers*. New York: Macmillan, 1988.

Clapp, Rodney. *Tortured Wonders: Christian Spirituality for People, Not Angels*. Grand Rapids: Brazos, 2004.

Cloninger, Claire. *A Place Called Simplicity: The Quiet Beauty of Simple Living*. Eugene, OR: Harvest House, 1993.

Collins, Kenneth J. *Exploring Christian Spirituality: An Ecumenical Reader*. Grand Rapids: Baker, 2000.

Collins, Kenneth J., and John H. Tyson, eds., *Conversion in the Wesleyan Tradition*. Nashville: Abingdon, 2001.

Cunningham, Lawrence S., and Keith J. Egan. *Christian Spirituality: Themes from the Tradition*. New York: Paulist, 1996.

Cutsinger, James S., ed. *Not of This World: A Treasury of Christian Mysticism*. Bloomington, IN: World Wisdom, 2003.

Dallen, James. *The Reconciling Community: The Rite of Penance*. New York: Pueblo, 1986.

Danielou, Jean, and Herbert Musurillo, eds. *From Glory to Glory: Texts from Gregory of Nyssa's Mystical Writings*. New York: Charles Scribner's Sons, 1961.

Davies, J. G. *Daily Life of Early Christians*. New York: Greenwood Press, 1969.

Davies, Oliver, ed. *Celtic Spirituality*. New York: Paulist, 1999.

Davis, Ellen F., and Richard B. Hays, eds. *The Art of Reading Scripture*. Grand Rapids: Eerdmans, 2003.

Dawson, John David. *Christian Figural Reading and the Fashioning of Identity*. Berkeley: University of California Press, 2002.

De Caussade, Jean-Pierre. *Self Abandonment to Divine Providence: The Sacrament of the Present Moment*. Translated by Kitty Muggeridge. San Francisco: HarperSanFrancisco, 1989.

De Waal, Esther. *A Life-Giving Way: A Commentary on the Rule of St. Benedict*. Collegeville, MN: Liturgical Press, 1995.

———. *Seeking God: The Way of St. Benedict*. Collegeville, MN: Liturgical Press, 1984.

Dowell, Samuel M., and Michael E. Lodahl. *Embodied Holiness: Toward a Corporate Theology of Spiritual Growth*. Downers Grove, IL: InterVarsity, 1999.

Downey, Michael. *Understanding Christian Spirituality*. New York: Paulist, 1997.

Driskill, Joseph D. *Protestant Spiritual Exercises: Theology, History, and Practice*. Harrisburg, PA: Morehouse, 1999.

D'Souza, Tony. *The Way of Jesus: A Contemporary Edition of a Spiritual Classic*. Grand Rapids: Eerdmans, 2004.

Duffy, Eamon. *The Stripping of the Altars: Traditional Religion in England 1400–1580*. New Haven: Yale University Press, 1992.

Dupré, Louis, and Don E. Saliers, eds., in collaboration with John Meyendorff. *Christian Spirituality III: Post-Reformation and Modern*. Vol. 6., *World Spirituality*. New York: Crossroad, 1989.

Endean, Philip. *Karl Rahner and Ignatian Spirituality*. New York: Oxford University Press, 2001.

Ephrem the Syrian, Saint. *Hymns on Paradise*. Introduction and translation by Sebastian Brock. Crestwood, NY: St. Vladimir's Seminary Press, 1990.

Evdokimov, Paul. *Ages of the Spiritual Life*. Original translation by Sister Gertrude, SD. Revised translation by Michael Plekon and Alexis Vinogradov. Crestwood, NY: St. Vladimir's Seminary Press, 1998.

Fedotov, Georgii P. *The Russian Religious Mind I: Kievan Christianity the Tenth to the Thirteenth Centuries*. Belmont, MA: Nordland, 1975.

———. *The Russian Religious Mind II: The Middle Ages, the Thirteenth to the Fifteenth Centuries*. Belmont, MA: Nordland, 1975.

———, ed. *A Treasury of Russian Spirituality*. Belmont, MA: Nordland, 1975.

Florovsky, Georges. *Creation and Redemption*. Vol. 3, *Collected Works of George Florovsky*. Belmont, MA: Nordland, 1976.

Forrest, Jim. *Praying with Icons*. Maryknoll, NY: Orbis Books, 2003.

Forsyth, P. T. *The Soul of Prayer*. 1916. Reprint, Vancouver: Regent College Publishing, 2002.

Foster, Richard J. *Prayer: Finding the Heart's True Home*. San Francisco: HarperSanFrancisco, 1992.

———. *Streams of Living Water: Celebrating the Great Traditions of Christian Faith*. San Francisco: HarperSanFrancisco, 1998.

Foster, Richard J., and Emilie Griffin, eds. *Spiritual Classics: Selected Readings for Individuals and Groups on the Twelve Spiritual Disciplines: A Renovare Resource for Spiritual Renewal*. San Francisco: HarperSanFrancisco, 2000.

Fowl, Stephen E., and L. Gregory Jones. *Reading in Communion: Scripture and Ethics in Christian Life*. Eugene, OR: Wipf and Stock, 1998.

French, R. M., translator. *The Way of a Pilgrim: And the Pilgrim Continues His Way*. New York: Crossroad, 1965.

Gadamer, Hans-Georg. *The Relevance of the Beautiful and Other Essays*. Cambridge, England: Cambridge University Press, 1987.

Gasquet, F. A., compiler. *Ancestral Prayers*. Springfield, IL: Templegate Publishers, 1996.

Glucklich, Ariel. *Sacred Pain: Hurting the Body for the Sake of the Soul*. New York: Oxford University Press, 2001.

Goldberg, Michael. *Theology and Narrative: A Critical Introduction*. Philadelphia: Trinity Press International, 1991.

Green, Joel B., and Michael Pasquarello III, eds. *Narrative Reading, Narrative Preaching: Reuniting New Testament Interpretaion and Proclamation*. Grand Rapids: Baker, 2003.

Griffin, Emilie. *Wonderful and Dark Is This Road: Discovering the Mystic Path.* Brewster, MA: Paraclete Press, 2004.

Groeschel, Benedict J. *Praying to Our Lord Jesus Christ: Prayers and Meditations through the Centuries.* San Francisco: Ignatius Press, 2004.

Hägglund, Bengt. *History of Theology.* Translated by Gene J. Lund. 1968. Reprint, St. Louis: Concordia, 1978.

Hall, Thelma. *Too Deep for Words: Rediscovering Lectio Divina.* New York: Paulist, 1988.

Harkness, Georgia. *Mysticism: Its Meaning and Message.* Nashville: Abingdon, 1973.

Hart, David Bentley. *The Beauty of the Infinite: The Aesthetics of Christian Truth.* Grand Rapids: Eerdmans, 2003.

Hauerwas, Stanley. *A Community of Character: Toward a Constructive Christian Social Ethic.* Notre Dame, IN: University of Notre Dame Press, 1981.

Hauerwas, Stanley, and Charles Pinches. *Christians among the Virtues: Theological Conversations with Ancient and Modern Ethics.* Notre Dame, IN: University of Notre Dame Press, 1977.

Hauerwas, Stanley, and Samuel Wells, eds. *The Blackwell Companion to Christian Ethics.* Malden, MA: Blackwell Publishing, 2004.

Herrick, James A. *The Making of the New Spirituality: The Eclipse of the Western Religious Tradition.* Downers Grove, IL: InterVarsity, 2003.

Hippolytus. *On the Apostolic Tradition.* An English version with introduction and commentary by Alistair Steward-Sykes. Crestwood, NY: St. Vladimir's Seminary Press, 2001.

Houston, James. *The Mentored Life: From Individualism to Personhood.* Colorado Springs: NavPress, 2002.

Irenaeus of Lyons, Saint. *On the Apostolic Preaching.* Translation and introduction by John Behr. Crestwood, NY: St. Vladimir's Seminary Press, 1997.

Johnson, Maxwell E., compiler and editor. *Benedictine Daily Prayer: A Short Breviary.* Collegeville, MN: Liturgical Press, 2005.

Jones, Cheslyn, Geoffrey Wainwright, and Edward Yarnold, SJ, eds. *The Study of Liturgy.* New York: Oxford University Press, 1978.

———, eds. *The Study of Spirituality.* New York: Oxford University Press, 1986.

Jurgens, William A. *The Faith of the Early Fathers.* 3 Vols. Collegeville, MN: Liturgical Press, 1979.

Kärkkäinen, Veli-Matti. *One with God: Salvation as Deification and Justification.* Collegeville, MN: Liturgical Press, 2004.

Kelly, J. N. D. *The Early Christian Creeds.* New York: David McKay Company, 1972.

Kenneson, Philip D. *Life on the Vine: Cultivating the Fruit of the Spirit in Christian Communion.* Downers Grove, IL: InterVarsity, 1999.

Kesich, Veselin. *The Passion of Christ*. Crestwood, NY: St. Vladimir's Seminary Press, 2004.

Kinnaman, Gary. *Experiencing the Power of the Cross*. Minneapolis: Bethany House, 2005.

Kopciowski, Elias. *Praying with the Jewish Tradition*. Grand Rapids: Eerdmans, 1997.

La Cugna, Catherine Mowry. *God for Us: The Trinity and Christian Life*. San Francisco: HarperSanFrancisco, 1991.

Lakoff, George, and Mark Johnson. *Philosophy in the Flesh: The Embodied Mind and Its Challenge to Western Thought*. New York: Basic Books, 1999.

Leech, Kenneth. *Experiencing God: Theology as Spirituality*. San Francisco: Harper & Row, 1985.

Lindbeck, George A. *The Church in a Postliberal Age*. Edited by James J. Buckley. Grand Rapids: Eerdmans, 2003.

———. *The Nature of Doctrine: Religion and Theology in a Postliberal Age*. Philadelphia: Westminster, 1984.

Lodahl, Michael. *The Story of God: Wesleyan Theology and Biblical Narrative*. Kansas City: Beacon Hill Press, 1994.

Longnecker, Richard N. *Into God's Presence: Prayer in the New Testament*. Grand Rapids: Eerdmans, 2001.

———, ed. *Community Formation: In the Early Church and in the Church Today*. Peabody, MA: Hendrickson, 2002.

Lossky, Vladimir. *The Mystical Theology of the Eastern Church*. Cambridge, England: James Clark, 1957.

———. *The Vision of God*. Bedfordshire, England: Faith Press, 1973.

Louth, Andrew, *The Origins of the Christian Mystical Tradition: From Plato to Denys*. Oxford, England: Clarendon, 1981.

Lovelace, Richard F. *Dynamics of the Spiritual Life: An Evangelical Theology of Renewal*. Downers Grove, IL: InterVarsity, 1979.

Luckman, Harriet A., and Linda Kulzer. *Purity of Heart: In Early Ascetic and Monastic Literature*. Collegeville, MN: Liturgical Press, 1999.

Macaulay, Ronald, and Jerram Barrs. *Being Human: The Nature of Spiritual Experience*. Downers Grove, IL: InterVarsity, 1978.

Madigan, Shawn. *Spirituality Rooted in Liturgy*. Washington, DC: Pastoral Press, 1988.

Maloney, George A., SJ. *The Breath of the Mystic*. Denville, NY: Dimension Books, 1974.

———. *Prayer of the Heart*. Notre Dame, IN: Ave Maria Press, 1981.

Mangalwadi, Vishal, and Ruth Mangalwadi. *The Legacy of William Carey: A Model for the Transformation of Culture*. 1993. Reprint, Wheaton: Crossway, 1999.

Manschreck, Clyde, ed. *A History of Christianity: Readings in the History of the Church*. Vol. 2, *The Church from the Reformation to the Present*. Englewood Cliffs, NJ: Prentice-Hall, 1964. Reprinted. Grand Rapids: Baker, 1981.

Markides, Kyriacos C. *The Mountain of Silence: A Search for Orthodox Spirituality*. New York: Doubleday, 2001.

Matthew the Poor. *Orthodox Prayer Life: The Interior Way*. Crestwood, NY: St. Vladimir's Seminary Press, 2003.

Matthewes-Green, Frederica. *The Illumined Heart: The Ancient Christian Path of Transformation*. Brewster, MA: Paraclete Press, 2001.

———. *The Open Door: Entering the Sanctuary of Icons and Prayer*. Brewster, MA: Paraclete Press, 2003.

Maximus the Confessor, Saint. *On the Cosmic Mystery of Jesus Christ*. Translated by Paul M. Blowers and Robert Louis Wicken. Crestwood, NY: St. Vladimir's Seminary Press, 2003.

McDonnell, Kilian, OSB. *The Baptism of Jesus in the Jordan: The Trinitarian and Cosmic Order of Salvation*. Collegeville, MN: Liturgical Press, 1996.

McGinn, Bernard. *The Flowering of Mysticism: Men and Women in the New Mysticism 1200–1350*. Vol. 3, *The Presence of God: A History of Western Christian Mysticism*. New York: Crossroad, 1998.

———. *The Foundations of Mysticism: Origins to the Fifth Century*. Vol. 1, *The Presence of God: A History of Western Christian Mysticism*. New York: Crossroad, 1991.

———. *The Growth of Mysticism: Gregory the Great through the 12th Century*. Vol. 2, *The Presence of God: A History of Western Christian Mysticism*. New York: Crossroad, 1996.

McGinn, Bernard, and John Meyendorff, eds. *Christian Spirituality I: Origins to the Twelfth Century*. Vol. 16, *World Spirituality*. New York: Crossroad, 1986.

McGrath, Alister. *Christian Spirituality: An Introduction*. Malden, MA: Blackwell, 1999.

McGuckin, John Anthony, ed. *The Book of Mystical Chapters: Meditations on the Soul's Ascent from the Desert Fathers and Other Early Christian Contemplatives*. Boston: Shambhala, 2003.

McIntosh, Mark A. *Mystical Theology: The Integrity of Spirituality and Theology*. Malden, MA: Blackwell, 1998.

Meisel, Anthony C., and M. L. del Mastro, translators with introduction and notes. *The Rule of St. Benedict*. New York: Image Books, 1975.

Melito of Sardis. *On Pascha*. Crestwood, NY: St. Vladimir's Seminary Press, 2001.

Meyendorff, John. *Byzantine Theology: Historical Trends and Doctrinal Themes*. New York: Fordham University Press, 1974.

———. *St. Gregory Palamas and Orthodox Spirituality*. Crestwood, NY: St. Vladimir's Seminary Press, 1974.

Modras, Ronald. *Ignatian Humanism: A Dynamic Spirituality for the 21st Century*. Chicago: Loyola Press, 2004.

Monk of the Eastern Church, A. *Orthodox Spirituality: An Outline of the Orthodox Ascetical and Mystical Tradition*. Crestwood, NY: St. Vladimir's Seminary Press, 1996.

Moreau, Scott. *Essentials of Spiritual Warfare: Equipped to Win the Battle*. Wheaton: Harold Shaw, 1997.

Moreland, J. P., and Scott B. Rae. *Body and Soul: Human Nature and the Crisis in Ethics*. Downers Grove, IL: InterVarsity, 2000.

Mottola, Anthony. *The Spiritual Exercises of St. Ignatius*. New York: Image Books, 1964.

Moutsoulas, Elias D. *The Incarnation of the Word and the Theosis of Man: According to the Teaching of Gregory of Nyssa*. Translated from the Greek by Re. Vonstantine J. Andrews, STM. Athens, Greece: Eptalofos S.A., 2000. eptalofos@ath.forthnet.gr.

Mulloy, Elizabeth. *Divine Love Song: Discover God's Passion for You in the Song of Solomon*. Grand Rapids: Chosen, 2003.

Murphy, Francis X. *The Christian Way of Life: Message of the Fathers of the Church*. Vol. 18, *Message of the Fathers of the Church*. Wilmington, DE: M. Glazier, 1986.

Neamr, Alan, translator of work written by a monk. *The Heritage Within: Spirituality in the Desert*. Kalamazoo, MI: Cistercian Publications, 1977, 1999.

Nemeck, Francis Kelly, and Marie Theresa Coombs. *The Way of Spiritual Direction*. Collegeville, MN: Liturgical Press, 1985.

Newport, John P. *The New Age Movement and the Biblical Worldview*. Grand Rapids: Eerdmans, 1998.

Nicodemus of the Holy Mountain, ed. *Unseen Warfare: The Spiritual Combat and Path to Paradise of Lorenzo Scupoli*. Revised by Theophan the Recluse. Translated by E. Kadloubovsky and G. E. H. Palmer. Crestwood, NY: St. Vladimir's Seminary Press, 1995.

Nikodimos, Saint of the Holy Mountain, and Saint Makarios of Corinth. *The Philokalia*. 4 Vols. Translated from the Greek and edited by G. E. H. Palmer, Philip Sherrard, and Kallistos Ware. London: Faber & Faber, 1979, 1981, 1984, 1995.

Norris, Richard A. Jr., ed. *The Song of Songs: Interpreted by Early Christian and Medieval Commentators*. Grand Rapids: Eerdmans, 2003.

Nouwen, Henri J. M. *The Way of the Heart: Desert Spirituality and Contemporary Ministry*. San Francisco: HarperSanFrancisco, 1981.

O'Connell, Marvin R. *Blaise Pascal: Reasons of the Heart*. Grand Rapids: Eerdmans, 1997.

Packer, J. I., and Loren Wilkinson. *Alive to God: Studies in Spirituality*. Downers Grove, IL: InterVarsity, 1992.

Pagitt, Doug, and Kathryn Pill. *Body Prayer: The Posture of Intimacy with God*. Colorado Springs: WaterBrook, 2005.

Pagitt, Doug, and the Solomon's Porch Community. *Reimagining Spiritual Formation: A Week in the Life of an Experimental Church*. Grand Rapids: Zondervan, 2003.

Payne, Leanne. *Restoring the Christian Soul through Healing Prayer: Overcoming the Three Great Barriers to Personal and Spiritual Completion in Christ*. Wheaton: Crossway, 1991.

Pecklers, Keith, SJ, ed. *Liturgy in a Postmodern World*. New York: Continuum, 2003.

Penner, Myron P., ed. *Christianity and the Postmodern Turn*. Grand Rapids: Brazos, 2005.

Peterson, Eugene H. *Christ Plays in Ten Thousand Places: A Conversation in Spiritual Theology*. Grand Rapids: Eerdmans, 2005.

———. *A Long Obedience in the Same Direction: Discipleship in an Instant Society*. Downers Grove, IL: InterVarsity, 1980.

———. *Subversive Spirituality*. 1994. Reprint, Grand Rapids: Eerdmans, 1997.

Pfatteicher, Philip H. *Liturgical Spirituality*. Valley Forge, PA: Trinity Press International, 1997.

———. *The School of the Church: Worship and Christian Formation*. Valley Forge, PA: Trinity Press International, 1995.

Pieper, Joseph. *A Brief Reader on the Virtues of the Heart*. San Francisco: Ignatius Press, 1991.

———. *The Four Cardinal Virtues*. Notre Dame, IN: University of Notre Dame Press, 1966.

Ponticus, Evagrius. *The Pratikos Chapters on Prayer*. Kalamazoo, MI: Cistercian Publications, 1981.

Preston, John, Nathaniel Vincent, and Samuel Lee. *The Puritans on Prayer*. Morgan, PA: Soli Deo Gloria Publications, 1995.

Raitt, Jill, ed. *Christian Spirituality II: High Middle Ages and Reformation*. Vol. 17, *World Spirituality*. New York: Crossroad, 1987.

Rea, Jana, with Richard J. Foster. *A Spiritual Formation Journal: A Renovaré Resource for Spiritual Renewal*. San Francisco: HarperSanFrancisco, 1996.

Regan, David. *Experiencing the Mystery: Pastoral Possibilities for Christian Mystagogy*. Collegeville, MN: Liturgical Press, 1994.

Richardson, Cyril C., ed. *Early Christian Fathers*. Vol. 1, *The Library of Christian Classics*. Philadelphia: Westminster, 1953.

Romano, Eugene L. *The Way of Desert Spirituality: The Plan of Life of the Hermits of Bethlehem*. New York: Alba House, 1998.

Rothschild, Fritz A., ed. *Between God and Man: An Interpretation of Judaism: From the Writings of Abraham J. Heschel*. New York: Free Press, 1959.

Rutba House, The, ed. *School(s) for Conversion: 12 Marks of a New Monasticism*. Eugene, OR: Cascade Books, 2005.

Russell, Norman, translator. Introduction by Benedicta Ward. *The Lives of the Desert Fathers*. Kalamazoo, MI: Cistercian Publications, 1980.

Ruth, Lester. *Early Methodist Life and Spirituality: A Reader*. Nashville: Kingswood Books, 2005.

Saliers, Don E. *The Soul in Paraphrase*. Cleveland, OH: OSL Publications, 1991.

Salisbury, Joyce E. *Perpetua's Passion: The Death and Memory of a Young Roman Woman*. New York: Routledge, 1997.

Schroeder, Celeste Snowber. *Embodied Prayer: Harmonizing Body and Soul*. Liguori, MO: Triumph Books, 1994.

Scotto, Dominic F. *The Liturgy of the Hours*. Petersham, MA: St. Bedes Publications, 1987.

Scupoli, Lorenzo. *Unseen Warfare: The Spiritual Combat and Path to Paradise of Lorenzo Scupoli*. Edited by Nicodemus of the Holy Mountain. Revised by Theophan the Recluse. Translated by E. Kadloubovsky and G. E. H. Palmer.

Seitz, Christopher R. *Figured Out: Typology and Providence in Christian Scripture*. Louisville: Westminster John Knox, 2001.

———, ed. *Nicene Christianity: The Future for a New Ecumenism*. Grand Rapids: Brazos, 2001.

Sheldrake, Philip. *Spirituality and History: Questions of Interpretation and Method*. 1992. Revised edition, Maryknoll, NY: Orbis Books, 1998.

———. *Spirituality and Theology: Christian Living and the Doctrine of God*. Maryknoll, NY: Orbis Books, 1998.

Silf, Margaret. *Sacred Spaces: Stations on a Celtic Way*. Brewster, MA: Paraclete Press, 2001.

Simeon the New Theologian, Saint. *On the Mystical Life: The Ethical Discourses*. Vol. 1, *The Church and the Last Things*. Crestwood, NY: St. Vladimir's Seminary Press, 1995.

———. *On the Mystical Life: The Ethical Discourses*. Vol. 2, *On Virtue and the Christian Life*. Crestwood, NY: St. Vladimir's Seminary Press, 1996.

———. *On the Mystical Life: The Ethical Discourses*. Vol. 3, *Life, Times and Theology*. Crestwood, NY: St. Vladimir's Seminary Press, 1997.

Smith, Huston. *The World's Religions*. San Francisco: HarperSanFrancisco, 1991.

Smith, James K. A. *Introducing Radical Orthodoxy: Mapping a Post-secular Theology*. Grand Rapids: Baker, 2004.

Sophrony, Archimandrite. *His Life Is Mine*. Crestwood, NY: St. Vladimir's Seminary Press, 2001.

Stavropoulos, Christoforos. *Partakers of the Divine Nature*. Minneapolis: Light and Life, 1976.

Stolz, Anselm, OSB. *The Doctrine of Spiritual Perfection*. New York: Herder and Herder, 2001.

Studer, Basil. *Trinity and Incarnation: The Faith of the Early Church*. Collegeville, MN: Liturgical Press, 1993.

Taft, Robert, SJ. *The Liturgy of the Hours in East and West: The Origins of the Divine Office and Its Meaning for Today*. Collegeville, MN: Liturgical Press, 1986.

Theophan the Recluse, Saint. *The Path to Salvation: A Manual of Spiritual Transformation*. Platina, CA: St. Herman of Alaska Brotherhood, 1996.

———. *The Spiritual Life and How to Be Attuned to It*. Safford, AR: St. Paisius Serbian Orthodox Monastery, 2003.

Thibodeaux, Mark E., SJ. *Armchair Mystic: Easing into Contemplative Prayer*. Cincinnati: St. Anthony Messenger Press, 1989.

Thomas, I. D. E. *Puritan Daily Devotional Chronicles*. Oklahoma City: Hearthstone, 1995.

Thomas, W. Ian. *The Saving Life of Christ and the Mystery of Godliness*. Grand Rapids: Zondervan, 1988.

Thompson, Robert W., ed. *The Teaching of Saint Gregory: An Early Armenian Catechism*. Cambridge, MA: Harvard University Press, 1970.

Tilley, Terrence W. *Story Theology*. Collegeville, MA: Liturgical Press, 1985.

Tugwell, Simon. *Ways of Imperfection: An Exploration of Christian Spirituality*. Springfield, IL: Templegate Publishers, 1985.

Underhill, Evelyn. *The Mystics of the Church*. New York: Schocken, 1971.

———. *The Spiritual Life*. 1937. Reprint, London: Hodder & Stoughton, 1996.

Valantasis, Richard. *Centuries of Holiness: Ancient Spirituality Refracted for a Postmodern World*. New York: Continuum, 2005.

Vanhoozer, Kevin. *The Drama of Doctrine: A Canonical Linguistic Approach to Christian Theology*. Louisville: Westminster John Knox, 2005.

Vanier, Jean. *Becoming Human*. New York: Paulist, 1998.

Vest, Norvene. *Friend of the Soul: A Benedictine Spirituality of Work*. Cambridge, MA: Cowley Publications, 1997.

Wallace, Dewey D., III, ed. *The Spirituality of the Later English Puritans: An Anthology*. Macon, GA: Mercer Press, 1987.

Wesley, John. *The Nature of Holiness: Wesley's Messages on Christian Experience*. Minneapolis: Bethany House, 1988.

Willard, Dallas. *The Divine Conspiracy: Rediscovering Our Hidden Life in God*. San Francisco: HarperSanFrancisco, 1998.

———. *Hearing God: Developing a Conversational Relationship with God*. Downers Grove, IL: InterVarsity, 1984, 1993, 1999.

———. *Renovation of the Heart: Putting on the Character of Christ*. Colorado Springs: NavPress, 2002.

———. *The Spirit of the Disciplines: Understanding How God Changes Lives*. 1988. Reprint, San Francisco: HarperSanFrancisco, 1998.

Williams, Brian A. *The Potter's Rib: Mentoring for Pastoral Formation*. Vancouver, British Columbia: Regent College Publishing, 2005.

Wilson, Jonathan R. *Gospel Virtues: Practicing Faith, Hope and Love in Uncertain Times*. Downers Grove, IL: InterVarsity, 1998.

———. *Living Faithfully in a Fragmented World: Lessons for the Church from MacIntyre's After Virtue*. Harrisburg, PA: Trinity Press International, 1997.

Wittmer, Michael E. *Heaven Is a Place on Earth: Why Everything You Do Matters to God*. Grand Rapids: Zondervan, 2004.

Yaconelli, Michael. *Messy Spirituality: God's Annoying Love for Imperfect People*. Grand Rapids: Zondervan, 2002.

Zelensky, Elizabeth, and Lela Gilbert. *Windows to Heaven: Introducing Icons to Protestants and Catholics*. Grand Rapids: Brazos, 2005.

Zimmerman, Joyce Ann. *Liturgy as Living Faith: A Liturgical Spirituality*. Scranton, PA: University of Scranton Press, 1993.

Zizioulas, John D. *Being as Communion: Studies in Personhood and the Church*. Crestwood, NY: St. Vladimir's Seminary Press, 1997.

Index